THE PATH TO FREE COLLEGE

THE PATH TO FREE COLLEGE

IN PURSUIT OF ACCESS, EQUITY, AND PROSPERITY

MICHELLE MILLER-ADAMS

HARVARD EDUCATION PRESS
Cambridge, Massachusetts

Paperback ISBN 978-1-68253-606-3
Library Edition ISBN 978-1-68253-607-0

Library of Congress Cataloging-in-Publication Data is on file.

Published by Harvard Education Press,
an imprint of the Harvard Education Publishing Group

Harvard Education Press
8 Story Street
Cambridge, MA 02138

Cover Design: Endpaper Studio
Cover Image: mikroman6/Moment via Getty Images

The typefaces in this book are ITC Legacy Serif and Atlan.

This book is dedicated to my mother,

Rachel Galperin

(1932–2016)

CONTENTS

Preface ix

1 **Why Free College?** 1

2 **The Promise Landscape** 29

3 **Affordability** 55

4 **Equity** 87

5 **Employment** 125

6 **Toward Free College for All** 159

Notes 183

About the Author 203

Index 205

PREFACE

I BEGAN WRITING this book amid the booming economy of 2019 and concluded it a year later in a very different world.

In 2019, unemployment was at a historic low and employers struggled to hire skilled workers. State finances had finally recovered from the fallout of the 2008 Great Recession, and most had returned to prerecession levels of funding for higher education. Income- and race-based gaps in college enrollment were narrowing, although gaps in degree completion remained, and college enrollment had leveled off due both to rising tuition prices and to a healthy jobs picture. Communities and states were forging ahead with the project of creating tuition-free college initiatives (sometimes called "Promise" programs) to meet their local needs. The free-college idea had gained traction within the Democratic Party and among the electorate, although concerns about cost and an absence of executive-branch leadership had halted progress at the national level.

A few months later, much had changed. By March 2020, the COVID-19 pandemic had brought the booming economy to its knees. Governors issued stay-at-home orders, and economic production and consumption dropped sharply. Schools and universities stopped in-person instruction, and existing Promise programs quickly moved their support services online to help eligible students make their way to college in the fall. Applications for federal financial aid to low-income students plunged. Unemployment rose to unprecedented levels, and the falloff in economic activity blew giant holes in state and local finances. Uncertainty reigned. No one could know when the spread of the coronavirus would end, and it was difficult to plan. Would school buildings reopen? Would college students show up if classes were held online? Should community colleges expect the influx of adult learners they had seen in earlier recessions?

The coronavirus pandemic had deep racial implications as well. Blacks, Latinos, and Native Americans were far more likely to contract or die from the virus than whites, directing attention to racial disparities in chronic health conditions, access to medical care, and employment patterns. The murder of George Floyd by a white police officer in Minneapolis in June 2020 was like a match to a flame, setting in motion a long-overdue reckoning not just with police practices but with systemic racism more broadly.

The twin phenomena of the COVID-19-induced recession and a widespread social movement for racial justice created, seemingly overnight, an altered context for free-college efforts. Now, the idea of free college was being driven forward not by employers' need for skilled workers but by workers' need for retraining. Now, the distributional benefits arising from free-college programs were not the stuff of academic debate but a possible avenue toward greater racial and economic equity.

The November 2020 presidential election was a watershed event. Joe Biden won a narrow victory, propelled into office by the Trump administration's poor handling of the pandemic. While the president and his party are on record in support of a national free-college initiative, a deeply divided electorate and a narrow Senate majority constrain the Biden administration. Even so, free college—especially of the two-year variety—remains an appealing option to help the nation meet the needs of unemployed and unskilled workers while furthering racial justice.

This book seeks to respond to this moment, but I came to the project for two other reasons. The first is the story of my family and how access to a first-rate education at almost no cost vaulted my parents from poverty into the middle class. The second is the story of my adopted hometown of Kalamazoo, Michigan, where a group of generous individuals with a new idea changed the future of higher education in the United States.

Both stories shed light on several fundamental realignments under way—the reality that a high school diploma is no longer sufficient for economic success, a rise in the price of college so relentless that college degrees are increasingly unaffordable for typical families, and a recognition that decades of efforts to close racial and income gaps in higher education have essentially failed. These three are related; more important, they are a recipe for perpetuating inequality and stifling the dreams of Americans young and old.

It was not always this way.

1938—Boston. Six people, three generations, in a two-room apartment. The mother, a Jewish immigrant from Russia, is raising four young girls and caring for her aged mother. Her husband has died, and two of her older children—the breadwinners—have moved to California for work. An adult son has died, and a baby has, too. When one of the girls falls ill, the doctor tells her mother it is rheumatic fever, the same disease that killed her son. The doctor says a warmer climate will be better for the child, so an older sister sends money to move the family west. The train ride takes five days. Eighty years later, the girls remember eating the hard-boiled eggs they had brought with them and marveling at the orange groves and palm trees out the window as they arrived at Union Station in downtown Los Angeles.

1942—Los Angeles. Another small house, this one home to ten family members. Four girls and their mother share a bed, and their brothers take the couch. The girls attend Los Angeles's then-excellent public schools, the children of immigrants all around them. No one talks about college. Their mother has only a few years of education and runs a liquor store to keep the family afloat. The oldest daughter graduates from high school at fifteen and goes to work at the Veterans Administration; it is wartime and jobs are plentiful. At work, she meets doctors and lawyers, professionals with children in college. Wanting to learn more, she takes a day off from work and rides the city bus to the University of California, Los Angeles, only a few miles away. At the age of ninety-three, my aunt still has vivid memories of that day: "When I came up the stairs and saw the beautiful green lawn—the area even smelled different—I decided I was going to go to college." Her mother, who knows nothing about college, nevertheless understands the value of education. She encourages her daughter to enroll right away, and the path has veered. A new story begins.

My aunt and her sisters attend and graduate from UCLA. They pay only nominal fees—the University of California system is basically free—live at home and ride the streetcar to class. They graduate with teaching credentials, then continue on for master's degrees. They marry similarly educated men—engineers, teachers—also born to poor Jewish families, also educated at California's public colleges and universities. Their children grow up in the middle class, barely able to envision the poverty of their parents' youth.

Two decades later, I enroll at the University of California. It is 1976, and tuition is $714 a year—around $3,000 in today's dollars. When I graduate four years later, the taxpayer revolt is underway. Proposition 13 is approved by voters in 1978, and the resulting limits on property taxes usher in drastic cuts to education. California's public schools, among the best in the nation in the 1960s, begin their sad decline. Tuition at public universities begins its steady climb. Today, as the next generation of my family enters college, annual tuition at the University of California is approaching $15,000 a year, with living costs, textbooks, and other expenses amounting to almost twice that amount.

In 1998, I move to Kalamazoo, a struggling midsized city in West Michigan. Seven years later, a group of wealthy individuals announce the Kalamazoo Promise, the first of a wave of place-based scholarships that cover college tuition for a large proportion of a community's young people. Students in the Kalamazoo Public Schools, an urban school district with high rates of economically disadvantaged and nonwhite students, learn they can go to college for free, just as my parents did. This changes the postsecondary aspirations of many of these young people, while also transforming their school district and community. The geographic accident of their living in a specific place at a given moment opens a pathway to upward mobility that runs through affordable higher education.

Can we create a world where such a pathway is available to all without the crushing burden of too much debt, where access to a valuable degree is a function of aspirations and ability, not of income? We are indeed on our way to this future, although the route looks much different than it did in the past. I write this book at a time of tremendous dynamism, with new forms of free college being introduced at a rapid pace and recent economic and social developments giving these efforts even greater impetus. But it is also a dangerous time. The speed of replication is so fast and public enthusiasm for free college so strong that there is the real potential for mistakes. We have already seen cases where promises were made that could not be sustained financially and design choices implemented that led to unintended consequences. These mistakes are avoidable, but only if we take the time to consider what we have already learned.

That is one of the goals of this book: to examine the landscape of free-college efforts, both current and past; distill the lessons they offer; and point a way forward that makes good on the promise of free college and restores opportunities that led families like mine out of poverty. But there is another goal—to make the case that free college is not just an investment in the success of individuals but that it also holds value for society. This dual-value proposition and its intergenerational impact played out in my personal history when access to an inexpensive, high-quality education brought benefits not just to my parents, but to their children and grandchildren, and to the state in which they lived. My story is just one among many, and in chapters 4 and 5, I tell the stories of several individuals I have met whose experiences illustrate the individual and societal implications of free college or its lack. These are true stories, and I am grateful to the individuals who were willing to share them.

Speaking of gratitude, this book would not have been possible without my two employers, Grand Valley State University and the W.E. Upjohn Institute for Employment Research, both of which provided financial support for this project. In my years of studying the free-college movement, I have had the privilege of working with many talented and generous individuals. At the Upjohn Institute, these include Tim Bartik, Dan Collier, Brad Hershbein, and Bridget Timmeney, all of whom devoted time and effort to help make this a stronger book. I am also indebted to those outside the institute who reviewed and commented on the manuscript, including Celeste Carruthers, Sara Goldrick-Rab, Emily House, Jennifer Iriti, Martha Kanter, and Chuck Wilbur, as well as leaders of Promise programs who helped ensure the accuracy of my work, including Krissy DeAlejandro, Saleem Ghubril, Greg Handel, Bob Jorth, David Rust, Sylvia Thompson, and Von Washington. My Upjohn Institute colleague Elizabeth Kellogg went above and beyond to ensure the quality of the manuscript. I am grateful to Nick Visscher for preparing the figures. I have benefited throughout from the guidance of Jayne Fargnoli, my editor at Harvard Education Press (HEP), who had the initial idea for this book and guided it to completion with insight and kindness. The editorial, production, and marketing staff of HEP was also a pleasure to work with; I am especially indebted to Jane Gebhart for her careful copyediting. The opinions expressed here and any errors are my own, but it is these relationships that have helped me learn and grow, and they are part of what keeps me excited about the free-college movement.

CHAPTER

1

Why Free College?

Not long ago, many colleges were indeed free;
much longer ago, elementary education was not.
There is no natural law that deems one thing
a public good and another a market-based
luxury. It is up to us to decide.

—E. Tammy Kim[1]

THIS BOOK BEGINS with a simple question. Why has the price of college become a major political issue in recent years? College prices, along with student loan debt, have been rising for decades, and both have received plenty of media attention. The value of a college degree in the workforce has also been well known for a long time.

The current free-college moment is not just the natural culmination of these long-standing trends. Three distinct concerns have interacted to move questions of college price and access firmly onto the local, state, and national policy agendas. There is also one new social fact that has vaulted the free-college movement to its current prominence.

The best known of these concerns is a seemingly unstoppable increase in the price of higher education that places it outside the reach of the middle class and has contributed to rising levels of student loan debt.[2] The reasons for tuition inflation are hotly debated, but declining state support for public colleges and universities, investments in amenities to attract students, and swelling administrative budgets all play a part—as do the shortcomings of the financial aid system itself. Rising prices for students hit especially hard at a time when a college degree or credential has become the gateway to a decent-paying job and when the proportion of college-educated workers in any given state is an important determinant of its economic success. In her 2016 book, *Paying the Price*, sociologist Sara Goldrick-Rab labels this interplay of greater demand for degrees, declining state aid, the failures of the financial aid system, and falling incomes "the new economics of college" and shows how it has placed tremendous burdens on college students and their families, even if these are not always well understood.[3]

Related to the issue of affordability are long-standing concerns about racial and economic equity in higher education. Decades of efforts to promote the educational attainment of low-income, Black, Latino, and indigenous students have fallen short, shining a spotlight on opportunity gaps and systemic racism that runs from preK through college and into the workforce. [4] Even while college enrollment has increased among these demographic groups, economic and racial divides persist in both enrollment and degree attainment.[5] Rising tuition, fees, and living expenses have made it more difficult to close these gaps, with research suggesting that tuition increases disproportionately reduce enrollment by low-income students. Equally troubling, there is some evidence that the economic returns to a college degree may be lower for poor students than for the nonpoor—a finding that could further deter underrepresented groups from college enrollment and completion.[6]

A third important dynamic behind today's free-college movement is worry among employers about the nation's supply of trained workers and the impact of a skills gap on productivity and competitiveness.[7] These concerns were aired loudly in the tight labor market that followed the nation's recovery from the Great Recession of 2008 and in states where out-migration and low birth rates led to forecasts of worker shortfalls, although a number of thoughtful critics have taken issue with the skills gap idea.[8] There is broader agreement on this, though: workers without college degrees never recovered from the 2008 recession, and there are concerns that the economic crisis following the 2020 pandemic will follow the same pattern.[9] Even if employers are not as desperate for workers as they once were, workers desperately need access to postsecondary degrees and credentials in order to survive a more competitive labor market.

Overlaying these three dynamics is the social fact of inequality. Income and wealth inequality in the United States has been getting worse since 1979, but conditions long accepted as the reality of living in a capitalist society have lately become less tolerable. As the US economy recovered from the 2008 recession, there was a growing sense that the game was not fair. The spoils of growth went to the wealthy, while the middle class, workers, and the poor continued to struggle.

Even as the economy was expanding, two-thirds of Americans polled in 2019 felt dissatisfied with "the way income and wealth are distributed in the US," and a similar percentage favored implementation of a wealth tax.[10] It is this relatively recent and broad-based preoccupation with fairness that has given political traction to free-college initiatives.

Accompanying and often exacerbating income inequality are racial disparities in fundamental measures of well-being, such as health, life expectancy, and wealth. Such disparities have been documented for decades, but in 2020 police violence pushed these aspects of systemic racism to the forefront of many white Americans' consciousness for the first time. Public opinion shifted rapidly; for example, 57 percent of American surveyed in June 2020 believed that Blacks are subject to the use of excessive force by police, up from 33 percent four years earlier.[11] While cash reparations for slavery remain unpopular among white Americans, support for them is growing, and there is rising interest in strategies that would reduce the Black-white wealth gap.[12]

In true American style, solutions to the challenges discussed above have come in an iterative fashion, first at the local level and, more recently, at the state level. Free-college programs are one such solution. Policy innovation around tuition-free college has been a bottom-up effort, with private and nonprofit actors leading the way and tremendous diversity among approaches. Much has been learned from these efforts. Free-college programs work best when they are simply structured, easy to understand, and embedded in a system of community supports that goes beyond the provision of a scholarship—although meaningful change is unrealistic when new financial resources are not also part of the package. If a Promise program reflects community values and addresses its needs, such an initiative can serve as a platform for transformative change and enrich opportunity for both individuals and communities.

Now attention has moved to the national level. Before 2016, support for the more generous versions of nationwide tuition-free college—specifically those that include four-year options—was confined to the left wing of the Democratic Party, although the antecedents of the free-college movement go back to John Edwards's run for the 2004 presidential nomination. In 2015, Vermont senator Bernie Sanders proposed making public universities tuition free and funding the program through a transaction tax on Wall Street trades—an idea one pundit called "powerful, wonderful, and profound."[13] That same year, Massachusetts senator Elizabeth Warren outlined a path to debt-free college based on her earlier work on student loan debt. When Hillary Clinton offered her own plan a few months later, it was clear the idea had moved squarely onto the Democratic Party agenda. Four years later, free college figured prominently in primary debates among Democratic presidential candidates almost from day one of the 2020 presidential campaign. Joe Biden's evolution on the issue has traced that of his party, moving from support for a modest community college-only approach to full-throated embrace of a more generous plan.

When I began thinking about this book in 2018, the odds of a national free-college program seemed long; today, those odds are shorter, although any free-college plan may still struggle to gain bipartisan support. Republicans, especially during the Trump administration, showed little interest in such an endeavor, yet the national political dialogue around free college has become louder. One reason is that speaking to the price of college responds to the concerns of both the Democratic voting base, especially young people and people of color, and a traditionally Republican-leaning business sector. I discuss options for national action around tuition-free college in the book's final chapter, but it is at the state and local levels where the real story lies.

THE ORIGINS OF THE PROMISE MOVEMENT

If the current free-college movement were given a birth date, it would be November 10, 2005, the night the superintendent of public schools in Kalamazoo, Michigan, announced to a crowded room that a group of anonymous donors would send virtually all the district's graduates to college tuition free. This was not the first tuition guarantee made to a group of students. I have written elsewhere about the intriguing story of Philomath, Oregon, and a communitywide scholarship program dating back to 1959.[14] In 1981, Eugene Lang promised college tuition to a class of sixth graders, launching what would become his "I Have a Dream" Foundation. Since 1993, Harris Rosen has been paying for college for high school graduates in the tiny Tangelo Park subdivision, located in the shadow of Orlando, Florida's amusement parks, and the Ayers Foundation had been granting scholarships to students in several rural Tennessee counties since 1999. A handful of other communities had waived tuition for students attending local community colleges. What these initiatives had in common was a focus on providing new opportunities for disadvantaged youth. The Kalamazoo Promise opened a new front in this arena, one that has had a profound impact on the free-college movement. We may never know precisely who the Kalamazoo Promise donors are, but their intermediaries, along with the structure of the program itself, tell us they were as concerned about their city as they were about the young people who live in it.

When the donors' gift was announced, Kalamazoo was grappling with economic challenges stemming from the loss of its key corporate leader, the Upjohn pharmaceuticals company, and a series of mergers and closings that had diminished the economic base. The school district, as is typical of most urban districts in the Upper Midwest and industrial Northeast, was shrinking as families relocated to the suburbs or left the state in search of better jobs. Enrollment in Kalamazoo Public Schools had fallen by half from its peak of almost nineteen thousand in the late 1960s, and the district had become home to growing concentrations of poor children and children of color. Free and reduced-meal eligibility (the metric for measuring economic disadvantage in K–12 schools) was about 70 percent, and nonwhites accounted for 60 percent of students. Michigan's system of small jurisdictional units, with nine school districts in a county of 250,000 residents, exacerbated the problem, as families could relocate by just a few miles to exit the urban core. In a place with a long history of quiet philanthropy, a group of wealthy individuals made a bet that they could reverse these outward flows. In doing so, the Kalamazoo Promise donors became the first philanthropists to suggest that a generous, open-ended investment in college scholarships based on residency and enrollment might change the fate of their hometown.

From these supremely local roots grew a national movement. The problems facing Kalamazoo were similar to those of many small and midsized communities throughout the nation. Hungry for solutions, cities of all sizes, in all regions, were attracted to the idea of simultaneously creating opportunities for their young people while making their communities more appealing. Many created tuition-free programs of their own, although most of these were less well resourced than the Kalamazoo Promise, which is set up to continue in perpetuity. In 2006, ten communities announced the launch of Promise programs, with another eight the following year. By 2010, more than forty communities had created scholarships based on the simple criterion of where students live (such programs are sometimes called place-based or community-based scholarships). One of these was Knoxville, where the Knox Achieves program began in 2008; it became the precursor for the Tennessee Promise that, in turn, sparked the introduction of two dozen statewide Promise programs. The period of most intensive growth in the Promise movement occurred between 2014 and 2017 as seventy new programs were created, many of them based at local community colleges.[15]

No one owns the "Promise" label, and it has come to mean different things to different people.[16] Advocacy organizations dedicated to increasing college access and success, most prominently the Washington, DC–based College Promise initiative, have applied the term to a broad range of financial aid and college access programs that, as of this writing, includes more than 320 institutions and communities. At the same time, "Promise" remains identified with a smaller group of place-based scholarship programs that are concerned with community transformation along with college access. As of 2020, the Upjohn Institute's Promise Programs Database listed 127 such community-based programs, along with another 65 tuition-free programs created by postsecondary institutions, primarily community colleges. (Statewide programs are not included in the Upjohn database.) At the same time, a database of College Promise programs created by the University of Pennsylvania Graduate School of Education's Alliance for Higher Education and Democracy (Penn AHEAD) contained 425 entries, including separate need- and merit-based grants in almost every state, scholarships offered by specific four-year institutions, and programs without financial benefits, such as guaranteed admission, college savings accounts, and dual-enrollment programs.[17] While seemingly unavoidable, the definitional uncertainty is problematic. Lack of a common understanding of the field impedes progress toward an understanding of best practices and makes a comparison of like programs difficult.

Even using a narrower definition, grouping Promise programs by their specific characteristics is a challenge, as each is designed to respond to local needs and is built from the ground up using local assets. So, in Hammond, Indiana, where city officials were concerned about low rates of home ownership, the College Bound program was created to provide scholarships to the children of homeowners. In Denver, where the city is booming but the public schools disproportionately serve low-income youth, the Denver Scholarship Foundation conditions scholarship awards on family income. In Richmond, California, the oil and gas company Chevron provided $35 million in seed funding for the Richmond Promise as part of a community benefits agreement tied to modernization of its local refinery. In Pittsburgh, the region's largest employer, the University of Pittsburgh Medical Center, provided a $100 million challenge grant to help launch the Pittsburgh Promise and increase the stock of homegrown talent. And in Dallas, the Dallas County Promise encourages local students to attend any campus of the community college district with the goal of promoting workforce readiness and equity. All five of these programs appear in both the Upjohn Institute and Penn AHEAD databases wearing the Promise label. Some are available to all students within a given jurisdiction (these are generally called universal programs), while others have some kind of academic requirement, usually a high school GPA threshold. Only a handful of Promise programs are explicitly need based, although almost all of them are designed to benefit economically disadvantaged students.

The next chapter takes on the task of categorizing this diverse set of programs. For now, it is sufficient to note that in this book I use the term "Promise" to refer to locally or state-bounded tuition-free college initiatives with goals that go beyond college access.

LESSONS FROM THE PAST

Tuition-free college is not a radical idea. Rather, it reminds us of an era when higher education in many parts of the United States was essentially free. The debate over free college also echoes an even earlier debate over whether high school should be universal and publicly funded.

Free and accessible public education, at least for white male children, has been a hallmark of the United States for most of its history. In the 1830s, Horace Mann in his role as secretary of the nation's first public board of education argued that a democratic society required access to education that is free and universal, nonsectarian (schooling had previously been delivered largely by religious authorities), available to all children regardless of race or social class, and reliant on well-trained professional teachers.[18]

The diffusion of the "common school" (forerunner of the public elementary school) during the nineteenth century, followed by the high school movement of the twentieth century, meant that the United States acted earlier than its European counterparts to increase educational attainment. These investments positioned the United States to benefit from higher skill levels in the form of technological innovation and economic growth, a story told by Claudia Goldin and Lawrence Katz in their book, *The Race Between Technology and Education*.[19] Of course, for much of this history, schools were segregated by race and unequally resourced, laying the groundwork for opportunity gaps by race not just in schooling but in the workplace.

The United States also led the developed world in the mass expansion of postsecondary schooling, although that progress skidded to a halt at the end of the twentieth century. Since then, postsecondary attainment in European countries has exceeded that in the United States. I address one of the most important reasons for this change—rising college prices—in chapter 3. First, though, we look to the past to see how both economic and political factors played a role in expanding educational opportunity, just as they do today.

High School for All

Today we take for granted that young people in the United States will attend high school. In truth, however, this is a relatively recent development. Until the late nineteenth century, school attendance in many states was optional, and most students completed their education by age fourteen. A political and legal movement driven largely by the economic transition from an agricultural to an industrial economy changed this, but only very slowly.

Beginning with a series of legal decisions in the late 1800s, the right to tax a community's citizens to support high school for all was established. Notably, one of the most important of these cases concerned Kalamazoo, a place that has played an outsized role in the spread of universal education. In 1859, Michigan's legislature passed a law authorizing larger school districts to elect school boards to govern their districts. The boards were given the authority to create high schools funded by local taxes if citizens of the district voted in favor of such a move. In anticipation of the law's passage, but without a vote, Kalamazoo established its first high school in 1858.

Kalamazoo Union High School operated with only minor opposition until 1873, when a prominent resident, former US senator Charles Stuart, and two other wealthy property owners initiated a lawsuit against the school district claiming that the 1859 law had been violated because no election to authorize the district had been held. Resentful of the tax burden placed on property owners, themselves included, Stuart also opposed the growing centralization of education and raised issues of equity (whether genuinely or not), expressing concerns that the high school education of the children of prosperous families was being paid for by taxes on everyone, including the poorer residents.

The case went straight to the heart of questions that guide today's free-college debate. Is education mainly designed to yield benefits for individuals and should it thus be the responsibility of the individual to pay for it? Or does investing in education have a public benefit, helping those who do not directly gain from it? Those arguing against a community's right to tax its residents to pay for high school believed that a common school education was sufficient for most young Americans and that those who aspired to more education should pay for it themselves—a belief echoed by some today. As many people recognized at the time, high school might be tuition free to those attending, but someone would be paying for it—the question was who.

The Kalamazoo school case was significant in part because of the prominence of the jurist who issued its ruling—Thomas Cooley, chief justice of the Michigan Supreme Court who would go on to serve as dean of the University of Michigan Law School and first chairman of the Interstate Commerce Commission. His argument on behalf of the legitimacy of publicly funded education was not primarily an economic one. Rather, Cooley argued that education was integral to citizenship and made a claim for "the right of the state to furnish a liberal education to the youth of the state in schools brought within the reach of all classes."[20] The case had important implications in Michigan and elsewhere, setting off a doubling in the number of high schools in the state, just as similar movements were occurring elsewhere. But the implementation of universal, publicly funded high school took time—more time than many realize. In 1910, only 9 percent of eighteen-year-olds had high school diplomas. By 1940, this rate had risen to 51 percent.[21] While high school attendance is now almost universal, completion is not—15 percent of all students (and higher proportions of Black, Latino, and Native populations) fail to complete a high school diploma.[22]

When free-college advocates speak today, they often reference the high school movement. The similarities are striking. The high school movement in the United States was a grassroots phenomenon, spreading from community to community in fits and starts. High school attendance did not become compulsory through the passage of state laws or other top-down action. Rather it was the result of families seeking greater social mobility for their children and local political and business leaders responding in order to give their communities a competitive edge. These intertwined motivations are also found in the free-college movement. Moreover, the process of expanding educational opportunity was politically fraught, with intense debates over the distribution of costs and benefits. And this newfangled idea took hold only very slowly, with almost a century elapsing between the Kalamazoo school case and the expectation that every young person in the United States would attend and graduate from high school.

College for Some

Unlike high school, and despite rapid rates of growth, college enrollment in the United States has never been a majority phenomenon. In 1900, only about 2 percent of the nation's population of eighteen- to twenty-four-year-olds enrolled in college. By 1949, with the surge in enrollment that followed World War II, 2.4 million students, or about 15 percent of eighteen- to twenty-four-year-olds attended college.[23] In fall 2019, US colleges and universities enrolled almost 20 million students, 12.5 million of them below the age of twenty-five.[24] This represents about 40 percent of the population in this age group.[25] Clearly the history of higher education in the United State is one of tremendous growth. But it is not just the expansion of postsecondary education that is important; equally notable are its secular and egalitarian nature and the role of government in establishing and funding postsecondary institutions—both traits that set US higher education apart from the European system.

Beginning with the Morrill Act of 1862 that established public land-grant colleges, the federal government played an important role in funding higher education. Related to this was the principle of broad access and an emphasis on secular over religious institutions. John Aubrey Douglass, a higher education scholar at University of California Berkeley, argues that the expansion of higher education was due to the combination of individuals' interest in their own success and society's interest in economic prosperity: "On the one side, the drive of individuals to succeed in an increasingly complex and technical marketplace created a new demand for postsecondary education. On the other side, state lawmakers and business interests increasingly recognized higher education as a means to improve the skills of the nation's labor force and the productivity of major sectors of its economy."[26] Land-grant colleges, for example, made it possible for states to offer practical training in fields like agriculture and engineering that the colleges of the time—still largely religious institutions serving the wealthy and focused on the liberal arts—failed to provide. What emerged was a decentralized system governed by states but reliant to a large degree on federal resources.

The Second Morrill Act of 1890 gave each state an appropriation to support its land-grant colleges. By giving federal land and funding to states with formally segregated education systems, the Morrill Act did little to reduce racial inequity. And while it expressly forbade racial discrimination in admissions for these institutions, it also provided a loophole by allowing separate institutions for Blacks if they were administered in a "just" manner. Seventeen institutions, located mainly in the Southeast, were established by this legislation and number among the 107 Historically Black Colleges and Universities (HBCUs) found today in nineteen states and the District of Columbia.[27] These institutions played a crucial role in accommodating Black students, as most Southern universities banned nonwhites from attending outright while those in the North employed quotas to restrict the number of African Americans or Jews who could attend.

World War II marked a major expansion of college going, thanks to a new federal investment that yielded both public and private benefits. The Servicemen's Readjustment Act of 1944, known informally as the GI Bill, was designed to reward veterans for their service and help integrate them into society. The GI Bill established new hospitals, offered veterans down-payment assistance for home purchases, and provided grants and stipends for college attendance. Along the way it democratized the landscape of higher education, propelled many veterans into the middle class, and enabled the United States to benefit economically from a massive increase in trained workers. In 1947, the year of peak usage for the GI Bill, veterans accounted for 49 percent of college admissions. By the time the original GI Bill ended in 1956, almost half (7.8 million) of 16 million World War II veterans had participated in some type of education or training program.

Black veterans were shut out of many of the benefits of the GI Bill. While the legislative language itself was race-neutral, a political compromise with Southern legislators put implementation in the hands of states so that Jim Crow laws could be maintained. This meant that ostensibly universal benefits were delivered through systems shaped by a long history of race-based exclusion. Redlining and other racist home-lending practices meant that Blacks were almost wholly unable to use their benefits to purchase homes, while legal segregation of colleges and universities narrowed their educational options. Southern flagship universities were not formally desegregated until around 1960, with the nation's military colleges taking even longer to accept Black students—the US Air Force Academy graduated its first Black students in 1963.[28] It wasn't until the 1960s that Black students began to enter predominantly white institutions in large numbers, and court-ordered desegregation did not occur until the 1970s. These structural features meant that the GI Bill had very different impacts on Black and white soldiers and the racial wealth gap decades later.[29]

This history holds important lessons for today's free-college debate. Even if free college is made available to everyone in a state or a community under the universal eligibility model that I prefer, its value will be filtered through unequal systems, whether these are underfunded K–12 schools or postsecondary institutions that serve high proportions of low-income students or students of color. Extra attention is thus required to ensure that universal programs have equitable impacts, a topic discussed further in chapter 4.

Federal involvement in higher education intensified with the onset of the Cold War, and especially the Soviet Union's launch of Sputnik in 1957. The United States responded by enacting the National Defense Education Act of 1958, legislation that committed federal resources to scientific and technological research, along with the teaching of science, math, and modern foreign languages. It also created the first low-income student loan program. The motivation here was more public than private; as Douglass writes, "At stake was the development of a high-quality work force and a competitive environment to attract and retain industries, as well as the expansion of the research prowess of a nation immersed in the cold war."[30]

The social upheaval of the 1960s brought about another wave of federal support for higher education. The Higher Education Act of

1965 emerged within the context of President Lyndon Johnson's Great Society programs and represented the first large-scale effort to provide financial assistance to low-income college students.[31] Renamed for Senator Claiborne Pell when the bill was reauthorized in 1972, Pell Grants today represent the largest share of federal investment in higher education, with research funding to universities and their faculty close behind. US funding for higher education since World War II can be characterized as providing targeted financial aid to specific populations—low-income students and veterans—and supporting research. In 2017, Pell Grants accounted for $27.7 billion, or 37 percent of the total federal higher-education investment. Research grants accounted for $26.5 billion, or 35 percent, while veterans' benefits (including various versions of the GI Bill) amounted to $13.6 billion, or 18 percent.[32]

The long history of federal investment in higher education underscores the idea of college as a public good. But that good has not always been shared equitably, especially when it comes to race, in large part because education systems in the United States are decentralized, designed and operated by states. Thus, much of our knowledge about the impact of tuition-free college, both historically and in the present, comes from state and local variations. We look at two historical examples here; contemporary statewide and local free-college initiatives are explored in chapters 3, 4, and 5.

California's free-college experiment

One of the nation's largest and longest-running free-college experiments unfolded in California over roughly a century, from the founding of the University of California in 1868 to the taxpayer revolt of the 1970s. The California system was based on a belief that all high school graduates should have the opportunity for postsecondary education or training. What emerged from this egalitarian conviction—one that also ensured from the beginning the right of women to enroll in college—was a landscape of tuition-free postsecondary institutions serving students of varying backgrounds and abilities. Ultimately, with the California Master Plan for Higher Education passed in 1960, this commitment evolved into a tripartite, statewide system made up of the University of California, the California State University, and the California Community College systems, each with its own mission and governing board. Until the 1970s, this system served mainly white students, since the state's massive influx of Asian and Latino immigrants did not begin until after the passage of the Immigration and Naturalization Act of 1965 that removed quotas based on national origin.

The University of California was founded as a tuition-free institution based on the promise implicit in the 1862 Morrill Act—that revenues from public lands granted to establish state universities would cover their operating costs. This assumption soon proved wrong, as funds fell short. Still, as other land-grant institutions began charging tuition in the late 1800s, the University of California remained tuition free, with costs covered by annual appropriations in the state budget. California also took the lead in creating a statewide system of junior colleges early in the twentieth century (the first public junior college in California was established in Fresno in 1910). The junior college mission was to offer university preparation and vocational or technical education for students not heading directly to university.

Like the expansion of high school and federal funding for higher education, the creation of California's higher-education system was driven both by individuals' demand for access and the state's interest in economic growth. As California's economy evolved from mining to agriculture to industry to high technology, its public education system played a critical role in supplying workers with increasingly high levels of human capital and providing the underlying research on which these industries rested.

World War II made California a major economic power—the state received about one-tenth of all federal government outlays during the war years[33]—and transformed the economy from its reliance on natural resources to higher-value-added defense industries, especially advanced manufacturing, shipbuilding, and aviation. Postwar economic surpluses put the state back on sound economic footing following the Great Depression. One of the major shock absorbers easing the transition from a wartime to a peacetime economy was a massive expansion of public higher education funded by the state. This also allowed the state's public institutions to serve the large number of returning soldiers—in the postwar period, no state had as large a veteran population as California.

The Sputnik launch in 1957 was a wakeup call for California, as it was for the nation. The sense that the United States was losing the space race because of the weaknesses of its educational system opened up an intense debate about reorganizing and reinvesting in education. These concerns are echoed today in conversations about economic competitiveness and the role of education in preserving the nation's technological edge—although the chief competitor to the United States today is China, not the Soviet Union.

The expansion of California's campuses in the 1960s had a strong political dimension. Businesses complained of shortages of skilled labor, especially in technical professions linked to the state's Cold War defense-related industries. Lawmakers sought to create new colleges in their home districts to help drive economic growth and serve their constituents. The allocation of resources was hard fought, with different regions facing off against each other in the struggle for new campuses and increased funding.

California's investments in its higher-education system bore fruit, although they created a conundrum for the state—how to reconcile shrinking budgets with rising demand for higher education. In the early twentieth century, around 5 percent of the state's college-age population enrolled in college. By the 1950s, this rate was 39 percent, compared to a national rate of 27 percent. Experts predicted that 50 percent of students would want to go to college by the 1970s. This projected increase, coupled with high in-migration and the baby boom, meant a surge in the absolute numbers of students needing to be served. In tough economic times, greater postsecondary capacity was needed to help workers retrain, and the institutions themselves served as essential sources of employment and economic stimulus for local communities. Yet budget concerns constrained the state's ability to fund the system it had created.

Free college in California foundered on the challenge of supporting such a dramatically expanding system, exacerbated by political changes culminating in the taxpayer revolt of the 1970s. On-campus protests against the Vietnam War, civil rights activism, and the free-speech movement of the 1960s alienated many California taxpayers from the student population, providing a platform for Ronald Reagan, the state's governor from 1967 to 1975, to develop the anti-elitist rhetoric that propelled him to the presidency in 1980.[34] A major inflection point came in 1978 with the passage of Proposition 13, officially called the "People's Initiative to Limit Property Taxation," that slashed property taxes. Opposed by business, labor, and government leaders, the initiative was nonetheless supported by two-thirds of voters struggling to pay the higher property taxes associated with rising home prices. Government revenue shrank by 40 percent as property taxes fell. One outcome was that general fund revenue was now needed to support local governments and schools, leaving less for higher education, and a prolonged period of systematic disinvestment in the state's postsecondary institutions began.

The disinvestment coincided with a period of rapid demographic change. From 1970 to 1990, California's Latino population almost doubled, from 13.7 percent to 25.8 percent, while the Asian Pacific Islander population rose from 2.8 percent to 9.6 percent. The white population fell from 89 percent to 69 percent, while the Black population remained fairly constant in the 7.0–7.5 percent range.[35]

As demand for college remained high, driven in part by new immigrant groups, tuition rates began to creep up, and California's historic commitment to free higher education came to an end. At the University of California, average tuition rates rose sixfold in inflation-adjusted dollars between 1980 and 2020, from an annual rate of $2,200 (in 2018 dollars) to just over $14,000 today. (On-campus housing and board adds $16,500 and health insurance another $2,800.)[36] The California state university system underwent a similar evolution, with inflation-adjusted tuition growing by more than a factor of ten to around $7,000 today. The community college sector held out the longest, maintaining free tuition until the 1983–1984 academic year, then increasing it steadily to its current rate of about $1,600 a year for a full course load, although a tuition waiver was available for low-income students throughout this period. (California's community college rates remain the lowest in the nation.)

Until 1996, California's public colleges and universities relied on affirmative action to create student bodies that mirrored the state's demographics. That year, voters passed Proposition 209 barring public institutions from granting preferential treatment to any individual or group on the basis of race, sex, color, ethnicity, or national origin. The state's flagship institutions took an immediate hit in terms of racial and ethnic diversity. In 2020, citing twenty-five years of data, the University of California Board of Regents unanimously declared its opposition to race-blind admissions: "To say that a color-blind model is the right structure for our university is not to say that we're color blind, but that we're blind to systemic racism and other structural challenges," said the board chair, pointing to the fact that Blacks, Latinos, Native Americans, and Pacific Islanders are more likely to live in areas with underresourced schools and to face discrimination and other structural barriers that can impede their ability to gain admission to the state's top public schools.[37] In November 2020, California's voters, asked to repeal Proposition 209, chose by a margin of almost 60 percent to keep it.

While the price of four-year institutions is still at a historic high, components of California's tripartite system are returning to an earlier era of affordability. In 2017, the legislature passed a College Promise bill (AB 19) that provided new resources to community colleges to use in a variety of ways, including to cover tuition for students not eligible for the tuition waiver. Many community colleges have also developed their own Promise programs, allowing students to attend tuition free after other forms of financial aid have been applied.

Looking back, it is clear the expansion of free higher education in California was driven by both political and economic needs. The outcome—a robust, affordable system providing multiple paths through postsecondary education—represented value not just to individuals but to the state as a whole. The California economy was boosted by education spending and the entrance of college-educated workers into the labor force, along with research and development that underpinned key industries. Ultimately, these investments proved unsustainable, as arguments over who would pay crested at a time of economic and societal unease. The California experiment is a political story, one in which the state has been unable to sustain educational and economic opportunity for all its residents. But it is not the only story.

Free college in New York City

A different kind of free-college experiment was underway over roughly the same period in New York City. From 1849 to 1976, public postsecondary education in New York was tuition free. There are important differences between the two cases: free college in California was intended to drive economic development as the state's population expanded, while in New York it was motivated by a lack of educational opportunity for all but the very wealthy. And while California's tripartite system accommodated students of all abilities and interests, New York's free-college opportunities were conditioned on academic merit. Still, as in California, questions of who benefited and who paid were deeply contested.

In 1847, wealthy businessman and reformer Townsend Harris proposed creating a public college to serve the city's young men. The Free Academy, renamed City College, opened its doors in 1849. At the time, there were no public high schools in New York (the first was established in 1878), and only the very wealthy attended the city's two private colleges—Columbia College, which became Columbia University, and the University of the City of New York, which became New York University. Not only did these institutions charge tuition, but between them they enrolled only 245 students.[38] Education for everyone else ended at the age of ten or eleven. The Free Academy was intended less as an engine of social mobility and more as an egalitarian force that would benefit both individuals and the city. "Make [it] the property of the people—open the doors to all—let the children of the rich and the poor take their seats together, and know of no distinction save that of industry, good conduct, and intellect," wrote someone, possibly Harris, in a response to critics of the plan.[39]

In its earliest years, the Free Academy functioned as an amalgam of high school, college, and vocational school. The average age of entering students was fourteen, and all were male—women were not admitted to City College until 1951, instead attending what would become Hunter College. Initially, students were drawn from the city's middle-class English, Irish, and German families, including its German Jewish population; in 1890, roughly one-quarter of graduates had Jewish surnames. But the mass immigration of Jews to New York around the turn of the twentieth century in response to oppression in Russia and Eastern Europe changed the character of the city's immigrant population and City College as well. By 1910, 70 percent of graduates were Jewish, mostly Eastern European. The outsize role of Jews at City College during the first half of the twentieth century—Jewish enrollment did not fall below three-quarters until the 1950s—is not a mystery. Jewish immigrants of the era were poor, and City College was free. The attraction of a college education as a path to assimilation and opportunity was strong, and during this period Jews went to college at two to three times the rate of non-Jewish Americans. Quotas discriminating against Jews at private institutions, along with their high tuition, meant that a disproportionate number of New York's immigrant Jews found themselves at City College.

The influx of immigrants supported the creation of additional campuses, all funded largely by New York City's taxpayers, and enrollment grew quickly even as admissions standards rose. This was free college for high-performing poor students who lacked other options. The strategy paid off for the institution, at least until the 1960s. In his 1994 history of City College, James Traub notes that between 1920 and 1970, more of its graduates went on to receive PhDs than those of any other college except for UC Berkeley, even though City College had no graduate program of its own, no research infrastructure, and "not even a very distinguished faculty."[40] The City University of New York (CUNY) system, created in 1961 through the merging of these various public colleges, became known as "the poor man's Harvard," counting thirteen Nobel Prize winners and twenty-six MacArthur "genius grant" awardees among its alumni.[41] More important, for many of its students, it accelerated the process of social mobility; as Traub writes, "It compressed into a few years a process that otherwise took a few generations."[42]

A second great migration in the mid-twentieth century brought a new round of changes to New York City and its publicly funded colleges. Between 1940 and 1960, the city's Black population rose from 450,000 to 1.1 million as Southern Blacks came North, while the Puerto Rican population grew from 70,000 to 720,000. The percentage of the city's population accounted for by these two groups rose from 6 percent to 25 percent in the span of two decades. The rapidly expanding Black and Latino populations were also poor but, unlike earlier immigrant groups, they could not access City College. Part of the reason was the dire condition of New York City's public school system that failed at the time to teach many of its graduates the basic skills needed for college. But another problem was the increasingly strict merit-based admissions criteria in place at City College. While the campus was located in the middle of Harlem, the spiritual home of Black America, in the 1960s probably only 2 percent of the college's population was Black.[43]

As in California, demographic change and the growing demand for a college education strained capacity and increased costs to taxpayers. CUNY responded by implementing instructional fees for some of its programs, while keeping the senior colleges tuition free. Admissions standards continued to rise, and by 1965, only students with high school GPAs of A-minus were able to gain entry.[44] Racial conflict intensified as the civil rights movement gained steam, and protests by Black and Puerto Rican students closed the campus for several weeks in 1969. Under fire from students and activists, the CUNY system adopted an open-admissions policy in 1970. The move to open admissions was, on its surface, the only possible response to what had become an intolerable degree of racial inequality; however, it also represented the culmination of deeper trends: the nation's century-long movement toward mass higher education, New York City's changing demographics, a growing sense of obligation toward the city's poor Black residents, and CUNY's own institutional growth imperative.[45] The new admissions standards led to a sudden increase in enrollment, which jumped by 55 percent between 1969 and 1975, and greater diversity. It also put the institution on a path to resembling other open-admission institutions in terms of low completion rates and a growing need for remediation for students coming from underfunded schools that had not adequately prepared them for success. City College still played an important role in social mobility; CUNY sociologists Paul Attewell and David E. Lavin, for example, found positive long-term effects for the children of women who attended City College after it became an open-admissions institution.[46] Still, its character had changed—no longer was City College the place ambitious, poor New Yorkers went to climb the income ladder. Instead, it became home to low-income students at all levels of ability seeking a path out of poverty.

Free college in California and New York foundered on fiscal crisis. In California, the fiscal crisis was created by the taxpayer revolt of the 1970s as voters opted to reverse a century of investment in education. In New York, the reasons were more structural. Middle-class flight from the city led to declining tax revenues, all in the context of the energy crisis and "stagflation" plaguing the larger US economy. In 1976, the city's near bankruptcy led to a federal bailout, the terms of which included drastic cuts in city services. Tuition-free education was among the casualties. CUNY's budget was cut by one-third; dozens of nontenured faculty members, many of whom taught remedial courses, were laid off; and the whole system shut down for a short time. While the institution remained open to all graduates of the city's high schools, criteria for admission to the most desirable colleges were tightened and the 125-year-old tradition of free tuition was ended. The path to decline was different in each case: California met a growing demand for education by expanding support until the cost of maintaining the system grew too high. New York City initially rationed supply until concerns about inequality overrode other priorities, leading the system to expand and quality to fall.

Why do these stories matter for today's free-college movement? Just as states and localities are seeking ways to become more economically competitive and provide greater opportunity to their citizens, so did California and New York rely on tuition-free college to meet their economic and political needs. Decisions about the structure of these opportunities determined who would benefit and who would be left out. Notably, California and New York both provided aid to their low-income students on a first-dollar basis (see chapter 2)—that is, before other grants were applied. This is a beneficial strategy for closing opportunity gaps, but it is expensive and has rarely been replicated within the current Promise landscape. Both systems foundered on rising costs and a breakdown in the political alliances that underpinned their creation. In both cases, it became clear that in the eye of a budget crisis, support for higher education is quick to land on the chopping block; budget analyst Harold A. Hovey has labeled this pattern the "balance wheel" in describing how states fund higher education in good economic times and cut funding when the economy is in trouble.[47] This history provides a warning as states and localities seek secure funding to guarantee longevity for their Promise programs. Funding streams that rely on annual budgeting are more vulnerable than those either embedded in the tax code or secured through existing funding mechanisms, such as lottery proceeds.

The differences between the California and New York experiments also raise an important issue for those who advocate nationwide tuition-free college. As we will see in the book's final chapter, a key challenge for tuition-free college at the national scale is overcoming existing differences in higher-education funding and structure among states. Currently, there are fifty different "systems" of higher education—in truth, more, because some states, including my home state of Michigan, lack any overarching state system. The question of how these systems can be treated equitably under a nationwide free-college initiative has barely been asked, let alone answered.[48]

While there are lessons to be learned from history, today's free-college debate comes with one huge caveat: the population of college goers today is vastly larger and more diverse than it was when college was last free.

POLITICS TODAY

Large-scale political and economic forces are driving today's free-college programs, especially at the state level, just as they did in California. In Tennessee, a Republican governor and legislature enacted the first universal, statewide scholarship program, the Tennessee Promise, in 2014 amid concern about the state's economic competitiveness. The Tennessee Promise and its companion Tennessee Reconnect program for adults without college degrees were embedded in a statewide post-secondary educational attainment goal. The scaling up of the Tennessee Promise from an earlier local program happened with support from the state's business community, and the program itself is designed to prepare workers for the twenty-first century economy, with scholarships restricted to technical certificates, diplomas, and two-year degrees.

In New York State, the Excelsior Scholarship, a tuition-free college program advocated by Governor Andrew Cuomo was billed quite differently—as a boon to middle-class families. Provisions of the Excelsior Scholarship, such as the requirement that students attend full-time and a cap on family income of $125,000 for receipt of the scholarship, targeted benefits toward students who are struggling with college prices but do not have access to federal need-based aid. The inclusion of public four-year options in this program further suggests that it is motivated less by immediate workforce concerns and more by ensuring that middle-income students have access to the college wage premium—the added increment of earnings that accrues to workers with degrees or credentials. Unfortunately, the program also includes a requirement that students must work in the state after graduation or repay their scholarship—a provision that has led to confusion and slowed uptake.

On the West Coast, in California and Washington, statewide Promise programs have focused more on equity. California's AB 19 created the California College Promise Grant (formerly known as the Board of Governors Fee Waiver) to allow low-income students and other designated groups to attend community college free of tuition and fees. The Washington College Grant program, passed in 2019, creates a uniquely generous first-dollar scholarship (applied before other forms of grant aid) for low- and middle-income students, with funding coming from business taxes on the two largest corporations headquartered in the state, Amazon and Microsoft.

Other statewide Promise programs run the gamut in terms of who they serve, but all are products of local political and economic forces. In Rhode Island, the Democratic governor who championed the Rhode Island Promise had to drop its four-year component in the face of opposition from a solidly Democratic legislature over cost concerns. In West Virginia, students accessing free community college are required to take a drug test before each semester, a provision seemingly unrelated to education but important to conservative legislators in the context of the state's opioid crisis. In Michigan, a Republican-controlled legislature deeply at odds with the state's Democratic governor nonetheless supported Michigan Reconnect, the governor's plan to allow adults without a college degree to attend community college tuition free. This support is rooted in concerns about workforce readiness in a state that lags the national average in terms of postsecondary attainment. In Arkansas, Kentucky, and Virginia, legislators have been willing to support Promise programs only for students majoring in high-demand fields.

The reasons and implications of these policy choices will be discussed later in this book, but for now, the message is simply that every Promise program is forged in a specific time and place, and the design choices made along the way shape program outcomes, distributional benefits, and likely longevity.

This is true at the local level as well. In Kalamazoo, the first-dollar structure created by the anonymous donors behind that community's Promise program has brought major benefits to low-income students, allowing them to retain use of their Pell Grants to cover living expenses, while serving as a catalyst for change in the school district and broader community.[49] This egalitarian model, though, is not the norm. In New Haven, a merit-based program advocated by program funders, including Yale University, serves a much smaller proportion of students enrolled in New Haven schools, but has been valuable to the community as those high-achieving, more highly educated students remain near or return to the community. The initial goal of stakeholders in Pittsburgh was to use their Promise program both as a carrot for improved academic achievement in the struggling Pittsburgh schools as well as a catalyst for local economic development. While the scholarship has helped move the needle on some key indicators of academic success, it has not led to the systems changes envisioned by stakeholders. The largest component of the Detroit Promise—the track that sends students to local community colleges—is designed with the area's workforce needs in mind, a point reflected in the close involvement of the Detroit Regional Chamber, the area's leading business group, in the program's operation.

Political interests and economic conditions are key drivers in the design of today's free-college programs, as they were in an earlier era. The history of high school expansion, higher-education funding, and the University of California and CUNY experiences suggests that as political, demographic, and economic factors change, support for expanding educational opportunity and expectations may change as well. This is an argument for designing and funding Promise programs for political and economic sustainability—a topic addressed in the next chapter.

CHAPTER

2

The Promise Landscape

HOW CAN WE make sense of today's complex landscape of free-college or Promise programs? As I noted in chapter 1, the definitional uncertainty that has accompanied the growth of the free-college movement is problematic if one is trying to compare models or generate usable evidence that might inform future program design. This chapter takes two different approaches to conceptualizing the free-college field. The first focuses on where such programs originate and what they seek to accomplish. The second looks at their structural features.

Throughout, we continue to examine how free-college programs can make good on their potential to transform systems. Promise programs differ from traditional scholarships in a variety of ways, the most important of which is that they seek to create public as well as private value. Historically, college financial aid has been awarded based on the attributes of individuals, whether these relate to financial need, academic merit, or some other measure of ability. The underlying assumption is that the investment represented by the scholarship will pay off for that individual in terms of both college affordability and higher lifetime earnings based on degree completion. Promise programs add a new element to this equation and rest on a different assumption—that is, by investing *at scale* in the postsecondary education of a large proportion of a community's (or state's) youth, and in some cases adults—the payoff will come not just for individuals but for the community or state as a whole. Promise programs most likely to yield these dual benefits—improved outcomes for both individuals and the states and communities in which they live—are rooted in a collective ethos and attract broad buy-in and support from diverse actors. Questions of program design are not just technicalities. Rather, it is these design choices that will determine if a Promise scholarship will produce the kind of alignment needed to drive change.

THE PURPOSE OF PROMISE PROGRAMS

It is hard work to create and maintain a Promise scholarship program, whether that work falls to local stakeholders, community colleges, or state government officials. Most Promise programs emerge from a critical need facing these stakeholders; someone animated the program, bringing the idea to public light, assembling coalitions, procuring funding, and structuring details of implementation. Sorting programs based on who did this work yields a three-part division, with programs that originate from groups of local stakeholders, those created by institutions of higher education, and statewide programs that are usually proposed by governors and funded by legislatures. The critical need driving each type of Promise initiative is different, and it makes sense to consider them separately.

Community-Based Programs

Most of the oldest and best-known Promise scholarship programs emerged from local leaders working together to expand college access for young people in their communities and transform their local economies. The Upjohn Institute, which first conceptualized place-based scholarship programs as a movement, defines them as

> geographically bounded, often along the lines of a school district, although boundaries may be larger, such as a county, or smaller, such as an individual school. Such programs usually include an enrollment and/or residency requirement for length of attendance within the school district or eligible entity. Because of this enrollment requirement, Promise programs function as early awareness programs. Families and children know upon entering a Promise community that scholarship resources will be available to them upon high school graduation. Finally, Promise programs seek to transform places, as well as individuals, and as such require community support from multiple stakeholders representing diverse sectors.[1]

Alignment among these sectors will be stronger if programs are structured to include all or nearly all students (see discussion of universality below).

Promise programs are often found in midsized cities struggling with economic decline. Here, local stakeholders see tuition-free college as a strategy to revitalize their communities. Promise programs are also found in larger cities like Detroit; Long Beach and Oakland, California; and Pittsburgh, and in small towns or rural communities like El Dorado, Arkansas; and Buchanan, Michigan. In all these cases, multiple community-based actors are partners in the design and implementation of the scholarship. Two recent big-city programs that involve key community partners, both launched in 2018, are in Dallas and Los Angeles. The Dallas County Promise is described as "a coalition of school districts, colleges, universities, employers, and communities that have joined forces to help more Dallas County students complete college and begin careers."[2] The Los Angeles College Promise is a partnership among the Los Angeles Community College District, Los Angeles Unified School District, City of Los Angeles, LA Chamber of Commerce, UNITE LA (a collaborative focused on aligning public education and workforce development systems), and private philanthropic organizations seeking to increase the number of community college graduates, university transfer students, and workforce-ready students throughout the Los Angeles region.[3]

Community-based programs have goals that fit into one or more of the following categories:

- Transforming K–12 school districts, often in concert with other education reform efforts, by building a college-going culture and creating broader awareness of the need for and benefits of a postsecondary degree.
- Increasing access to postsecondary credentials and degrees by reducing financial barriers to higher education through the provision of scholarship funding. This goal is also supported by college awareness, readiness, and success programs to help students overcome the nonfinancial barriers to successful postsecondary education.
- Promoting community and economic development by aligning actors throughout the community in support of Promise program goals and use it as leverage to create a more desirable and vital community. This includes slowing or reversing middle-class flight that has led to concentrated poverty in many urban school districts.

While the notion of individual opportunity is embedded in these goals, they go beyond that, seeking to transform systems and create value for the community as a whole. This speaks to the dual value of Promise programs in building assets for both individuals and systems. To accomplish this task, a broadly representative group of stakeholders needs to be at the table. Organizations involved usually include the school district, local postsecondary institutions, youth-supporting nonprofits, municipal or regional government, philanthropic organizations, and the business sector. For these locally based programs, aligning the priorities and resources of these multiple stakeholders is often as big a challenge as raising the necessary funds.

Community-based tuition-free college initiatives are almost always funded by local actors, such as philanthropic entities, businesses, and individuals. Examples include the anonymous donors behind the Kalamazoo Promise; Pittsburgh's largest employer and many of its other businesses and foundations that fund the Pittsburgh Promise; and a single corporation that has underwritten the El Dorado Promise. Many community-based programs have active fund development efforts and dedicated staff to carry them out. Some benefit from a flow of public resources, although few are solely funded by public entities. Examples include Michigan's Promise Zones that blend local, private resources with a dedicated portion of a state tax, and a handful of programs that rely all or in part on municipal financing.

Institution-Based Programs

The population of Promise programs has grown rapidly in recent years because many community colleges have made themselves tuition free, building on preexisting federal and, in some cases, state grant aid. These programs tend to be less expensive and easier to launch than communitywide initiatives, and are generally funded through college foundations that, in turn, rely on a range of philanthropic commitments. Growth in institution-based programs has been especially pronounced in California, where dozens of programs were created in the wake of Assembly Bill 19, passed in 2017, but the model has earlier roots.

The "Educate and Grow" scholarship at Tennessee's Northeast State College was introduced in 2001 to provide incentives for academic achievement, create a well-educated workforce, and encourage local economic development. Over thirteen years, it awarded $2.2 million to fourteen hundred students, wrapping up in 2016 when the Tennessee Promise made it superfluous. School Counts! programs in various states, beginning with two in New Jersey in 2004, required students to achieve certain benchmarks related to attendance, punctuality, attitude, and effort, rewarding them with certificates and, in some cases, tuition-free attendance at their local community college. Ventura College introduced its own Promise in 2006; this one-year scholarship was designed to make it easier for students in the local catchment area, a coastal city north of Los Angeles, to afford community college.

Of course, community colleges in the United States have long played an important role in delivering both societal and individual benefits, serving as regional economic development engines and pathways for upward mobility. Community colleges in several states were tuition free for much of their history, and prices in the sector remain low relative to four-year institutions. In all but a few states, Pell Grants cover tuition, meaning that for low-income students, community college was and remains tuition free. So why have community colleges felt the need to introduce their own Promise programs? There are several reasons, although the diversity of these programs makes it difficult to generalize.

In creating single-institution Promise programs, community colleges are seeking to encourage postsecondary education for students who may not have been on a college-going path and improve the success rate of those already enrolled. To this end, many single-institution programs involve supports to enhance student success around academic and nonacademic needs. The tuition component of these programs is often minimal, as many community college students qualify for some level of need-based aid. (Because Pell Grants have not kept pace with inflation, many low-income students will still struggle to afford fees, textbooks, materials, transportation, and other living expenses.) Even if a "last-dollar" promise—one where the scholarship is awarded after other forms of grant aid—does not bring new financial benefits to low-income students, it can serve as an important vehicle for conveying the message that everyone will benefit from postsecondary education or training. Chuck Wilbur, who leads the Michigan Promise Zones Association, calls this the "Promise wrapper" effect.[4] Even without new money, the promise of tuition-free college, made early and often, can catalyze efforts to enhance academic preparedness, increase awareness of available scholarship resources (such as Pell Grants), and boost FAFSA completion and college enrollment.

Some community colleges are partners in cross-sectoral initiatives that fit better under the community-based category above. For example, Long Beach Community College is a partner in the Long Beach

Promise and collaborates closely with the city, school district, and local four-year university to create a set of higher-education pathways for local youth. This is a qualitatively different kind of endeavor than a single-institution program created by a community college.

Many four-year institutions also offer scholarships to specific groups of students, and some of these are structured to benefit the local community. Ivy League colleges with large endowments have long provided free tuition and sometimes room and board to students from low- to moderate-income families. Most Ivy League institutions cover the full cost of attendance for students from families earning roughly less than median household income and provide tuition-only scholarships for those with incomes up to twice that level. But these are elite institutions that recruit nationally and internationally, and students rarely remain local upon graduation. Of course, these institutions benefit their communities by attracting high-value human capital in the form of faculty and administrators, and in offering relatively high-paying jobs to local residents.

Other four-year programs look more like the community-focused Promise model described above: the University of Michigan, while it continues to court students from out of state and abroad, has developed several full-tuition scholarship programs to recruit high-achieving, low-income students from around the state; one of these is Wolverine Pathways, targeted specifically to low-income school districts adjacent to two University of Michigan campuses.[5] The University of Rochester, a private institution, offers the Rochester Promise, a tuition-free scholarship program for graduates of the local school district. The award requires admission to the university and family incomes less than twice the area average. In the words of the vice provost, one goal of the program is "to ensure that dozens of young Rochester citizens recognize the University of Rochester not only as *one of the nation's best universities*, but also as their *neighborhood college*."[6] Even so, these programs fit awkwardly within the Promise universe not just because the number of students served is small and admission is contingent on both academic performance and financial need, but also because they are driven by institutional rather than community needs. Tuition-free programs offered by community colleges, on the other hand, are centered on institutions that are considered "open admission." And community college graduates tend to stay in the region after degree or credential completion. Such programs thus have very different effects than four-year university-sponsored scholarships and share many features with locally based Promise programs.

State Programs

As word of the Kalamazoo Promise spread, it reached two prominent community members in Knoxville, Tennessee. Randy Boyd, CEO of a pet products conglomerate, dreamed of making Knoxville the most pet-friendly city in the nation. Then Knox county mayor Mike Ragsdale wanted to provide tuition-free college to area residents to strengthen the region's workforce. Together they launched a place-based scholarship program, Knox Achieves, that became the model for the nation's first statewide program, the Tennessee Promise.

The Tennessee Promise, in turn, sparked the creation of new statewide Promise programs in two dozen states. These differed from an earlier model—statewide merit-based scholarship programs, of which the Georgia HOPE Scholarship is the best-known example. Beginning in 1993, Georgia HOPE offered high-achieving students at all income levels the opportunity to attend a public university in the state. The idea spread rapidly, and by 2004, twenty-five states had similar merit-based aid programs.[7] Details varied, but students are usually required to graduate from high school with a 3.0 GPA and enroll directly at an in-state institution where they attend tuition free. Research suggests that merit-based programs, while increasing enrollment, especially at in-state institutions, mainly serve students already on the path to college and preserve long-standing racial and income-based disparities in college attainment.[8]

The Tennessee Promise is different. Designed to support a statewide attainment goal known as the Drive to 55 (referring to the idea that 55 percent of state residents should have a college degree or credential by

2025), the Tennessee Promise is open to any high school graduate without regard to academic achievement or financial need. The program, profiled in chapter 5, is closely tied to Tennessee's workforce needs, supporting students earning two-year degrees and shorter-term certificates. It also enjoys buy-in from the business community, members of which have been enlisted in a statewide mentoring program to promote student success.

By 2019, two dozen states had introduced or passed legislation to create statewide College Promise programs. In a 2018 survey of the field, the Century Foundation found that about half the statewide programs had universal eligibility requirements while the other half based eligibility on some measure of academic merit.[9] Most of the programs covered two-year colleges only, and all but one awarded funds on a last-dollar basis. Several states require scholarship recipients to remain in the state for a given number of years following degree completion—a provision that may increase the economic benefit to the state but that adds confusion and complexity to program rules. Most of these scholarships are available to students at all income levels, although a few have set fairly high income ceilings, and a few that predate the current Promise movement (including Indiana's 21st Century Scholars Program and Oklahoma's Promise) are structured to serve low-income students.

There is tremendous variation in the structure, purpose, and funding of statewide Promise programs, just as there is in the local arena. At one extreme in terms of generosity and flexibility is Washington State's program, signed into law in May 2019. It has several provisions that are unique among statewide Promise programs. In addition to an innovative funding structure (see below), it is flexible, allowing both recent high school graduates and adults without college degrees to attend any in-state higher-education institution and choose any field of study. And it is awarded on a first-dollar basis, before other forms of financial aid, allowing lower-income students to use their need-based assistance for other college-going expenses.

Washington State's program is not universal—technically it is an expansion of the chronically underfunded state need grant—but its income caps are generous, covering full tuition for low-income students and providing some benefit to everyone below the state's median income. In 2019, New Mexico's governor proposed an ambitious program to send all its full-time undergraduates to college for free—a truly universal plan, without income cap or financial need requirement. Last-minute legislative changes meant that for now, the New Mexico Opportunity Scholarship is limited to students (including adults) attending community colleges, but the hope is eventually to cover both two-year and four-year institutions.

At the other end of the spectrum are targeted programs, such as the Arkansas Future Grant that requires recipients to enroll in a STEM or high-demand program of study, participate in mentoring and community service activities while enrolled, remain in the state for three years after graduation, and be employed within six months of degree completion. If these requirements are not met, the scholarship will convert to a loan. Uptake on the grant in its first two years was so low that state lawmakers chose to revise its provisions to make them more flexible.[10] The New York program (profiled in chapter 3) also has a series of requirements that limit its impact, including the requirement that students be enrolled full-time and remain in the state after graduation for the same number of years they receive scholarship funding.

As with local Promise programs, statewide tuition-free initiatives seek to address a range of problems, including college affordability, access, attainment goals, and workforce needs. As they have proliferated, some observers have raised alarm at what they see as regressive funding models that privilege nonpoor students.[11] While it is true that the last-dollar structure of most statewide Promise programs brings limited new financial resources to Pell-eligible students, there is evidence that such programs still benefit them by delivering an early and clear message that a college degree is affordable and inducing them to access already-available financial resources.[12] As a result, more students are brought into the process of applying for financial aid—one result of the Tennessee Promise is that the state now leads the nation in the rate of FAFSA filing.

Statewide programs also vary in their funding sources. Tennessee created a trust from lottery proceeds to fund the program. New Mexico, New York, Oregon, and Rhode Island all fund their Promises through annual budgetary appropriations, making them vulnerable to cutbacks if legislative support or state resources wane—a real possibility in the post-COVID-19 economy. California's Assembly Bill 19 gives community colleges the choice of using state monies to eliminate tuition, while Washington State turned to its two largest employers—Microsoft and Amazon—and with their support enacted a 67 percent increase in the state business and occupation tax to fund free college. The tax applies only to "advanced computing businesses with revenue of more than $100 billion," of which there are exactly two.[13]

These three types of programs—community-based, institution-based, and statewide—constitute the Promise landscape. This conceptualization is not as broad as some, although it embodies a great deal of heterogeneity. Most important, it encompasses programs that seek to go beyond financial aid to institutional and community transformation. We turn now to a second way of understanding the Promise landscape that relates to structural decisions around program design.

THE STRUCTURE OF PROMISE PROGRAMS

A second way to understand the landscape of Promise programs is to look at their structure—more specifically, how they address the three big questions of program design: which students will be eligible for the scholarship, which postsecondary institutions may they attend, and how much funding will be involved. A fourth critical question explored in subsequent chapters is how programs address barriers to college that go beyond its price. It is the answers to these key questions that create incentives for students, families, school administrators, and community members, and it is the behavior of these actors that will determine a program's outcomes.

In part because the Promise movement is so new and the research base so limited, there is no acknowledged best way to craft a Promise program. Program design ranges from an exercise in improvisation, leveraging intuition and politics, to more careful choices informed by a still-limited evidence base. Decisions about program structure are often driven by cost and funder beliefs rather than critical need. Community-based and statewide programs are also shaped by state and local politics. But by sorting programs along these three key structural features, one can assemble groups of like programs that may have similar effects.

Who Benefits?

The first critical design element of a Promise program is which students will qualify for the benefit. To date, eligibility has fallen into three categories.

Universal

Programs without academic merit or financial need requirements can be called "universal," although they are not truly available to everyone because they almost always entail a minimum enrollment and residency requirement. Some community-based programs require that students spend at least four years of high school in a specific school district to receive any level of benefit, with a sliding scale allocating larger scholarships to those who have been enrolled for a longer period. The Kalamazoo Promise and El Dorado Promise, for example, both provide 65 percent coverage of tuition and fees for graduates who have spent four years in the district and 100 percent of tuition and fees for those who have spent the entire K–12 period, with a sliding scale in between.

Sliding scales are designed to reward long-term attachment to a school district or community, but they add complexity to messaging, and longer residency requirements can disadvantage low-income students who tend to move more often than higher-income students. The Pittsburgh Promise in 2018 eliminated its sliding scale, replacing it with a simpler four-year residency and enrollment requirement. Some Promise programs have opted for shorter residency requirements; for example, the Detroit Promise requires that students reside and attend school within the city for two years to qualify for its community college scholarship. And most statewide programs ask only that a student be a state resident, although a few require graduates to remain in the state for a given number of years after completing their degree.

Academic requirements

A second approach to eligibility involves applying a marker of academic success, usually high school GPA and sometimes attendance. This is based on the rationale that for students to succeed in college, they must be academically prepared and have strong "soft skills," especially regarding attendance. This approach is backed by research showing that a certain level of high school academic achievement predicts college persistence and success.[14] Some Promise programs also use academic requirements as incentives for higher achievement and better behavior, although recent research suggests this is not a particularly effective tool.[15] Of course, it is difficult to know precisely where the cutoff should be, and there is limited research to suggest the ideal level. The typical merit-based program might require a high school GPA of 2.5, although several programs have set the bar higher at 3.0, making these local programs indistinguishable from earlier statewide merit programs, while others have chosen a seemingly random 2.3. Many programs with GPA requirements also have attendance rate policies (often 90 percent high school attendance), and there may be additional requirements such as community service. A few programs, the Pittsburgh Promise among them, provide a bridge or extension program for students who fall just below the cutoff, enabling them to demonstrate their success in community college and then transition to four-year scholarship eligibility. GPA minimums work to the disadvantage of lower-income students who tend to have lower academic achievement levels, but they will quite naturally increase a program's success rate once students are in college because the population receiving the scholarship is better prepared academically for the college experience.

The 192 programs in the Upjohn Institute's database as of August 2020 were divided as follows between those with universal eligibility and those with academic requirements: 109 of the programs had no academic or other merit requirements, while 82 conditioned receipt of the scholarship on some type of academic success.

Financial requirements

While financial need is the determinant of eligibility for federal Pell Grants and plays a role in some statewide programs, it has had less relevance in the place-based scholarship movement. About one-fifth of Promise programs in the Upjohn database require some evidence of economic need, such as being available only to students who are economically disadvantaged or who are first-generation college goers. A handful of programs, including the Denver Scholarship Foundation, combine both financial need and minimum academic requirements in awarding scholarships.

In their first decade, Promise programs focused on recent high school graduates (although the Kalamazoo Promise's ten-year time frame for usage—an atypical feature—allowed young adults to take advantage of it). More recently, states and localities have experimented with Promise programs for adults without college degrees. More than one-third of college students are age twenty-five or older, and adults make up an even higher percentage of the community college population.[16] The adult component of the Tennessee Promise, called Tennessee Reconnect, recognized the need to support adult learners, particularly in the context of the state's workforce development goals. Several other states, including Washington and New Mexico, have extended their Promise benefits to adults, and another group of states is experimenting with pilot programs to serve adults in higher education.[17]

What Are the Postsecondary Options?

The second critical design question—and the one with the greatest impact on cost—is which postsecondary institutions a Promise program will cover. There is tremendous variation on this question. Some programs allow students a wide range of postsecondary options, while others limit attendance to a single community college. This second category is growing. While they used to represent about half the programs in the Upjohn Institute database, single-institution programs now constitute two-thirds of them, or 129 of 192. Many programs fall between these extremes by, for example, restricting attendance to a select group of local institutions, in-state institutions, or public institutions only. For example, the Kalamazoo Promise allows students to attend one of fifty-nine public and private colleges and universities within Michigan, while the Detroit Promise provides support for students at one of six regional community colleges and almost all the state's four-year colleges and universities. Most statewide programs limit scholarship use to two-year institutions, with a few notable exceptions in New York (the Excelsior Scholarship) and Washington State.

Ideally, the decision about which postsecondary institutions to include will be driven by the critical need to which a program is designed to respond. Offering a greater range of choices provides larger incentives for students and families, and offering four-year options may be essential for communities seeking to attract new residents. Limiting attendance to two-year institutions, especially local institutions, can be an effective strategy for building the local workforce, since students who attend a local community college will be more likely to remain in the community after graduation. In practice, however, Promise program decisions about eligible postsecondary institutions are often driven by cost considerations. Two-year programs that are awarded on a last-dollar basis (see next section) can be very low cost when a school district enrolls a high proportion of economically disadvantaged students, since Pell Grants will cover the tuition prices at community college in most states. Programs with a small number of postsecondary choices also limit students' ability to find the right fit for higher education—a determinant of future persistence and success. And they can drive students on the margin—those who could succeed in a four-year setting but choose a two-year institution because of a Promise scholarship—to settings where completion rates are lower, thus possibly hurting a student's likelihood of degree attainment.

How Much Funding Is Involved?

The final key question in the design of a Promise program is how much funding is provided and for what purposes (e.g., tuition and fees only, room and board, or other living expenses). Most Promise programs cover only tuition and fees, although a few allow students to cover the full cost of attendance or provide a stipend for textbook purchases or other nontuition expenses.

Some Promise scholarship programs commit to covering the full cost of tuition and mandatory fees, whatever that amount may be, at any eligible institution to which a student can gain admission; the Kalamazoo Promise is one example. Other programs provide a fixed annual amount; the Pittsburgh Promise is an example of this approach, although the amount offered has changed as the program has evolved. All programs are limited in terms of the number of credits, type of degree, and/or number of years of study they will cover. Almost no Promise programs cover graduate study.

Another critical attribute is whether a scholarship is awarded on a first-dollar or last-dollar basis—that is, before or after other forms of grant aid. The Tennessee Promise, for example, guarantees free community college tuition after Pell Grants are calculated, which makes it less inexpensive and hence politically more feasible. Only a handful of Promise programs, including the Kalamazoo Promise and the El Dorado Promise, are structured as first-dollar programs. Programs like the Pittsburgh Promise that are last-dollar but cover the full cost of attendance (tuition and fees, plus room and board) function similarly to first-dollar programs in that most students will receive the maximum scholarship. And several statewide programs are piloting last-dollar-plus models or basic needs grants that provide additional funds to students whose tuition is already covered by Pell Grants.

The three questions discussed above interact to create scholarship programs that have very different types of effects. To capture their impact, the Upjohn Institute created two measures—"intensity" and "saturation"—for inclusion in its database.[18] Intensity refers to the size of the incentive created by the scholarship program, while saturation refers to the proportion of a community's students that are likely to be eligible for the scholarship. (A colloquial way to think about the difference is that intensity measures the size of the carrot while saturation reflects how many students will be receiving those carrots.) Together, intensity and saturation will determine not only the expected magnitude of impacts but also the extent to which impacts are likely to be felt broadly across the student population.

As the Promise movement has evolved, new efforts have been made to define and categorize the programs it includes. University of Pennsylvania researchers Laura Perna and Elaine Leigh locate place-based scholarship programs as one category within a larger movement and use a statistical technique called cluster analysis to identify similar programs.[19] The College Promise initiative takes an even broader approach, including in its definition many programs that enable students to attend college tuition free, such as dual-enrollment initiatives. From a research perspective, lack of clarity around the Promise term can create confusion. If scholars believe they are investigating the same topic but are actually studying different things, their findings will be less valuable to the field. It is also hard to reach conclusions about the relative effectiveness of different types of program structures without clear definitions.

Is it possible to make a judgment call about what constitutes an ideal Promise program or, put more bluntly, are some Promise scholarship programs better than others? This is the wrong question. To begin with, it is impossible to answer in the absence of a discussion of resources; first-dollar programs are always preferable to last-dollar programs but are rarely affordable. Beyond that consideration, communities have different needs, and the diversity of Promise program design reflects this variation in local dynamics. A program that limits scholarships to the children of homeowners might make sense in a city that is trying to increase its home ownership rate, while it would have little point elsewhere. Communities seeking to promote postsecondary access for low-income youth would be ill-advised to include strict academic, residency, or minimum credit requirements as they reduce participation by the very population the program is trying to serve. Stakeholders hoping to revitalize a public school district will want to limit funding to graduates of that district and not include those who attend the area's private or charter schools. And adding a high minimum GPA requirement to a scholarship that only allows recipients to attend a community college is a recipe for undermatching.

In short, whether a program is effective or not will depend on stakeholder goals and how well the program's design is tailored to meet them. The Promise universe contains examples of strong and weak program design, and there is plenty of room for more research to better understand how design decisions affect outcomes and impact.

THE DIFFUSION OF THE PROMISE IDEA

There is one more piece of the puzzle when it comes to understanding the Promise movement. Reportedly, when the anonymous donors behind the Kalamazoo Promise introduced it in 2005, it never occurred to them that other communities might want to emulate their idea. Yet, just a few years later, dozens of communities had enacted their own place-based scholarships. How did the Promise idea spread? The following account provides insight into not just the mechanisms through which expanding groups of stakeholders adopted the place-based scholarship model, but also how both good and bad design principles have been enshrined in practice and then perpetuated.

The political science literature is rich with stories of policy diffusion where an innovative idea introduced in a single community spreads from place to place, ultimately finding its way into state or even national policy. Tuition-free college is a prime example. Everett

M. Rogers, a leading scholar of policy diffusion, identifies four elements in the process, all of which are relevant to the Promise movement.[20] First is the notion of *innovation*—policies most likely to diffuse are those that represent truly new ideas or practices. The innovation in this case is the idea of bounding a scholarship by place rather than by student characteristics. This was a new approach, and it attracted national attention when introduced in Kalamazoo in 2005. Second is the role played by *communication systems*—how is the new idea transmitted from one individual or group to another? Mass media is the most rapid means of informing potential adopters about the existence of an innovation, but interpersonal communication is also important. Both played a role in the initial spread of the Promise idea, with national media outlets covering the Kalamazoo Promise and other early programs, and leaders in other communities learning about them, reaching out, and forming networks across communities. A third ingredient is the *social system* involved—who facilitates the diffusion process? The Promise model touches on multiple social systems, including community development practitioners, educators, philanthropy and business leaders, and other advocates interested in questions of college access and financial aid. All these constituencies have played a role in diffusing the Promise idea through various conferences, publications, and online communications. Finally, there needs to be *time for the innovation to spread* from awareness to adoption. Rogers was writing before the era of internet communications and social media; these tools have been essential in creating communities of practice and sharing of information about Promise programs across geographically distant places. They have also dramatically sped up the process of policy diffusion.

From its introduction in Kalamazoo in 2005, the place-based scholarship model and the idea that tuition-free access to college can transform communities and educational systems has diffused broadly. Using the narrower of the definitions presented at the beginning of the chapter, the Promise movement now includes about two hundred local- and institution-based programs located in more than half the states in the nation. Statewide initiatives can now be found in more than twenty states. What may be most striking is that rapid growth has occurred without any central direction, leadership, or funding. In recent years, the College Promise initiative has come to serve as an umbrella for tuition-free college programs, but the Promise landscape remains a prime example of bottom-up innovation, with local actors seizing on a concept and adapting it to their own needs.

How has this process of adoption and adaptation played out? Political scientists Charles Shipan and Craig Volden identify four distinct mechanisms of policy diffusion: learning, competition, imitation or emulation, and coercion.[21] The primary dynamic behind the diffusion of tuition-free college programs to date has been emulation, although learning has become increasingly important as the evidence base for Promise programs has grown. And there is certainly an element of competition, especially at the state level, as a growing number of states devise programs to expand access to and through postsecondary education.

One of the advantages of the Promise idea when it comes to diffusion is its simplicity. Rogers has noted that "many adopters want to participate actively in customizing an innovation to fit their unique situation" and argues that an innovation diffuses more rapidly, and its adoption is more likely to be sustained, when it lends itself to reinvention. The place-based scholarship model is uniquely appealing in this regard. The premise is simple: cities and states can simultaneously provide young people with greater opportunity while making themselves more attractive to residents and businesses. This basic formula lends itself to endless adaptation and variation, as communities and states explore how to leverage their assets to meet their needs. It is no surprise that the idea has spread quickly over a relatively short time, now framed in an even more appealing way through the shorthand of "free college."

It is, on the other hand, surprising that such widespread policy diffusion has occurred in the absence of strong evidence about impact. There is clearly high demand to find alternatives to the debt-laden path to college affecting so many families, and policy makers may simply be responding to this need. But why is so little known about the effects of Promise programs a full fifteen years after the launch of the Kalamazoo Promise? For one thing, the impacts of Promise programs are generally slow to materialize. While some indicators, such as school district or college enrollment, may get a quick boost from the announcement of a place-based scholarship, other potential outcomes, such as higher incomes for scholarship recipients or population change for a city or state are truly long-term outcomes, requiring a decade or more to detect. Another reason is that while large sums of money have been spent on Promise programs, research and evaluation efforts have received only limited attention and funding. Most of the research into the outcomes of Promise programs has been supported with philanthropic resources that take time to procure and that generally focus on only a small part of the movement. Individual Promise programs, often strapped for funds, have rarely invested in robust evaluation components that could yield not just insight into outcomes, but information needed to refine and improve programs themselves. Even when resources are available, it is sometimes difficult to obtain the data needed to uncover causal relationships between Promise programs and their outcomes. Finally, the heterogeneity of program design and difficulty of generalizing about results across communities have hindered the research effort. All this has meant that new Promise programs continue to be created without access to a solid base of research or best practices, with stakeholders driven by instinct and hope, rather than data and evidence.

Much of the learning that has taken place about the Promise idea, design considerations, and research-based outcomes has occurred at PromiseNet, an almost-annual convening of stakeholders engaged in Promise work. The story of PromiseNet illustrates the strengths and weaknesses of the Promise enterprise as embodying both tremendous grassroots energy and extreme heterogeneity.

For those of us engaged in work related to the Kalamazoo Promise, it had become clear by the fall of 2007 that something needed to be done. The tiny staff of the Kalamazoo Promise (then numbering two), the slightly larger group of individuals engaged in Promise research at the Kalamazoo-based Upjohn Institute, and the overstretched administrators of the Kalamazoo Public Schools were spending far too much of their time meeting and speaking with visitors to the community who were eager to learn about the Kalamazoo Promise. In December of that year, the Upjohn Institute convened representatives from a handful of Promise programs, including those in Pittsburgh, Denver, and Washington State, to discuss how information about the Promise idea could be shared more efficiently. The group decided to host a meeting six months later, inviting the people with whom they had been in contact over the preceding year or two. Expectations were that a few dozen people would travel to Kalamazoo in June 2008 for a two-day learning and networking opportunity, but when the first PromiseNet meeting was held, more than two hundred people from thirty states attended. Nine more conferences took place over the next decade, with conferences in Denver; Pittsburgh; New Haven; Washington, DC; and Berkeley, as well as four more in Kalamazoo. Through these repeated meetings, Promise stakeholders have come together to share their experiences and knowledge, to network, and to learn from each other.

Perhaps the most intriguing aspect of PromiseNet is that no one is in charge of it. There is no PromiseNet organization, no office, no staff, and no funding. Communities step forward and assume a leadership role focused on hosting, with volunteers representing multiple communities planning the content. The PromiseNet web address migrates from server to server depending on the host organization. There have been sporadic efforts to link Promise communities more closely, but these have generally not been successful. The main reason seems to be the intensely local focus of the Promise movement and resource constraints, with stakeholders preferring to remain focused on the success of their programs rather than on building a national network.

Yet despite this decentralized structure, PromiseNet has helped build networks and propel collective knowledge. The work of College Promise has accelerated this process, providing a point of contact for aspiring Promise communities and creating new, more formalized networks among researchers and others. The Campaign for Free College

Tuition, another advocacy and networking organization, focuses its efforts on sharing best practices among states interested in tuition-free college. Regional organizations have also been influential. The Upjohn Institute, a nonpartisan research institute with which I am affiliated, has since 2006 carried out rigorous research into the impacts of the Kalamazoo Promise and other place-based scholarships, advised other communities on the cost and design of planned Promise programs, and promoted collaborative research spanning multiple Promise communities. WestEd, a San Francisco–based research, development, and services nonprofit with expertise in education, has carved out a coordinating role related to California's rapidly expanding population of Promise programs, many of them launched by the state's community colleges. PennAHEAD is a university-based research entity that supports a rising generation of academic researchers and coordinates closely with the College Promise initiative. MDRC, a social policy research organization headquartered in New York City, provides technical support to communities through its College Promise Success Initiative and shares best practices around student support strategies with the Promise movement more broadly.

While more emphasis on learning in the Promise field would be welcome, the heterogeneity of program structure and definitional disagreements make this difficult, as lessons learned in one setting are not necessarily applicable in a different context. Much of the rigorous research into program outcomes has focused on the older and more generous initiatives—usually those with four-year options for students—whereas much of the action in the growth of the Promise field is in institution-based programs or those that offer exclusively two-year options. Thus, lessons learned to date are of only limited relevance, and a much larger and more differentiated research effort is required for learning to truly take place.

Why do we need more learning? If Promise programs continue to be created in a vacuum, with limited understanding of the connection between design and outcomes, the Promise movement will surely disappoint. The same is true if planning is driven more by resource constraints and political exigencies than by underlying needs. Good program design must begin with a clear understanding of critical need: what is a locality, community college, or state seeking to accomplish with the introduction of a Promise program? Promoting college access and success, ensuring greater equity of outcomes, or successfully meeting workforce needs each require different approaches to program design and implementation.

Research is also essential to promote the understanding of Promise programs as qualitatively different from traditional scholarships. While it may be defensible in narrow cost-benefit terms to dedicate scarce resources to low-income students with the potential to succeed in college—an alternative that has been advocated by some critics of the Promise model—tuition-free college made available to a broader group of students seeks not just to help individuals but also to create value for people other than scholarship recipients. So, for example, a systems change in a K–12 school district to create a more robust college-going culture will help all the students enrolled in that district. Innovative supports at the postsecondary level can help nontraditional college goers complete degrees and credentials. Free-tuition programs can catalyze political buy-in across a community—or even a state, as we will see in chapter 5—to increase economic vitality through the creation of a better-trained workforce. It is this emphasis on transformation and the joining of individual and collective priorities that sets Promise programs apart from traditional financial aid.

Place-based scholarships seek not just to help students get to and through college. They are also designed to transform the systems that serve those students and improve the communities in which they live. For many local Promise programs, the motivation for making college tuition free is as much about community revitalization as it is about college access. And because most local Promise programs are based in poor communities or school districts, access to higher education for low-income students and students of color—in other words, their impact on equity—is a natural preoccupation and programmatic focus. For state

Promise programs, postsecondary attainment and workforce concerns play an important role, but statewide programs are also designed to lift the burden of rising tuition from at least a portion of the population. The next three chapters address these motivations behind the Promise movement: affordability, equity, and employment. All of these embody the public and private dimensions discussed above. These motivations are, of course, intertwined, but if we are to understand how best to design a Promise program, we must examine them separately.

CHAPTER

3

Affordability

NOTHING HAS MOTIVATED the free-college movement more than rapidly rising college prices and burgeoning student loan debt. College prices have long outpaced inflation, yet serious discussion of reducing them is a recent phenomenon. Why now? One reason is the changing economy. A college degree or credential has become a key to success in the twenty-first century economy, and demand for college has risen accordingly. At the same time, wage stagnation and an inexorable climb in tuition have placed that valuable commodity out of reach for many, with the impact falling heavily on low-income students and people of color.

Promise programs represent one strategy for addressing college affordability and student loan debt. In this chapter we first examine the data around the price of higher education. We then consider the question of how Promise programs can help with affordability and assess whether they are achieving this goal.

THE PRICE OF COLLEGE

Measuring college affordability is harder than it seems. To begin with, affordability is not the same thing as cost. Prices charged to students and families capture only a portion of the true cost of providing a degree or certificate, and that portion has risen over time as state and federal funding of higher education has failed to keep pace with rising expenses. The value of a college education still far outweighs what people pay for it: on average, holders of bachelor's degrees will earn at least half a million dollars more than high school graduates over their lifetimes.[1] For associate degrees and certificates, the returns are lower but still positive. But the prospect of higher lifetime earnings is not what drives decisions about whether or not to pursue a degree or credential. It is, rather, the price that students and families are being asked to pay.[2] And these prices are difficult to measure.

It is widely understood that attending college incurs expenses beyond tuition. Mandatory fees, books, transportation, and, of course, living expenses all figure into what students will need. Federal law requires colleges to publish numbers for the overall cost of attendance, and while these may be accurate for a student paying for on-campus room and board, such calculations are more difficult when that is not the case. A study carried out by the Wisconsin HOPE Lab (which is now the Hope Center for College, Community, and Justice at Temple University) found that published estimates of living expenses can, in fact, be far off base.[3] Forty-one percent of the four-year colleges included in the study reported a cost of living that was at least 20 percent above or below the actual cost of living in the county where the college was located.[4] The authors fault vague federal rules as contributing to this problem. When published estimates are too low, students often find they are short of funds. When estimates are too high, students may take out more loans than they need.[5] And incorrect estimates contribute to confusion about the real price of college, an information gap that has been shown to shape students' postsecondary choices.[6]

The issue of financial aid also complicates the task of measurement. If aid levels are rising in line with prices, the high price of college is less problematic than it would be otherwise. Of course, aid affects students at various income levels in different ways; even if financial aid in the aggregate is keeping pace with rising prices, which it is not, many students will still be left behind. Another drawback of the current financial aid regime is that students do not find out how much aid they will receive until quite late in the game—sometimes just weeks before starting college. One big advantage of Promise programs is that they send an early message about college affordability by guaranteeing tuition coverage for eligible students.

There are several types of postsecondary institutions, and prices range widely among them. Most reporting sources, including the College Board data presented in figure 3.1, distinguishes among private four-year institutions, public four-year institutions, and public two-year institutions, but even within these sectors, there are large variations. (Private, for-profit institutions are generally not included in the College Board reporting.) Sometimes institutions with higher sticker prices can actually be cheaper to attend than those with lower published prices. An extreme example is found at the nation's most selective institutions where full-ride scholarships covering tuition, room, and board are offered to students from families with household incomes below the nation's median.

Keeping these measurement challenges in mind, we can look at tuition rates over time at these three types of institutions to get a sense of rising sticker prices. In figure 3.1, we see tuition and fees rising for all three classification categories, with the steepest rise and highest prices in the private nonprofit sector.

To show the rate of increase in tuition and fees for these three types of institutions, the College Board uses an indexed approach, with the index set at 1 for 1988–1989 (see figure 3.2). Even the lowest-priced sector—public, two-year colleges—has seen a doubling of tuition over twenty years, while the price has tripled at public, four-year colleges.

FIGURE 3.1 Published tuition and fees in 2019 dollars, 1989–2019

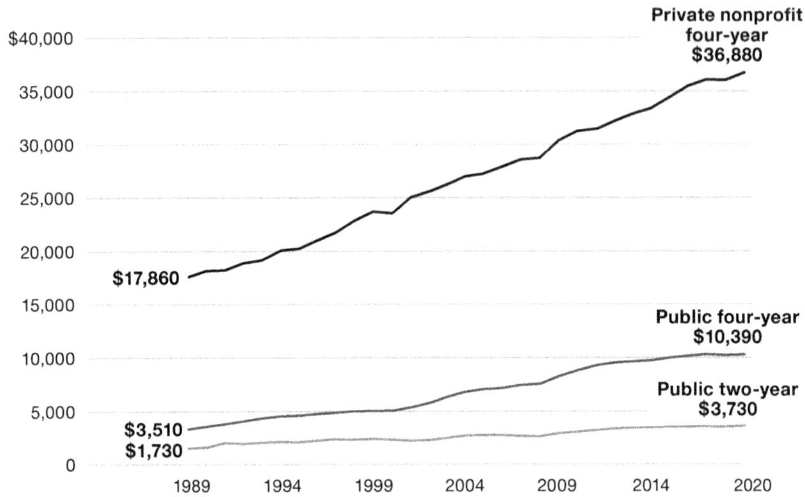

*Currency in 2019 dollars

Source: Trends in College Pricing. Copyright © 2019. Figure 3. The College Board. www.collegeboard.org.

FIGURE 3.2 Inflation-adjusted published tuition and fees, with 1989–90 set at index of 1

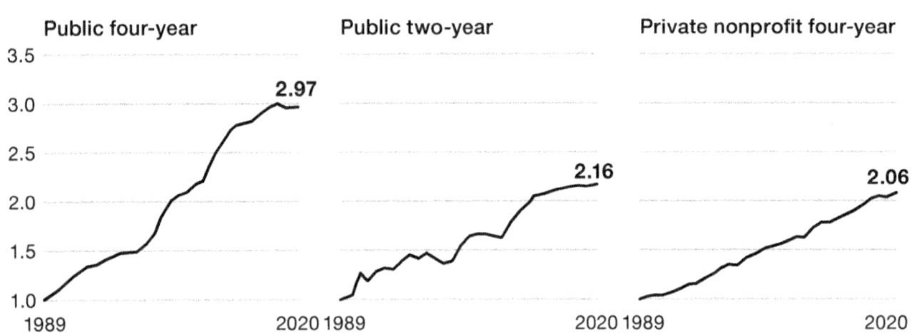

Source: Trends in College Pricing. Copyright © 2019. Figure 48. The College Board. www.collegeboard.org.

College Board data also provide some answers to the important question of whether financial aid is tracking rising prices. Every year, the organization publishes net price information, both for tuition and fees, and for a broader category that also includes room and board. The net price is what students pay after receiving grant aid, primarily Pell Grants but also institutional aid. This calculation also sometimes includes tax credits and deductions available for educational expenses.

Figures 3.3, 3.4, and 3.5 show changes in net prices at the three types of institutions. The figures tell three different stories about how well financial aid is keeping up. (Note that the scale of the three figures is different.) The dotted line represents net price; a flat line shows prices remaining constant. If the dotted line slopes upward, the price for students has been rising. These figures present averages, and what individual students receive will vary in line with their circumstances.

In figure 3.3, we see that while published prices at private institutions have risen dramatically over the past twenty years, aid has almost kept up, with net prices for both tuition and fees and for the full cost of attendance rising only modestly.

FIGURE 3.3 Net prices at private, nonprofit four-year institutions

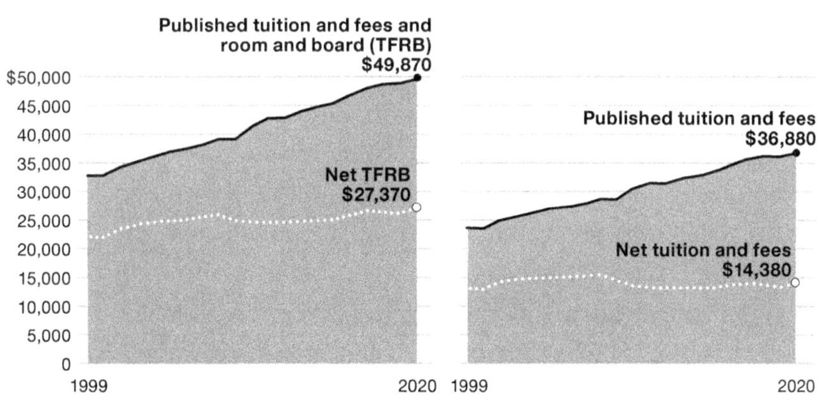

Source: Trends in College Pricing. Copyright © 2019. Figure 10. The College Board. www.collegeboard.org.

FIGURE 3.4 Net prices at public four-year institutions

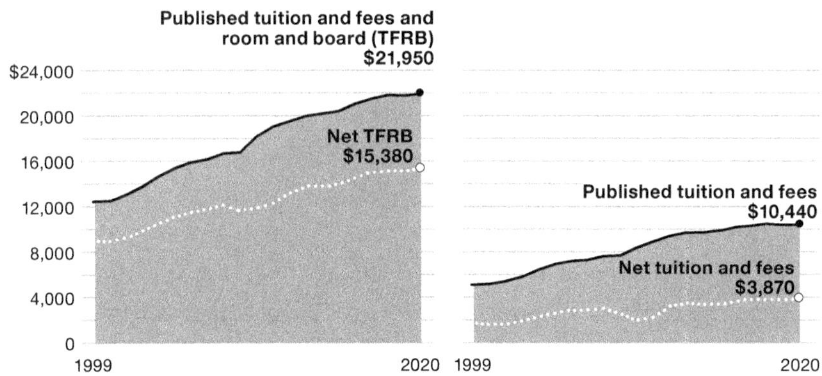

Source: Trends in College Pricing. Copyright © 2019. Figure 9. The College Board. www.collegeboard.org.

Figure 3.4, covering the all-important public, four-year sector, shows net prices for the full cost of college (tuition, fees, room, and board) almost doubling, suggesting that aid levels are falling short.

Figure 3.5, covering public two-year colleges, shows financial aid basically keeping pace with increases in published rates both for tuition and fees as well as for room and board. The lowest line—the net price of tuition and fees—dips below zero, suggesting that aid provides more than enough resources to cover tuition, leaving students, on average, with some excess resources after tuition bills are paid.

These three figures show net prices well below sticker prices at all three types of institutions, but still rising in the four-year sector. Only in the public, two-year sector is the cost of attendance on a net basis as low as it was twenty years ago.

The College Board's methodology and its presentation of data have been the subject of some criticism. There is little to argue with in the reporting of published tuition rates, but calculating the full price of college, as well as the adequacy of aid, is less objective. In June 2019, a group of fourteen Democratic senators, including four of whom were

FIGURE 3.5 Net prices at public two-year institutions

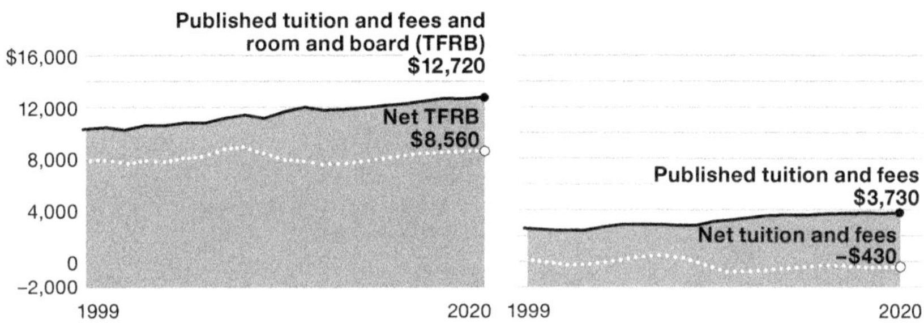

Source: Trends in College Pricing. Copyright © 2019. Figure 8. The College Board. www.collegeboard.org.

presidential candidates at the time, criticized the College Board's calculation methods for nontuition costs.[7]

Still, the diverging picture painted by this net price data suggests that concerns about college prices are felt most acutely by students attending four-year public institutions—many of them middle class and ineligible for federal grant aid. In this category, the share of the cost of attendance covered by Pell Grants has been declining since the 1970s. Figure 3.6 shows that forty years ago, Pell Grants covered around three-quarters of the full cost of attending a public, four-year institution, whereas by 2019, they covered less than one-third. This shift has been driven both by rising prices and by stagnation in the rate of increase for Pell Grants, which are not indexed to inflation. Changes made in the 2016 to 2019 period, in which the maximum Pell Grant rose from $5,815 to $6,195, did little to redress this underlying mismatch between college prices and grant aid availability.

By whatever measure, the price of attending college has risen relentlessly over the past two decades or more. Financial aid, on average, has generally kept pace with tuition increases at public, two-year institutions, but has fallen short of accommodating rising living expenses—a key barrier for low-income students. Middle-income families who must

FIGURE 3.6 **Share of attendance costs covered by maximum Pell Grant award**

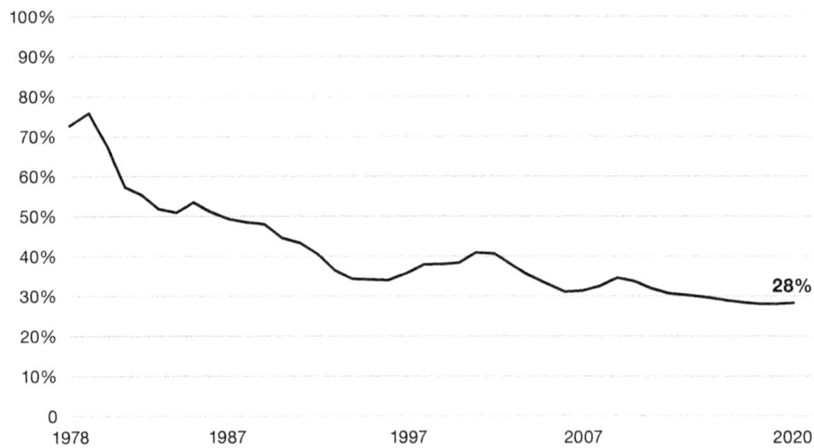

Source: CBPP bases on college pricing data from College Board.

rely on loans rather than grants to meet rising tuition are also among those struggling the most with college costs.

These two problems—the declining affordability of a college degree for middle-class students and the declining value of the Pell Grant for low-income students—are not always disentangled in discussions of college prices. Taken together, they mean that higher education is less attainable for large swaths of the population, damaging both individuals' economic prospects and the vitality of the broader economy. But the two problems have different impacts, and strategies to address them look different. For the low-income population, an increase in the value of Pell Grants is a key strategy. For the middle-income population, different strategies are needed, and Promise programs can fill some of this gap.

WHAT'S BEHIND RISING COSTS?

Explanations for the rising price of college are contested, and like so much in society today, the argument runs largely along partisan lines.

Those on the left identify cutbacks in state aid for higher education and the failure of Pell Grants to match rising tuition, while those on the right focus on administrative expenses and a race to the top around amenities designed to attract students. While all three factors have contributed to the problem, a serious review of the evidence shows declining state aid is the key driver of higher tuition.

Declining State Aid

As discussed in chapter 1, the higher-education sector has been nurtured by state funding from its earliest days. Even after recession-related cutbacks, states (and, to some degree, localities) still contribute more than half the costs of teaching and instruction at public colleges and universities. With a role this large, reductions in state support inevitably squeeze the operation of these institutions.[8]

We have already encountered the story of declining state support for public education in California. In that case, funding cutbacks were due largely to political dynamics in favor of lower property taxes. But trends in the macroeconomy are often the cause of changes in state support for higher education. The Great Recession of 2008 is the most recent example. A series of reports from the Center on Budget and Policy Priorities demonstrates the degree to which state support for public education fell following the recession. This research also shows that, even a decade later, in almost all states, funding had failed to return to prerecession levels.[9]

The combination of reduced funding and rising enrollment (the number of full-time equivalent students rose by 8 percent in the eight years after the recession) put colleges and universities in a bind. The solution, if one can call it that, was to cut academic resources and student services but, more importantly, to raise tuition. In the ten years after the 2008 recession, annual published tuition rates at four-year public colleges rose by 35 percent, with increases of more than 60 percent in a handful of states. In Louisiana, tuition doubled.[10]

One corollary of the reduction in state funding is that the balance between federal and state support for higher education has shifted.

Historically, states provided much more funding to higher education than the federal government—65 percent more, on average, in the 1987 to 2012 period. State budget cutbacks, coupled with the growth in Pell Grants (the chief form through which the federal government supports higher ed) as enrollments increased, mean that state and federal contributions are about equal for the first time in many years.[11]

And, of course, the balance between state funding and tuition has shifted as well. Data from the State Higher Education Executive Officers Association show that in 2008, state support amounted to $8,512 per full-time equivalent (FTE) student, compared to average tuition paid of $4,712 (with numbers adjusted for inflation). By 2018, states were contributing $7,853, while tuition accounted for $6,788 per FTE.[12]

Financial aid practices at private colleges and some flagship public universities have also contributed to rising tuition. We have already learned of the failure of Pell Grants to keep pace with tuition increases, and an opaque and confusing financial aid process itself disadvantages low-income students. One other issue worth mention is tuition discounting—the practice of offering a select group of students a price that differs from an institution's published, or "sticker," price, a system that resembles the differential pricing found in airline ticketing. This has meant that sticker prices, especially at private colleges, have risen to stratospheric heights. Most students do not, in fact, pay these prices, yet they serve as a deterrent that keeps many low- and moderate-income students from even applying. Overall, they serve to complicate the narrative around college prices, and for those who do not have the social capital to navigate this complex landscape, they can screen students out.

Colleges offer discounts for a variety of reasons. They may want to encourage high-performing students to attend, thereby raising the institution's academic profile, or they may be trying to increase the diversity of their student population. These discounts are not scholarships—rather, they are reductions in the tuition actually charged a student, delivered through institutional need-based or merit-based aid.[13] The practice is especially widespread at private colleges. The National Association of College and University Business Officers has tracked tuition discounts at private, independent colleges for almost twenty-five years. Its most recent report found that while published tuition rates had increased by 46.9 percent between 2008 and 2018, the price actually paid by incoming freshmen at these institutions had risen by only 18.4 percent. Over 90 percent of incoming freshmen at private, independent colleges received some form of financial aid from the institution they attended, and across the sector, discount rates were around 50 percent.[14] Students are highly sensitive to these discounts and other marketing initiatives, both of which may serve to shift their choice of college.

With tuition discounting, institutions can continue to raise their rates and charge full tuition to some students while offering discounts to others. Some private institutions have become tired of the game and have opted to reduce both tuition and discount rates in a process known as a tuition reset.[15] But the ability to publicize one set of rates while actually charging lower rates overall is another factor behind rising sticker prices.

Administrative Budgets

Critics who focus on burgeoning administrative budgets as drivers of higher college prices have a point. There is no doubt that administrative spending has risen at all types of postsecondary institutions, as has the number of administrators. A 2017 article in *Forbes* cited the following statistics: in 1980–1981, administrative spending comprised 26 percent of total educational spending by American colleges, while instructional spending comprised 41 percent. Three decades later, the two categories were almost even, with administrative spending making up 24 percent of schools' total expenditures and instructional spending accounting for 29 percent.[16] And while it is difficult to find accurate numbers, the Delta Cost Project found that the number of full-time faculty and staff has declined relative to the number of administrators at almost every type of postsecondary institution.[17]

The more interesting question is why administrative budgets have grown so fast. Some of the increase has been driven by federal and state regulations with which higher-ed institutions must comply.[18] My own university employs administrators focused on health compliance, research compliance, grants compliance, Title IX compliance, and Americans with Disabilities Act (ADA) compliance, along with a legal staff, grants and contracts specialists, and an "enterprise risk manager." Changes in the nature of the student population also require new forms of administrative support. Colleges and universities seeking to create student bodies that more closely match society may invest in resources to support students with disabilities, hire equity and inclusion officers to ensure that nontraditional students feel welcome on campus, create new resources for first-generation college goers, and develop on-campus centers or programs that provide affinity groups for specific populations, such as LGBTQ+, Black, Latino, or Asian students. Colleges and universities also invest in tutoring centers, health centers, counseling centers, and career centers to meet student needs and promote degree completion. Technological change and the advent of remote learning even prepandemic has also led to high costs related to expanding information technology resources. Robert Kelchen has shown that most of the increase in higher-ed administration has come not at the top in the form of highly paid deans and assistant deans, but among lower-level student and academic affairs staff members charged with activities such as advising.[19]

Amenities

A third factor behind tuition inflation is investments in amenities designed to attract students. Some observers have called this trend an arms race, a "battle between universities to attract potential students with the shiniest facilities, the most exotic study abroad programs, the widest variety of *a cappella* groups."[20] While investments in amenities do indeed help attract new students—a growing challenge as demographic trends shrink the pool of high school graduates—they also require more staff and higher budgets. Criticism over amenities spending does not come just from conservative sources. In 2015, Senator Elizabeth Warren critiqued the trend in a speech to the American Federation of Teachers, saying, "Some colleges have doubled down in a competition for students that involves fancy dorms, high-end student centers, climbing walls and lazy rivers—paying for those amenities with still higher tuition and fees."[21]

While real, it is important to put amenities spending in context. As the eligible college-going population contracts and tuition rises, it becomes increasingly difficult for all but the highest-profile institutions to attract students. Acceptance rates at most Ivy League institutions may be in the single digits, but overall college enrollment is in decline, and institutions must compete on multiple fronts.[22] Universities without large endowments seek to attract a greater share of this shrinking pie not with costly scholarships but with relatively inexpensive investments in the physical environment. There is a role for athletics spending here as well. Athletics programs and all they require are costly, but it has been argued that they increase the visibility of institutions and thus help their enrollment.[23]

Of these three explanations, data analyses such as one carried out in 2015 by the public policy organization Demos show that cutbacks in state funding are the main culprit for increased prices.[24] There is a tight correlation between reduced levels of state support for higher-education institutions and higher tuition rates. The result has been a shift in the burden of paying for an education at a state university from the state to the individual. The scale of spending on administrators and amenities is simply not large enough to have driven this change, although it has certainly contributed.

Cutbacks in state funding have affected public higher-education institutions more acutely than private institutions because of their relative reliance on public monies. Some states also offer grants or loans that can be used at private institutions, and these, too, have been cut. The level of state funding for higher education is both a political and an economic decision. In the years following the 2008 recession, almost every state demonstrated a preference for balancing state budgets through spending cuts rather than tax increases. And even as the nation's economy recovered, funding for higher education failed to return to prerecession levels in most places.[25]

It has been especially difficult to restore funding in states where legislatures are controlled by Republicans, as almost two-thirds of them are.[26] In Michigan, a Democratic governor was elected in 2018 in part on the promise of increasing spending on education, but her budgetary plans ran up against a Republican-dominated legislature intent on keeping revenues flat. In the governor's 2019–2020 budget proposal, a nominal increase in higher-education funding was approved, but when adjusted for inflation, state funding for public universities had actually declined 12 percent in nine years.[27] As of 2018, only three states—Hawaii, Wyoming, and North Dakota—had increased spending on higher education over 2008 levels, with California's spending holding steady. In the other forty-six states, spending remains below prerecession levels, in some cases, dramatically below.[28] And the COVID-19 pandemic's effects on state finances will undoubtedly compound this problem.

Some state legislatures have sought to moderate the increase in college prices through the use of tuition caps—mandated ceilings on the rate of tuition increase. Caps can take the form of flat-dollar amounts or year-to-year percentage increases. A typical cap might look like Michigan's, where the 2017–2018 budget limited universities to no more than a 3.8 percent increase (or $475) in tuition and fees in order to receive state performance funding dollars. An important caveat is that tuition caps affect only tuition and mandatory fees, leaving the door open for price increases through other avenues, such as increases in room and board.[29]

In 2018, seventeen states either had enacted or were considering tuition caps for at least one postsecondary sector.[30] Some states have frozen tuition rates for their public institutions. In a state with decentralized tuition-setting authority and low levels of state funding (Michigan is a prime example), tuition caps can backfire, which explains why individual colleges and universities regularly violate them—if a proposed tuition increase will bring in more tuition dollars than the institution receives in state performance funding, breaking the rule will benefit the school's bottom line.[31] An academic study of the impact of several tuition-restraint strategies showed that tuition caps work best in states where tuition-setting authority is centralized.[32]

How do Promise programs fit into this landscape of rising prices and declining state aid to higher education?

PROMISE PROGRAMS AND COLLEGE AFFORDABILITY

Promise programs make college more affordable, but they do so in an unusual manner—by circumventing tuition prices through scholarships granted to a designated group of students. Which students benefit and by how much will depend on the program design choices discussed in chapter 2. The question, then, is not *whether* Promise programs make college affordable, but *for whom* do individual Promise programs reduce costs.

It should be noted that the college affordability discussion around Promise programs is really a discussion about public colleges and universities. Almost no statewide Promise programs and only a handful of local programs include private institutions among their eligible destinations, and when private colleges are included, the amount of money available is more of a gesture than a real step toward affordability. No Promise program covers the full price of private college, although some (such as the El Dorado Promise) will allow students to take the maximum public tuition amount to any institution of their choosing, while others (such as the Kalamazoo Promise and the four-year track of the Detroit Promise) have worked out agreements with a set of private institutions to grant scholarships from their own funds to eligible students.

So, with a focus on public institutions, we can now examine which decisions matter most for understanding the impact of Promise programs on affordability.

While the maximum amount of the scholarship is obviously important when it comes to improving affordability, equally important is the form the scholarship takes. One aspect of this is whether it is a fixed amount or if its value rises as tuition increases. Promise programs that commit to covering tuition and fees, whatever they may be, will be highly effective in protecting recipients from rising prices. A program that offers students a fixed-dollar scholarship may have a meaningful impact on college costs today but will lose purchasing power over time. It also makes the message to students and families less powerful—a young student or a family with low financial literacy can far more easily understand the idea that college will be tuition free than they can assess the impact of, say, a $5,000 scholarship some years in the future.

A second important aspect of affordability is what a Promise scholarship will pay for. Most programs limit scholarship use to tuition and fees, although a few cover the full cost of attendance and a handful of others provide additional allowances for books and other expenses. This question interacts with the first- versus last-dollar distinction described in chapter 2. Promise programs that allow low-income students to use their Pell Grants first, then add Promise dollars on top, will make a bigger dent in rising college prices than those that use the Promise to close any financing gap once Pell Grants are applied. Last-dollar scholarships that cover only tuition and fees will be very helpful to middle-income students who do not have access to Pell Grants; however, they will bring little or no new money to low-income students whose costs will be largely covered by Pell. The next chapter explores ways in which last-dollar programs benefit low-income students even if they do not provide them with funding.

A third important issue concerns student eligibility. Scholarships that are awarded based on some measure of academic achievement (usually high school GPA and/or attendance) will be of value for students who meet these criteria; however, they will reach a smaller proportion of the population than universal-eligibility programs. This is the idea captured in the Upjohn Institute's saturation index described in chapter 2. While such programs enhance college affordability for some, others in the same school district, city, or state will be left out of the price-reduction mechanism altogether.

Finally, there is the question of income limits on Promise scholarships. These are designed either to focus benefits on low-income students or to prevent affluent students from receiving funds they presumably do not need. Income limits are found in both statewide and local programs; of the programs included in the Upjohn Institute database, roughly 20 percent, or about 40 of 192, have an income requirement or its equivalent. Most community-based Promise programs eschew income ceilings because they are located in communities or school districts with high poverty rates. In such a setting, there is a trade-off worth making: a few higher-income students may benefit from the scholarship, but not many, because of the makeup of the school district. In exchange, the Promise program is able to offer benefits to everyone, simplifying the free-college message and broadening community support. In some cases, stakeholders avoid income limits because they hope to use their Promise program to retain middle-income families in a school district or draw them to a city. For statewide programs, all students in the state are eligible, meaning that benefits are not restricted to lower-income school districts; hence, income ceilings are sometimes added, as they have been in New York, Washington State, and at times in Oregon.

How successful have Promise programs been in addressing the issue of college affordability? Drawing general conclusions is neither realistic nor helpful. The design decisions embedded in specific free-college programs determine who benefits and in what ways. These distributional questions are not widely understood and are best illustrated by exploring the details of specific Promise programs.

The remainder of this chapter is devoted to analyzing four Promise programs that have college affordability among their goals. We look at two local programs—the El Dorado (Arkansas) Promise and the Pittsburgh Promise—and two statewide programs—the Oregon Promise and New York State's Excelsior Scholarship—to illustrate the relationship between program design and its impact on college prices.

Community-Based Programs: El Dorado Promise and Pittsburgh Promise

The El Dorado Promise and the Pittsburgh Promise, the provisions of which are summarized in table 3.1, are both among the earliest

TABLE 3.1 Characteristics of selected community-based Promise programs

	EL DORADO PROMISE	PITTSBURGH PROMISE
Date established	2007	2008
Student eligibility	Graduates of El Dorado High School who have attended for at least four years (scholarship amount prorated for length of attendance).	Graduates of Pittsburgh Public Schools who have attended and resided in the city for at least four years. Students must have a cumulative high-school GPA of 2.0 and a 90 percent attendance rate.
Eligible postsecondary institutions	Any accredited public or private college or university in the United States.	Any accredited higher education institution in Pennsylvania; students with GPAs of 2.0–2.49 must start at local community college and, if successful, may transition to full benefits.
Structure of scholarship	First dollar (awarded before other forms of grant aid) up to maximum in-state public university tuition; sliding scale related to length of attendance; covers tuition and mandatory fees only.	Last dollar (awarded after other forms of grant aid) up to $5,000 a year for up to four years; covers full cost of attendance.
Funding	Philanthropic contribution from Murphy Oil Corporation.	Businesses and foundations, with original challenge grant from University of Pittsburgh Medical Center (UPMC).
Duration	In place for current kindergarten class; no end date announced.	In place for current kindergarten class; no end date announced.

programs to follow in the wake of the Kalamazoo Promise. Both also have strong affordability impacts. Beyond that, they vary in important ways. A comparison of the two offers a window into the key approaches to student eligibility that characterize the Promise movement—whether all students are eligible, or whether students must meet a defined measure of academic success to receive the scholarship. Community-based Promise programs are divided roughly between these two approaches, while institution-based and statewide programs are more likely to have universal eligibility.

The origins of the El Dorado Promise illustrate the idiosyncratic mechanisms of policy diffusion discussed in chapter 2. In the spring of 2006, a member of El Dorado's business community shared a *Wall Street*

Journal article about the Kalamazoo Promise with colleagues at a meeting of the town's industrial council. This was just a few months after the Kalamazoo program had been announced, and while no results had been reported yet, the business leaders were excited by the idea. They approached the area's largest employer, Murphy Oil Corporation, a longtime supporter of education in the community.[33] Its CEO, Claiborne Deming, sent a team to Kalamazoo to learn more. The El Dorado Promise was launched in January 2007 with a $50 million gift from Murphy Oil. Modeled closely on the Kalamazoo Promise, its terms are the most generous of any Promise program.

El Dorado is a small town in southern Arkansas, located only twenty minutes from the Louisiana border. Its roots are in oil—El Dorado was at the center of the region's oil boom in the 1920s and by 1930 was the wealthiest town in America.[34] Today it is the headquarters of the Arkansas Oil and Gas Commission, along with natural resource industries based in oil, chemicals, and timber. The population of around eighteen thousand is served by a school district of just over four thousand students, around two-thirds of whom are economically disadvantaged. The district is demographically diverse, with a student population that is 48 percent Black, 37 percent white, and 10 percent Latino.

The funders of the El Dorado Promise share the same goals as those of other Promise programs—helping students access higher education, strengthening the school district, and transforming the economy. There is evidence that all these goals are being met. Rigorous research into the impact of the program has found positive achievement effects in the K–12 setting and significant increases in both college going and degree attainment.[35] The impacts became evident almost immediately; in 2006, the year before the Promise was announced, around 60 percent of El Dorado graduates attended college. In 2007, the first year that funding was available, that rate had jumped to about 80 percent.[36] Today, 84 percent of Promise-eligible graduates go on to higher education, compared to a statewide rate of just 50 percent.

Possibly the most significant impact from the standpoint of the funders has been a boost to local economic development. Beginning with the passage of a local sales tax in 2007 (renewed in 2015), with proceeds to be used for downtown development, and continuing through the creation of an award-winning downtown arts district and music festival, the El Dorado Promise has served as a foundation for community transformation on many levels.[37] In May 2020, in the midst of the COVID-19 pandemic, Murphy Oil Corporation announced it would be moving its headquarters to Houston. The company has confirmed that funding for the El Dorado Promise will continue, but the loss of the town's major corporate leader is undeniably a blow from a broader economic development standpoint.[38]

College affordability has been strongly enhanced by the El Dorado Promise. Its first-dollar structure, an unusual provision, has a big impact on affordability, as does the commitment to cover in-state public tuition and fees as they increase. Because students receive their Promise scholarships first, those who qualify for Pell Grants retain use of those resources to help cover living expenses. This has made it more affordable for low-income students to attend college. The program is also uniquely flexible, allowing students to use their scholarships—capped at the maximum public in-state tuition rate—at any accredited institution nationwide. This provides a range of choice for students unmatched by any other Promise program. In practice, most recipients stay in Arkansas, with four institutions accounting for more than half of Promise recipients; about 20 percent go out of state, a rate similar to that before the Promise.[39] In 2013, a decision was made to offer the scholarship to any student who attends El Dorado schools, whether or not they live within the district boundaries. This is a rare approach for a community-based Promise program, most of which require both enrollment and in-district residency as a condition for the scholarship.

The generosity and flexibility of the El Dorado Promise has paid off when it comes to college enrollment and completion. A recent study found that the El Dorado Promise led to an 11.4 percentage point increase in postsecondary enrollment and a 10.7 percentage point increase in bachelor's degree completion (there was no change in associate's degree completion). Students of color and students with below-average GPAs saw the biggest gains in college enrollment, while students of color and students with above-average GPAs saw the biggest gains in bachelor's completion.[40] These results are similar in magnitude and direction to those of the Kalamazoo Promise, which is not surprising given the close similarities between the two programs. (The Kalamazoo Promise is discussed in detail in chapter 4.)

The Pittsburgh Promise has taken a different approach to affordability. It is less flexible than the El Dorado Promise, but it has some uniquely generous provisions and has benefited from a series of programmatic changes designed to better serve students. The Pittsburgh program was also announced in 2007, although in this case the funding was not yet in hand. The program's advocates—initially the mayor and the school superintendent, and later the city's largest employer, the University of Pittsburgh Medical Center (UPMC), that contributed $10 million and then an additional $90 million challenge grant to anchor the program—wanted to use the scholarship as an incentive for higher academic achievement. To this end, they limited scholarship recipients to students graduating from Pittsburgh Public Schools with GPAs of 2.5 or above and attendance rates of 90 percent. There was a brief phase-in period over the program's first few years with eligibility criteria stepping up to this level. At the same time, program stakeholders recognized that some students with the potential to succeed in a postsecondary setting would be left behind by these requirements, so they created the Promise Extension Program for students with GPAs between 2.0 and 2.49; these students can use their scholarships to attend the local community college and, if successful, become eligible for the full scholarship.

Over the years, the Pittsburgh Promise has revised its terms in several ways. Some of these changes were required to accommodate available financial resources, while others were designed to better serve the district's students. The maximum annual amount of the Pittsburgh Promise scholarship has been reduced twice (in 2015 and 2018) from a high of $10,000 to its current level of $5,000 a year. At the same time, what the scholarship can be used for has been broadened, with students able to apply it not just to tuition and fees but to the full cost of attendance. While the Pittsburgh Promise has a last-dollar structure, it covers the full cost of attendance, making it function more like a first-dollar program with most eligible students able to claim the full amount of the scholarship.

In 2018, the sliding scale for eligibility that awarded the maximum scholarship amount only to students who had been enrolled in the school district since kindergarten was eliminated and replaced by a flat, four-year high school residency and enrollment requirement—students who meet this are eligible to receive the maximum $5,000 award, while those who enter the district after ninth grade are ineligible for funding. This program change represented a recognition that residency requirements tend to work against lower-income students who experience greater mobility in and out of school districts than higher-income students.[41]

One thing that has not changed are the program's high school GPA and attendance requirements, but the Pittsburgh Promise has created some alternative paths for students who fall short in these areas. In addition to the extension program, the Pittsburgh Promise announced in 2014 that any high school student could use Promise funds for vocational training during their high school years.[42] This initiative has the potential to provide valuable technical certification and work skills for students who might not otherwise meet the program's academic requirements and offers a path to students seeking a less academic form of postsecondary training.

The Pittsburgh Promise has sought to address other aspects of affordability through a series of agreements with some of the state's higher-education institutions that have opted to become "preferred partners." This means they offer Pittsburgh Promise recipients discounted room and board along with proactive, targeted student support resources. Essentially, the Pittsburgh Promise used its bargaining power and bully pulpit as a scholarship provider to leverage additional resources to help students manage their living expenses and increase their likelihood of success.

Research into postsecondary outcomes for Pittsburgh Promise students has shown that as a result of Promise eligibility, Pittsburgh Public School graduates are about 5 percentage points more likely to enroll in college. Much of this increase has been concentrated in the four-year sector where cost constraints were high before the program. The Pittsburgh Promise has increased in-state enrollment, with recipients 10 percentage points more likely to select a Pennsylvania institution. And there have been positive effects on retention, with recipients 4 to 7 percentage points more likely to enroll and persist into a second year of postsecondary education.[43]

How much do these two local programs help with rising tuition prices, and who benefits most? Table 3.2 summarizes the key affordability metrics mentioned above. In El Dorado, benefits are diffused widely because of universal eligibility, while the first-dollar structure is especially helpful to low-income students. In Pittsburgh, benefits are concentrated on higher-achieving students, while the full-cost-of-attendance provision means that students attending four-year institutions generally receive the full amount. Those starting out at a community college also have a greater ability to manage the costs of transferring to a four-year institution. Over the medium term, El

TABLE 3.2 **Affordability metrics for selected community-based Promise programs**

	EL DORADO PROMISE	PITTSBURGH PROMISE
Maximum annual award (as of 2020)	$10,000–$12,000, depending on number of credits taken	$5,000
Type of award	Covers tuition and fees as they increase	Fixed amount
Structure of scholarship	First dollar, covers tuition and fees	Last dollar, covers full cost of attendance
Student eligibility—academic	Universal, with enrollment requirement	Limited by academic requirements with some provisions for other students
Student eligibility—income	None	None

Dorado's commitment to covering tuition and fees, whatever they may be, will have a larger affordability impact than Pittsburgh's fixed-dollar structure that will lose value over time. That being said, neither program is guaranteed to continue beyond the current class of kindergarteners, and the Pittsburgh Promise in particular has faced funding challenges that have called its continuation into question a number of times.

While there are distinctions between the two programs, it is important to recognize that both are at the generous end of the scale of Promise programs, ranking "high" on the Upjohn Institute's Intensity Index that captures the size of the incentive created by the scholarship program. Most Promise programs, especially those based at single two-year institutions, have much less impact on affordability than those with robust four-year attendance options. As Promise program stakeholders consider their various goals, affordability will undoubtedly be among them. Four-year options and first-dollar structures or their equivalent are important components of addressing affordability; however, even programs with these attributes may differ in their impact on students, and a careful assessment of who will benefit should be an integral part of program design efforts.

State Programs: Oregon Promise and Excelsior Scholarship

The differences among local Promise programs are mirrored at the state level, as shown in table 3.3. Of the two programs discussed here, one has a minimum GPA requirement, while the other does not. Oregon has intermittently applied an income ceiling, while New York's is firmly established. In Oregon, this was primarily a cost-saving measure, while in New York it is designed to prevent affluent students from using scholarship funding. A third important difference between the programs discussed here is where students can use their scholarships, a distinction that has a strong impact on college affordability.

The Oregon Promise, launched in fall 2016, was the second of the current wave of statewide Promise programs after the Tennessee Promise (see chapter 5). The two initiatives have similarities as well as some important distinctions. Both restrict scholarship usage to two-year programs,

TABLE 3.3 Characteristics of selected statewide Promise programs

	OREGON PROMISE	EXCELSIOR SCHOLARSHIP (NEW YORK)
Date established	Announced 2015; implemented for Class of 2016.	Announced 2016; implemented for Class of 2017.
Student eligibility	High school graduates with 2.5 GPAs or GED recipients with equivalent scores. Income ceiling in 2017, 2018, and 2020 academic years.	High school graduates or GED recipients who have resided in New York State for one year, with family incomes below $125,000.
Eligible postsecondary institutions	In-state community colleges	New York State public colleges and universities (64 SUNY campuses, 17 CUNY campuses, plus a few others).
Structure of scholarship	Last dollar, for up to four years, tuition only	Last dollar for up to four years; covers tuition and mandatory fees only.
Funding	State budgetary appropriation.	State budgetary appropriations.
Duration	Year-to-year depending on funding	Three-year phase-in funded; future funding depends on state budgets.

mainly community colleges, and both are last-dollar programs, but they take different approaches to the question of student eligibility. In Tennessee, all high school graduates are eligible. In Oregon, students must have resided in the state for at least twelve months and graduate from high school with a cumulative 2.5 GPA. In the program's second and third years, an income ceiling was added, and income limits were tightened further in response to the COVID-19 pandemic. Taken together, these provisions have made the Oregon Promise of greatest benefit to middle-income students. More affluent students are now ineligible, and lower-income students mainly use their Pell Grants to cover community college tuition, although the program offers up to $1,000 in additional support annually for students whose tuition is fully covered by other grants. In addition, high school GPA requirements for Promise eligibility tend to favor higher-achieving (and thus nonpoor) students.

Recent research has shown that the implementation of the Oregon Promise increased two-year college enrollment in the state by roughly 4 to 5 percentage points for the first two cohorts of eligible students.

In the first year, this increase was due largely to reduced enrollment at four-year colleges, although by year two, postsecondary enrollment statewide had increased.[44] Research also bears out the expectation that nonpoor students benefit most from the program. Internal analyses have found that 53 percent of all aid in the program's first year went to students who did not receive a Pell Grant. Only 7.9 percent of first-year funding went to the poorest quintile of students, while the wealthiest quintile received 30.1 percent of projected state resources.[45] By year three, these patterns were well established, with Oregon Promise students less likely to be Pell eligible or first generation than the average community college attendee.[46] As in Tennessee, the Oregon Promise seems to have boosted FAFSA completion rates and brought additional Pell Grants into the state—an important by-product of statewide Promise programs that will be discussed in the next chapter.[47]

With the introduction of the Oregon Promise and its GPA-bounded model, two approaches were now available to states embarking on Promise program design. In 2016, New York added a third option with big implications for college affordability—the inclusion of four-year institutions in the Excelsior Scholarship. New York is also by far the largest state to implement a statewide Promise program, suggesting that such initiatives can be carried out on a large scale.

The Excelsior Scholarship is targeted squarely at middle-class students and their families. It is a last-dollar program, meaning that it brings the greatest benefits to those above the Pell cutoff, and it has an income cap of $125,000 (slightly lower income caps accompanied the program's introduction). These two provisions direct the program's impact toward families with incomes from about one to two times the median—a group that earns too much to qualify for need-based aid but still struggles with college affordability.

The Excelsior Scholarship is very much a part of Governor Andrew Cuomo's emphasis on middle-class issues. (The *New York Times* wrote in 2017 that the governor, who had long espoused liberal issues, such as a higher minimum wage and juvenile justice reform, had "taken a deep plunge into the center of the pool . . . rolling out a 'middle-class agenda' and a 'middle-class recovery act,' promising to address 'middle-class wages,' 'middle-class anxiety' and 'middle-class frustration.'"[48]) In 2018, the governor won reelection to a third term, decisively defeating both a high-profile primary challenger and his Republican opponent. He followed up on his reelection with a "Tax Fairness for the Middle Class" campaign, announced early in 2019, to cut middle-class taxes and permanently enshrine a cap on property taxes. The Excelsior Scholarship is the free-college component of this agenda.

Under the program, students may attend any of the state's two-year or four-year public colleges and universities tuition free after Pell Grants and any other grant aid. A separate provision was offered to assuage supporters of private colleges, with students eligible to receive scholarships of up to $6,000 a year applied toward their tuition. Private colleges, which are required to bear half the cost of the scholarship, must opt into the program, and only about a third of the state's private institutions had done so at the time of this writing.

While free-college advocates welcomed the inclusion of four-year options in the Excelsior Scholarship, some of its provisions were worrisome. Chief among these is the requirement that scholarship recipients must remain in the state for the same number of years for which they receive funding or have their grant converted into a loan. While such a residency requirement is appealing politically, it introduces a major administrative burden, is unrealistic in light of individuals' circumstances such as marriage or job relocation, and cuts against the goal of creating more upward mobility for New York's young people.[49] Most important, it creates complexity in messaging, adding fine print that many recipients will not fully understand and amplifying uncertainty about the real value of the program. This provision, alongside a requirement that students must take a full course load and complete their degrees on time, further disadvantages low-income students and focuses the scholarship's benefits on middle-class students with a greater ability to attend college full-time.

All these stipulations limited uptake of the program in its first few years. In 2017, the state denied 68 percent of the applications it received, with most rejections due to an insufficient number of credits earned. In part as a result, only 3.2 percent of the 633,543 undergraduate students in New York received the scholarship.[50] Because of the size of the state, however, the number of scholarship recipients is still large—there were approximately 22,000 recipients in 2017–2018, with the expectation of 30,000 by 2019–2020. This can be compared to the number of annual recipients in Oregon, which ranged from about 5,500 to 7,000 in its first few years. The governor's office has pointed out that many students in New York State already attend college tuition free through other state grant aid programs or Pell Grants; its estimate is that 53 percent of students attend tuition free.[51] It remains to be seen if any adjustments will be made to the Excelsior Scholarship in light of the limited uptake. The COVID-19 pandemic-induced fiscal crisis also adds pressure to statewide programs reliant on annual budgeting processes. New York State has backed away from an earlier plan for the Excelsior Scholarship's income ceiling to rise from $125,000 to $150,000, and Oregon Promise grants were also subject to cuts as the state confronted a hole in its budget.[52]

For students who can meet the requirements of the Excelsior Scholarship, it represents an effective affordability strategy. The program's credit-hour rules prioritize on-time completion, meaning that if one can adhere to them, a four-year degree can in fact be completed in four years tuition free. There are no data yet available about completion rates, but the Excelsior Scholarship provides a good illustration of how program rules embed (whether intentionally or not) specific priorities and create incentives for certain types of students and not others.

Table 3.4 summarizes the provisions of the Excelsior Scholarship and the Oregon Promise in relation to the affordability metrics outlined above. Neither program has incorporated one of the key findings of more than a decade of observation and research—that simplicity is a critical element of a successful Promise program. Accessing the Oregon Promise involves a cumbersome application process and several additional verification steps (although some of these are being simplified),

TABLE 3.4 Affordability metrics for selected statewide Promise programs

	OREGON PROMISE	EXCELSIOR SCHOLARSHIP
Maximum annual award in 2020	Awards range from $1,000 to $4,005 per year (in 2020–2021) for full-time students, minus a $50 copay per term	$5,500 in 2020–2021
Type of award	Last dollar	Last dollar
Structure of scholarship	Tuition at community colleges in Oregon.	Tuition and fees at public two-year and four-year colleges in New York State
Student eligibility—academic	2.5 GPA	Universal
Student eligibility—income	EFC less than $22,000 (for 2020)	$125,000

while shifting rules around family income have introduced an element of uncertainty that works against clear messaging. The Excelsior Scholarship has a host of requirements that also add complexity and reduce usage; these include the requirement that students already enrolled in college be attending full-time to be eligible (thereby further tilting benefits toward middle-class students) and the provision that students must remain in the state after graduation. In chapter 5, the discussion of the Tennessee Promise will show how simplicity and clear messaging can work to the advantage of statewide programs.

Implicit in the Promise idea is that, by increasing affordability, scholarship programs will also increase degree attainment. There is a growing body of knowledge about the impact of local Promise programs (primarily those with four-year options) on degree attainment, but the statewide movement is still too new for robust findings in this area. It is clear, though, that statewide programs are already incorporating one of the lessons widely acknowledged at the local level—that money alone is not enough to ensure success. Even in Oregon, where scholarship benefits are targeted toward higher-achieving students, program stakeholders recognize that additional student support may be needed for degree completion.[53] New York State, too, may at some point acknowledge that strict eligibility requirements impede uptake and possibly completion. These lessons about student support needs and the efforts that must accompany the provision of scholarship dollars become even more important when we move to the topic covered in the next chapter—how Promise programs can address long-standing equity gaps in college access and success.

Political discourse at the national level (see chapter 6) and innovation around college affordability appears to be driven largely by middle-class concerns about the rising price of college. Middle-class students with family incomes above the Pell cutoff are clearly disadvantaged when it comes to managing college costs. Without access to need-based federal aid, and with family incomes too low to easily manage rising prices, they have turned to borrowing, creating a student loan debt bubble and raising alarm about a full-blown debt crisis. It is not surprising that political leaders at both the state and national levels are responding to a concern of many of their constituents by embracing the free-college idea.

The danger is that policy innovation without a clear understanding of design choices and their impacts can run the fatal flaw of overpromising and underdelivering. The Excelsior Scholarship is one example—when actual recipients of the scholarship in its first few years fell short of projections, the response in the press and the public was distinctly negative.[54] In Oregon, too, financial constraints that led to the imposition of an income ceiling were not well received.[55]

As we will see in the next two chapters, it is not just middle-class concerns that are driving the Promise movement. Other constituencies also see place-based scholarships as avenues through which community needs can be met. Chapter 4 looks at the role of Promise programs in promoting racial and economic equity, while chapter 5 examines how Promise programs can help employers meet the needs of a changing workforce. Whatever their imperfections in reaching these goals, Promise programs are essentially reinventing a system of community support for higher education that collapsed in the United States in the

1970s. It is this idea of college as a public good that runs throughout the Promise movement, whether the immediate rationale is improving the labor market, enhancing racial and economy equity, or making college more affordable.

CHAPTER

4

Equity

IN THE SPRING of 2019, US federal prosecutors charged fifty people in a bribery scheme they dubbed "Operation Varsity Blues." The goal of the scheme was to help affluent parents secure admission for their children to some of the nation's top universities. The parents, several of them high-profile entertainers or financiers, had used their wealth to stack the deck in their children's favor. Working with a college admissions consultant, they helped their children cheat on admissions tests (sometimes without the students' knowledge), obtained falsified diagnoses of disabilities, embellished résumés, faked athletic accomplishments, and bribed university officials and coaches. Payments, which ran to the hundreds of thousands of dollars, were disguised as charitable contributions and funneled to universities through the consultant's nonprofit foundation.[1] Legal consequences, when they came, were minimal, with most sentences falling far short of what prosecutors had recommended.[2]

One impact of the scandal was to open to public scrutiny the secretive world of competitive college admissions. The scheme was especially brazen, and the revelations shocking and sometimes even entertaining, as when parents altered photos to add their children's faces to the bodies of athletes.[3] But the practices bore a striking resemblance to many of those long used by families with financial means to help their children gain admission to the college of their choice. Paying for test preparation and retakes, hiring consultants to help write admissions essays, fostering athletic achievement in high-demand sports, seeking diagnoses of learning disabilities to procure testing accommodations, making donations to universities with the expectation that one's child will be admitted in exchange—practices like these are completely legal and have been used for many years.

The admissions scandal is only the most extreme case of the unlevel playing field on which the educational process unfolds. From lack of access to quality prekindergarten (preK) through underfunded public school systems, to a college application and admission process rife with practices like legacy admissions, low-income students face opportunity gaps at every step of the way.

Community-based Promise programs, most often found in less-advantaged school districts or cities, can help level this playing field. But these programs are not just about creating opportunity for low-income individuals. Rather, they change the systems experienced by these individuals. By sharing with students and families a simple message early on that college is attainable and expected, Promise programs can set in motion school changes that support a college-going culture, enlist community organizations in promoting student success, and provide new financial and support resources for students accessing higher education. In the process, Promise programs help build more equitable systems along the college-going pathway. This is an uphill fight, as the layers of privilege laid bare by the college admissions scandal begin at birth, and educational settings are constrained in their ability to address the root causes of inequality. Yet, the free-college movement represents a new front in equity-oriented educational policy, even if it is not always framed that way.

In this chapter, we look first at the facts surrounding inequality and higher education, then explore how Promise programs can help address these issues. One of these facts is that low-income students, especially those with strong academic records, *already have* tuition-free access to higher education through a combination of Pell Grants, state aid in some places, institutional scholarships, and/or tuition discounts. But there is often little awareness on the part of poor students or their families that these resources exist and limited knowledge of how to access them. This suggests that our current formulation of college as a private good, one that people can readily access to increase their own well-being, is flawed. Promise programs help correct these flaws by creating community or statewide systems of college access that include not just funding but also information and supports delivered early and often. States and communities have the incentive to do so because robust college going and credential or degree attainment across all income and racial groups is in the public interest. This chapter concludes with a look at several Promise programs that have equity goals at their core.

UNEQUAL ACCESS, UNEQUAL OUTCOMES

Inequality in higher education runs along both racial and economic lines. Blacks, Latinos, and Native Americans access and complete college at a lower rate than whites, as do individuals from low-income backgrounds and those who do not have parents with college credentials. Distinguishing between race and socioeconomic status when it comes to opportunity gaps is difficult, as the coincidence of race and poverty means that Black and Latino students are overrepresented among low-income and first-generation college goers. When looking at college access and attainment patterns by income and race, we must recognize that not all students of color are poor and that many poor students are white. At the same time, it is also essential to acknowledge the extra burdens faced by low-income students of color because of the history of racism in America and inequalities embedded deeply within our educational system.

It makes little sense to consider racial and economic disparities in higher education in a vacuum. Gaps in college enrollment and completion are the culmination of unequal resources and outcomes all along the educational continuum, from preK through high school graduation. Recent research suggests that K–12 achievement gaps may be driven more by concentrated poverty than by race, but whatever the balance of these factors, low-income students and students of color are less likely to have high-quality preK experiences than white and middle- or high-income students.[4] They arrive at kindergarten having had more limited exposure to school-valued skills and are more likely to lag in key markers of educational achievement such as third-grade reading scores. By high school graduation, the gaps are even more apparent. As figure 4.1 shows, the national high school graduation rate in 2017–2018 was 85 percent. Asian/Pacific Islander and whites exceeded this rate, with rates of 92 percent and 89 percent, respectively. The rate for Latinos was 81 percent; for Blacks, 79 percent; and for American Indian/Alaskan Natives, 74 percent. Of students from low-income homes, 80 percent graduated from high school.[5]

There is limited rigorous research on how Promise programs affect high school graduation rates, although there is some evidence of impact on K–12 achievement (discussed below). Graduation rates are slow to change, and many factors contribute to a student dropping out. For students who are unsuccessful in high school, the promise of

FIGURE 4.1 High school graduation rates by race and income, 2017–2018

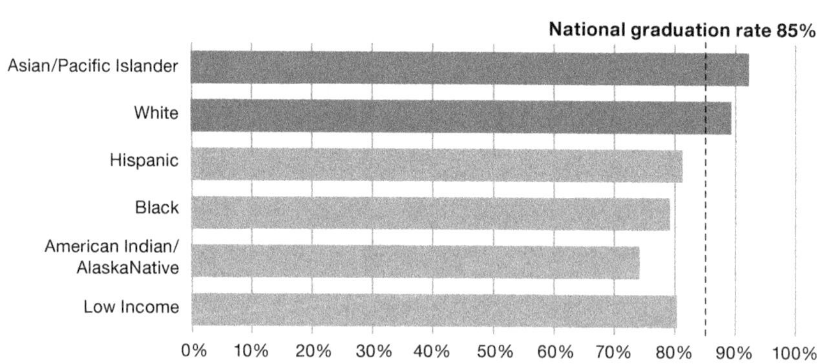

Source: National Center for Education Statistics.

tuition-free college may not be a powerful enough lever to shift their trajectory. This is especially true for scholarship programs that have complex or restrictive eligibility requirements.

Postsecondary Enrollment

Racial and economic gaps in high school completion (and earlier) persist into the postsecondary sphere. Yet there are signs of hope in this picture, with pronounced equity gains in postsecondary enrollment over the past forty years.

In 1976, white students made up 84.3 percent of all students enrolled in degree-granting institutions. By 2017, that percentage had dropped to 56.0 percent (see figure 4.2).[6] The reason is increased enrollment by nonwhite populations, including Asians/Pacific Islanders (where enrollment rose from 1.8 to 7.1 percent), Blacks (9.6 to 13.6 percent), and Latinos (3.6 percent to 18.9 percent), as well as the addition

FIGURE 4.2 **Proportion of college enrollment by race/ethnicity, 1976 and 2017**

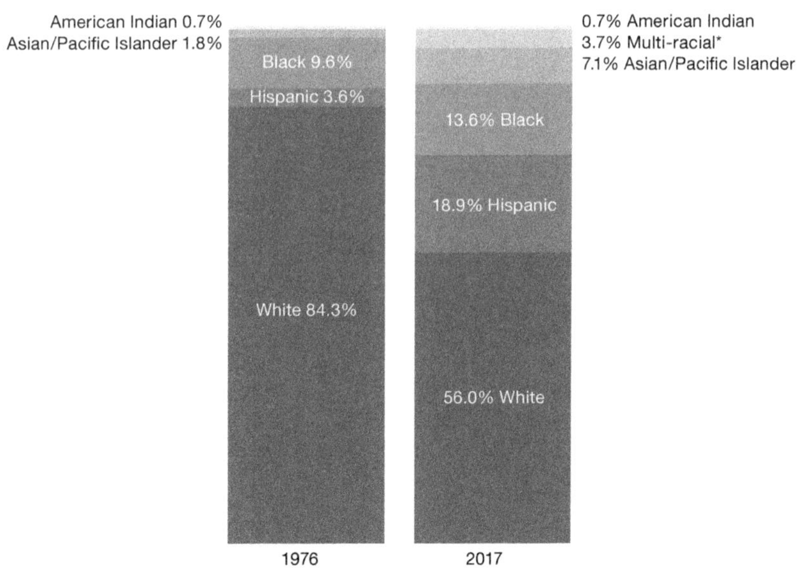

*Multiracial was included as a category in 2010 and later.
Source: National Center for Education Statistics.

of a multiracial category that today accounts for 3.7 percent of enrollees. College enrollment by Blacks and Latinos now almost exactly matches their representation in the general population, although there are still significant disparities in the quality and selectivity of institutions attended by these racial groups, especially when it comes to the level of investment in student support.[7]

Of the 2.9 million students who completed high school or a GED in 2017, 67 percent had enrolled in college by the following October.[8] As figure 4.3 shows, white students slightly exceeded the national average, enrolling at a rate of 69 percent, a few percentage points higher than in 2000. Asian students far exceeded the average, with an immediate college enrollment rate of 87 percent, up from 74 percent in 2003 when data collection began for this population. The most dramatic increase was seen in the Latino population whose immediate enrollment rate rose to 67 percent in 2017 from only 49 percent in 2000. The rate for Black students, 58 percent, showed no discernible change from 2000.[9] This rate is not reported for the American Indian/Alaska Native population, whose overall college enrollment rate is only about 20 percent.[10]

Gaps in immediate college enrollment are also large when disaggregated by income. In 2016, 70 percent of high school completers enrolled in college. As figure 4.4 shows, the enrollment rate was 83 percent for students from high-income families, compared to 64 percent

FIGURE 4.3 College enrollment by race/ethnicity groups, 2000–2017

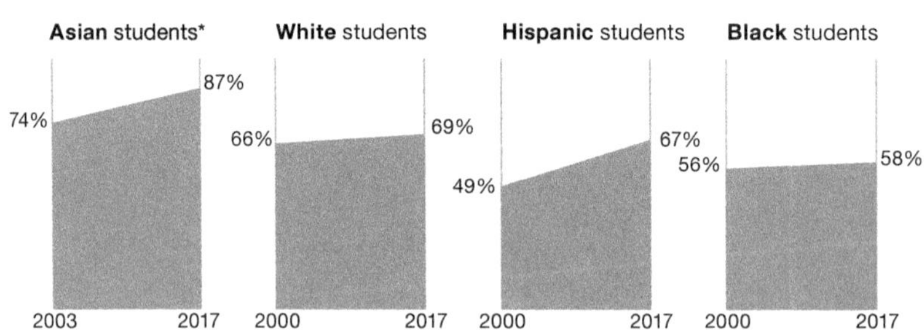

*Data collection began in 2003 for this population.
Source: National Center for Education Statistics.

FIGURE 4.4 College enrollment by income 2000–2016

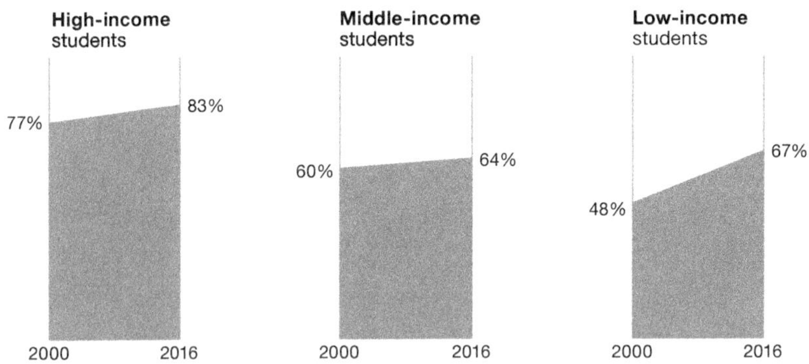

Source: National Center for Education Statistics.

for middle-income and 67 percent for low-income students. These gaps have narrowed somewhat since 2000 but remain pronounced.[11]

The National Center for Education Statistics (NCES) in its Condition of Education report provides a longer-term perspective: low-income students from the ninth-grade class of 2009 were less likely than high-income students to enroll in college within one year of high school graduation—53 percent of the poorest students either never enrolled in college or delayed their enrollment, while only 11 percent from the top-earning families did so.[12] Similar gaps appear when looking at immediate college enrollment based on type of high school. Students from higher-income schools enrolled in college at the national rate of 69 percent, while those students from low-income schools (defined as those where at least half the population is eligible for the federal free and reduced-price lunch program) enrolled at a rate of 55 percent.[13]

The impact of Promise programs is most evident in this area of postsecondary enrollment. Research from Kalamazoo, El Dorado, Pittsburgh, Say Yes to Education, and Knox Achieves, along with data from the Tennessee Promise, show that simple, robust free-college programs lead to increases in postsecondary enrollment across racial and economic groups.[14] Some of this research is discussed below.

Postsecondary Completion

Results are less encouraging when it comes to degree completion. Sixty percent of first-time, degree-seeking students who enrolled at four-year institutions in 2010 completed degrees within six years of enrollment. In a pattern that should be familiar by now (see figure 4.5), Asian and white students outperformed this average, with completion rates of 74 percent and 64 percent, respectively. Latino and Black students lagged the average, with completion rates of 54 percent for Latinos and 40 percent for Blacks. In every category, women outpaced men by 6 to 10 percentage points.[15]

Similar gaps appear at two-year institutions, although completion rates are lower overall (see figure 4.6). Thirty percent of first-time, full-time students seeking associate degrees or certificates beginning in 2013 graduated within three years. Latino students matched this average with a 30 percent graduation rate. Blacks lagged with a 23 percent rate, whites and Asians slightly exceeded the rate, with 32 percent and 36 percent, respectively.[16]

FIGURE 4.5 College completion by race/ethnicity in 4-year institutions

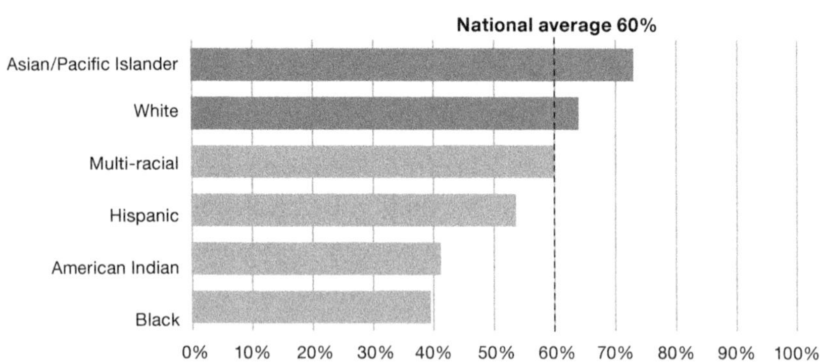

Note: Data from 2010 starting cohort, students graduating within 6 years after start.
Source: National Center for Education Statistics.

FIGURE 4.6 College completion by race/ethnicity in 2-year institutions

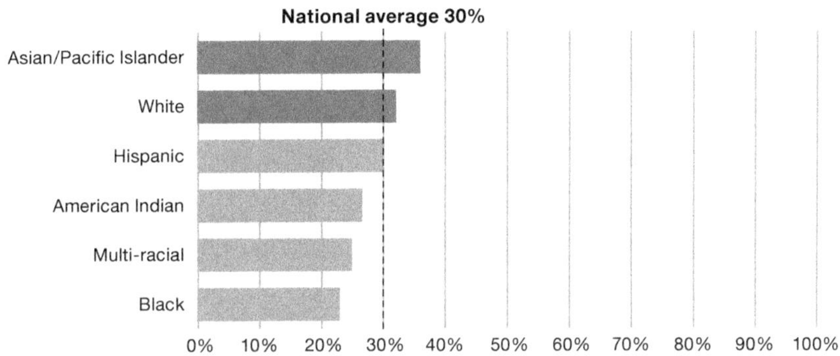

Note: Data from 2013 starting cohort, students completing within 3 years after start.
Source: National Center for Education Statistics.

Although there exist well-documented challenges with measuring community college success rates—for example, how to account for transfer students—evidence still reveals racial disparities.[17]

The story gets more complicated when looking at college completion by socioeconomic status. Family income plays a large role in the type of postsecondary institution students attend, and different types of institutions have very different completion rates. Lower-income students are more likely to enroll at open-admission community colleges, while higher-income students are overrepresented at four-year institutions. In part, this is a function of financial resources—while Pell Grants still exceed total community college tuition in most states, they fall far short of covering tuition at most public four-year institutions, meaning those institutions are less affordable for low-income students. But patterns of institutional "choice" are also affected by barriers built into the college application process (including standardized testing, FAFSA completion, and college application fees) that hinder low-income and first-generation students. These barriers contribute to undermatching in which higher-achieving poor students often enroll at institutions that are less competitive than those to which they could gain admission.

Where students go to college matters a great deal. As selectivity of institution rises, so do resources, with performance reflected in metrics such as year-to-year retention and degree completion. A student enrolled at a community college will be less likely to complete a degree than if that same student enrolled at a four-year institution. So, completion rates must be examined not just through the prism of income but also with attention to the important variable of type of institution attended. Low-income students who enroll in college are more likely to begin their studies with an associate degree as opposed to a bachelor's degree (42 percent versus 32 percent). The wealthiest students, by contrast, are far more likely to enroll in four-year institutions than seek a two-year degree (78 percent versus 13 percent). Wealthy students are also much more often enrolled at highly selective public or private institutions, and almost never choose for-profit options (only 2 percent of the wealthiest students attended a for-profit institution).[18]

Bachelor's degree attainment is measured in federal and institutional data over a six-year time frame. Sixty-seven percent of students who started college at a public four-year institution in 2013 had completed a degree six years later, compared to 40.8 percent of students who first attended a community college. Students choosing for-profit institutions fared equally badly, completing at a rate of 42.4 percent. Those who started at private, nonprofit four-year institutions completed at the highest rate—76.5 percent.[19] To some extent, these rates reflect variations among the student population entering different types of institutions—community colleges and for-profit schools are disproportionately attended by low-income students who may be less prepared for college than their middle-income peers. The private college sector is not necessarily more competitive than the public four-year sector in terms of admission, but class sizes are smaller and more wraparound supports are available. Of course, sticker prices are also much, much higher. The college completion impact of Promise programs has been studied in only a few communities, with encouraging results from Kalamazoo and El Dorado discussed in the following pages.

The discussion of racial and income gaps in college could go on much longer. It turns out, for example, that students from different demographic groups tend to major in different fields, which means their college wage premium—the higher salaries they earn over their lifetime, thanks to their college degrees—will also vary later on.[20] But no matter how you slice the data, racial and socioeconomic gaps in college going and progression are pronounced. Thus, it is no surprise that educational attainment levels continue to show disparities by race (see figure 4.7). In 2019, 36 percent of Americans over the age of twenty-five had completed a bachelor's degree or higher. The rate for whites (40.1 percent) slightly exceeded the national average, while that of Blacks (26.1 percent) and Latinos (18.8 percent) lagged behind it. The demographic group most likely to complete a bachelor's degree or higher was Asians, with 58.1 percent holding such degrees.[21] Degree attainment matters because, in the neutral language of the NCES, it is "associated with higher median earnings and higher employment rates."[22]

Why do these gaps exist? One obvious reason is the high price of college, discussed in chapter 3, and the fact that Black and Latino

FIGURE 4.7 Americans age 25 and older who have completed a bachelor's degree or higher

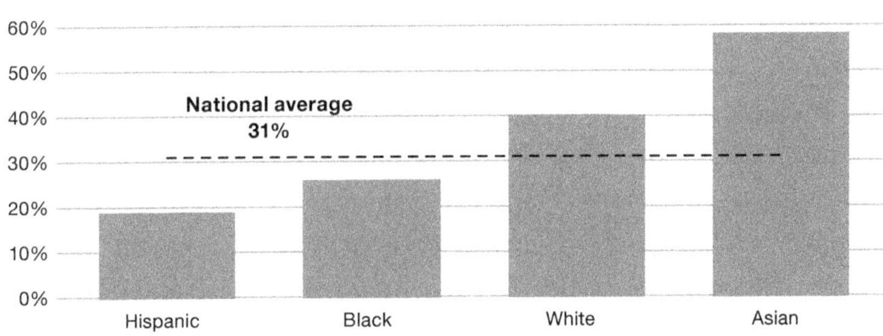

Data from 2016

Source: US Census Bureau Educational Attainment in the United States: 2019 Table Package.

families are more likely to be low income than white or Asian families. Rising college prices are barriers to college enrollment and completion even for the nonpoor population, but they pose more formidable challenges to prospective students from low-income backgrounds. Academic achievement gaps that run along racial and economic lines also contribute to differences in college-going rates and the type of institution attended by poor and nonpoor students.

Informational and procedural barriers to accessing higher education constitute another reason for economic and racial gaps in higher education.[23] The high school to college transition is fraught with complexity, from SAT or ACT preparation to FAFSA completion and verification, to understanding college prices, to sorting through the vast range of options to determine the best postsecondary fit. The need for college knowledge extends into the postsecondary setting, where students will find a new set of challenges to address.

Young people growing up with a college-educated parent or who attend better-resourced high schools where most students are college bound will have access to guidance and support in navigating these complicated transitions. One of the strongest predictors of whether a child will go to college is the educational attainment of his or her parents (mothers in particular). Research exploring this relationship points not just to the higher earnings of college-educated parents that make postsecondary education more affordable, but also to greater access to cultural capital and social networks that smooth a child's path to college.[24] Young people who lack these advantages at home are more highly reliant on what their schools and communities can provide, and here the disparities are stark. Private schools and those serving affluent communities look completely different than low-income urban or rural schools when it comes to college-access resources. The ratios of guidance counselors to students are shockingly low at high schools with large numbers of poor students, and college visits, Advanced Placement classes, dual enrollment, or standardized test preparation are meager or lacking (see the sidebar "MJ's story").[25]

→ MJ'S STORY

MJ* stood out in class in the fall of 2007. Not only was she one of only a handful of nonwhite students, she was also one of the very smartest, earning a near-perfect grade. MJ's subsequent academic performance was equally outstanding, despite the challenges of being a Black student at a largely white university, along with the financial stresses that accompany most low-income students on their journey through higher education. A few years later, when she received her bachelor's degree, MJ was named the department's outstanding student. I watched with admiration as she navigated the path from college to graduate school to a career, earning a master's degree from a top public university, becoming an in-school social worker, and successfully juggling the challenges of work and motherhood.

Only years later, over lunch during a visit to her alma mater, did I think to ask MJ how she had come to be at my university rather than at a more selective institution. I was not surprised to hear that she had never thought of applying to one of the private, liberal arts colleges in the region, or one farther afield—schools where she would very likely have received generous financial aid and encountered a more supportive environment. For first-generation college students like MJ, the sticker price of private colleges is a major deterrent. On the other hand, I was puzzled to learn that my former student had been admitted to the state's top-two public institutions and chosen not to attend either. Both are within a couple of hours of her home, but she had never even visited the campuses.

"I had the intelligence and academic ability to excel, but I just did not have the money to make it happen," she explained. "During my senior year of high school, my family moved five or six times and was focused on survival. Going on campus tours and visiting dorms were not priorities or even possibilities when we couldn't even make it around our own town." In short, MJ chose her college for the simple and practical reason that she could get there using public transportation. The family did not have a car, and there was no one to take MJ on a college visit or to orientation. Being at a college only a city bus ride away would enable her to help her mom and younger siblings on the weekends.

Would a Promise program have led MJ to a better college match? Perhaps. At a minimum, it would have created a focus on college going in her high school, with the potential for exploring a broader range of alternatives. There might also have been a college coach on hand who could have helped her navigate the process and learn more about the true cost of college. MJ points out that she was only sixteen years old for most of her senior year: "Looking back it seems really crazy that I had to make all of these adult decisions about finances and logistics."

A Promise program could have smoothed MJ's path to college, but it would not have addressed the socioeconomic challenges that made her journey so difficult or the ever-present racial bias in high school and college that constitute an added burden for students of color.

MJ has been successful in leveraging her degree into a profession, although she sometimes wishes she had explored more options. She believes she would have thrived at a Historically Black College or University (HBCU) and would love to have had the resources to go on for a PhD. Her story reveals how even the brightest of students can face barriers caused by poverty, race, and the absence of a robust system of supports. It underscores, too, why Promise programs must go beyond scholarships if they are to be effective.

*MJ is a pseudonym.

The recruitment and admissions policies of colleges and universities can exacerbate these disparities, as Anthony Carnevale and his colleagues at Georgetown University found in a study of the admissions practices of the nation's most selective public universities.[26] Standardized test scores may be biased against Black and Latino students and, according to some research, are also poor predictors of college performance.[27] It is comparatively easy to game the system if a student has access to resources to invest in test preparation, takes tests multiple times, or strategically retakes specific sections of tests. In recognition of these biases, some universities have moved away from relying on standardized test scores, making SAT or ACT optional and placing a greater emphasis on the high school GPA, which has been shown to be a more reliable guide to college success. The COVID-19 pandemic has accelerated the move toward test-optional admission—a welcome development from an equity standpoint if it continues.

Efforts to close racial and economic gaps in college enrollment have been underway for years, with a more recent focus on closing gaps in completion. Promise programs are a part of this effort, although stakeholders have not always clearly articulated equity concerns.

PROMISE PROGRAMS AND EQUITY

It is difficult to target free-college programs to reach specific racial or demographic groups in the same way that Pell Grants reach low-income students. Community-based Promise programs cover entire school districts or cities, meaning that local students of all races and income groups benefit. That being said, the choice of school district or community—almost always low income, many enrolling high percentages of Black and Latino students (especially in urban areas)—means that benefits are directed toward disadvantaged populations, even if not narrowly targeted by race or income. Similarly, the growth of institutional programs at community colleges that serve lower-income populations than four-year schools accomplishes the same goal of supporting lower-income learners, many of them students of color.

Promise programs smooth the pathway to higher education not just by providing financial resources but also by increasing access to information about college and stimulating efforts along the K–12 continuum to improve students' college readiness. Promise programs can have important economic benefits for low-income school districts if they lead to increased enrollment, thereby generating new funding. They can also strengthen high-poverty urban school districts relative to more-affluent surrounding districts.

The most direct equity impact of Promise programs is to increase the amount of grant aid available to students. One hard fact about Promise programs, both state and local, is that they are structured as grants rather than loans.[28] In localities with first-dollar programs (of which there are very few), students have access to Promise dollars before other forms of financial aid, retaining use of their Pell Grants. Programs covering the full cost of attendance have a similar impact, bringing new money to almost all recipients. Under the prevailing last-dollar model that covers tuition and fees only, new funding goes largely to nonpoor students, although it is exceedingly valuable for this population since moderate-income students are among those least able to pay for college without heavy borrowing. Another financial impact of free-college programs is to bring more Pell-eligible students into the student financial aid and college-going system through early, simple messaging about college affordability and changes in school and community norms and support.

Promise programs set expectations around college going and provide the kind of navigation that children of college-going parents or those who attend affluent school districts already enjoy. The scholarship component of a Promise program is almost always accompanied by efforts to strengthen the K–12 college-going culture. At the high school level, this might include new or reallocated college counseling resources (sometimes paid for by the Promise program itself); the expansion of Advanced Placement offerings to help students prepare for college-level work; schoolwide college admissions testing and practice testing, with fees paid by the school district; college visits or fairs; and expanded resources for FAFSA completion. Earlier along the educational pathway, school districts with Promise programs tend to increase college and career planning in middle school and emphasize college awareness in elementary settings through, for example, signing ceremonies for kindergarten students. They also can serve as catalysts for wraparound community-based support for basic needs, such as mental and physical health, tutoring, and afterschool or summer programming.

A third important equity-related function of Promise programs is to strengthen school districts themselves, drawing in new students, making it less attractive for existing students to exit, increasing financial resources, and strengthening programs and extracurricular offerings. This point is especially relevant for community-based Promise programs found in urban, high-poverty settings. In places like Buffalo, Cleveland, Kalamazoo, Pittsburgh, New Haven, and Syracuse, public school districts serving a region's urban core have for decades experienced out-migration, rising concentrations of poverty, and shrinking financial resources. Often these districts have declined because surrounding school districts have siphoned off students and resources, a trend compounded by white and middle-class flight to the suburbs and more recently by the schools of choice and charter school movements.[29] Promise programs can make urban school districts (as well as rural, high-poverty districts that suffer from some of the same trends), more attractive to students and families, both through the financial incentives that come with long-term attendance and through the new initiatives and student supports that accompany the introduction of Promise programs.

More grant funding, better college navigation support, and the strengthening of school districts serving low-income students all hold the potential for improving equity outcomes in college access and completion. Whether explicitly or not, free-college programs are also asking community members to think of college as a public good—something that strengthens the community as well as individual opportunity—and to invest in strategies that support student needs and attainment. Whether or not programs actually achieve these goals will depend on their structure and implementation.

What makes a Promise program effective in narrowing equity gaps? One of the most important characteristics is who benefits. Universal programs—those covering all students graduating from a given school district or within a particular state—will do a better job of extending opportunity to historically disadvantaged populations than programs targeted on some measure of academic merit. Merit-based scholarships with 2.5 or 3.0 high school GPA requirements will screen out lower-income, first-generation, Black, and Latino students at disproportionate rates because of academic achievement gaps that run along racial and economic lines. Advocates of merit-based requirements argue that it is not equitable to set up poorly prepared students to fail in a postsecondary setting, but navigation supports around "right fit" postsecondary programs, including short-term credentials and apprenticeship programs, as well as supports at the college level, can open paths to successful degree attainment and improved workforce outcomes even if a student's high school academic performance falls short.[30]

Some people argue that free-college programs would have even stronger equity impacts if targeted toward students with financial need, and this argument has some validity.[31] Notably, there is very little need-based targeting within the Promise movement. Promise programs are intended to send an early, clear message about college affordability to entire school districts, cities, or states, and adding an income requirement complicates this effort. Promise programs also seek to transform not just individual opportunity but also systems, so broader reach is preferable to a narrower focus. Finally, there is ample evidence that universal social programs enjoy greater political support and staying power than those focused on serving the poor.

Student eligibility is not the only important design element shaping a Promise program's equity impacts. First-dollar programs, or those that cover the full cost of attendance, will bring more money to low-income students than last-dollar programs. Last-dollar scholarships to be used only at two-year institutions are especially bad at tapping new financial resources for poor students, since in almost every state a student's Pell Grants will cover the full cost of community college tuition.[32] Some programs have innovated around the idea of "last-dollar-plus" structures (Oregon, discussed in the previous chapter, is one example) where students who receive no tuition support from a Promise program get a stipend to cover some additional expenses. But these amounts are a far cry from the size of new resources directed toward low-income students through first-dollar programs.

A third critical design feature when it comes to equity is simplicity. More students will be engaged by simple programs than by those with more complex requirements, thanks largely to ease of messaging. Even a last-dollar, community-college-only program with clear messaging can bring benefits to low-income students—one example (discussed in the next chapter) is the Tennessee Promise, where a program that is not particularly generous financially has brought about record-high FAFSA completion rates, meaning that many more low-income students are receiving the federal grants to which they were already entitled.

A fourth element with implications for equity is whether and how support services are delivered in grades K–12 and in college. It is not enough to provide first-generation and low-income college goers with a scholarship.[33] High school and college performance depends heavily on what happens in earlier grades, with researchers able to trace ripple effects from elementary and middle school interventions into high school and the postsecondary sphere.[34] Support is essential in high school if students are to find the right match for their abilities (undermatching is a chronic problem for low-income, high-achieving students), complete their FAFSAs, meet deadlines for college application and enrollment, and adjust to new expectations in a higher-education setting.

Promise programs often serve as catalysts for expanding support services to students. Sometimes this task is left to schools, colleges, and communities, with the implicit assumption that these supports will arise spontaneously in response to the introduction of a Promise program. In other cases, support services are embedded within the structure of a Promise program. Examples of each approach are offered in the case studies below. In several communities, including Denver, Lynchburg (Virginia), and La Crosse (Wisconsin), Promise programs pay for high school-based Future Centers that serve as one-stop college access and advising resources. In Tennessee, a large-scale mentorship program is integrated into the Tennessee Promise (see chapter 5 for more details). At the postsecondary level, some communities are experimenting with coaching models where students receiving scholarships are required to meet regularly with a college coach and offered incentives to do so. (The details of such an effort in Detroit are discussed in chapter 5.)

In a critique of statewide tuition-free college programs published in 2018, The Education Trust identified some additional dimensions of equity-focused tuition-free college in its "Framework for Equity-Driven Free College Policy." These included whether living expenses and fees are covered, whether four-year institutions are included, whether benefits are extended to adults and returning students, whether GPA and credit accumulation requirements are imposed, and, of course, whether the aid needs to be repaid.[35] While these criteria are important, there is no statewide program that meets all seven of them, and the fifteen state programs active when the report was published met, on average, fewer than four. The main reason state programs fail on these particular equity measures is cost. Providing first-dollar aid and covering bachelor's degree programs are tremendously expensive propositions, and very few Promise programs, state or local, do so. With state leaders having witnessed hard-fought battles to implement even minimal Promise programs, it seems unlikely they will pursue the more generous type of funding proposed by this report. Thus, state policy makers should consider the Education Trust criteria aspirational rather than practical.

Three of the design features mentioned above—universal eligibility, simplicity, and robust support services—can, in contrast to the Education Trust criteria, be incorporated into any kind of Promise program. As for financing, first-dollar programs are few and far between because of their high cost, but new ways to funnel additional resources to students are being tried. These four equity-related criteria are examined in more detail below through a comparison of two local Promise programs and several recently introduced statewide programs.

Community-Based Programs: Kalamazoo Promise and Say Yes Buffalo

Both the Kalamazoo Promise and the growing family of Say Yes to Education programs rank high on the intensity scale presented in chapter 2, as should be evident from the provisions summarized in table 4.1. The genesis of these programs differs, as does their structure, especially when it comes to the delivery of support services, but they both have the potential to reduce equity gaps.

The Kalamazoo Promise, the first of the current generation of place-based scholarships, emerged from the thinking of a group of anonymous donors interested in the economic vitality of their city. The Say Yes model now in place in four communities evolved in partnership with a national organization, Say Yes to Education, that was created by financier George Weiss in 1987. For its first two decades, Say Yes operated along the same lines as the "I Have a Dream" Foundation that was founded even earlier. Both encouraged wealthy individuals to guarantee college tuition to individual cohorts of students at selected elementary schools. Beginning in 2006, Say Yes transitioned to a community-based model that provides a scholarship guarantee

TABLE 4.1 Characteristics of selected community-based Promise programs

	KALAMAZOO PROMISE	SAY YES BUFFALO
Date established	2005; Class of 2006 first to receive scholarships.	2012; Class of 2013 first to receive scholarships.
Student eligibility	Graduates of Kalamazoo Public Schools who have attended and resided in the district for at least four years. Scholarship amount prorated by length of attendance; must be enrolled by 9th grade.	Residents of the City of Buffalo who have graduated from a public or charter high school in the city beginning in 2013, and completed federal and state financial aid forms on an annual basis. Scholarship amount prorated by length of attendance; must be enrolled by 9th grade.
Eligible postsecondary institutions	59 public and private colleges and universities in the State of Michigan plus some apprenticeship programs.	74 in-state public institutions (SUNY/CUNY), along with more than 100 private colleges and universities nationwide that provide scholarships from their own resources when attendees meet family income guidelines (combined family income below $75,000).
Structure of scholarship	First-dollar tuition and fees grant covering tuition and mandatory fees. Sliding scale (65%–100%) related to length of attendance. Covers up to 130 credits that may be used any time within 10 years of high school graduation.	Last-dollar tuition and fees grant covering tuition. Sliding scale (65%–100%) related to length of attendance. Students eligible for maximum Pell receive $2,000 per year toward other expenses if they reside on campus. At private colleges and universities, tuition is waived when family income is below $75,000 (some institutions have a higher threshold). For families with incomes above $75,000, an award of up to $5,000 is provided annually.
Funding	Funded by a group of anonymous local donors.	Funded by individuals, businesses, foundations, and New York State. Endowment campaign to raise $100 million by 2023 underway secured by $25 million anonymous donation.
Duration	In perpetuity	Short-term fund-raising secures program through high school class of 2022; endowment development underway to secure program in perpetuity.

and support services to potentially every graduate of a school district. The model has diffused slowly, launching in Syracuse in 2008, Buffalo in 2012, Guilford County (North Carolina) in 2015, and Cleveland in 2019.[36] This discussion will focus on Say Yes Buffalo, generally considered the most successful of the Say Yes communitywide programs.[37]

The Kalamazoo and Buffalo programs also vary when it comes to the four equity considerations outlined above. Both offer universal eligibility, but the Kalamazoo Promise has a first-dollar structure, making it one of the highest-intensity Promise programs in the nation. Generous funding is supported by very simple rules for accessing the scholarship, including an application form that is only a page long. Say Yes programs are last-dollar but provide some additional financial resources to low-income students. Accessing the scholarship is also a more complex process. The biggest difference between the programs, though, is in the delivery of support services. Kalamazoo is an example of the "money as catalyst" model, where provision of a large and simple scholarship is intended to generate new levels of community-based supports for students. Say Yes embeds these supports within its model. Both programs make important contributions to equity.

Kalamazoo, Michigan, is an unusual place. With a metro population of around 250,000, centered on a city of 75,000, it reflects all the major structural trends that have plagued larger cities since the 1970s. I have told this story elsewhere, how loss of industry and growth of the suburbs hollowed out the urban core; how the school district located in that core faced declining enrollment for twenty years, while serving higher concentrations of poor students and students of color; and how the acquisition of the city's largest employer led some of its wealthiest philanthropists to devise a strategy that could fundamentally reverse these trends.[38]

In Kalamazoo, great wealth and great poverty live quite literally side by side. The downtown hosts a symphony orchestra, an art museum, and other first-rate arts organizations with large endowments, along with well-funded family and community foundations. Hospitals, a medical school, and a vibrant health sciences sector have replaced some of the lost manufacturing of the past. Two colleges and a university bring people to Kalamazoo from all over the world, and rents for two-bedroom apartments in the city's newest buildings start at $3,000 a month. Yet just a few blocks in almost any direction, one can find poverty rates that rival those of the nation's most distressed cities. Seventy percent of students in Kalamazoo Public Schools (KPS) are economically disadvantaged, and the district is home to one of the state's largest populations of homeless children. Violent crime numbers are low because of the small population, but the crime rate has periodically landed Kalamazoo on the list of Michigan's most dangerous cities.[39]

Introduced in this context and limited to graduates of the public school district serving the urban core, the equity concerns of the Kalamazoo Promise are hard to miss. The Promise is designed to address two dimensions of equity—that of the individual and that of the community. At the individual level, the scholarship offers new postsecondary opportunities for students who attend KPS (see the sidebar "Roy's Story"). Its first-dollar structure and simplicity of the application process reduce barriers to college access. The range of postsecondary institutions and programs that students can attend—fifty-nine in-state public and private institutions offering everything from short-term certificates to bachelor's degrees, along with a handful of vocational apprenticeships—provide flexibility, while a ten-year time frame for usage does the same.

At the community level, the scholarship is a means of strengthening KPS relative to surrounding, more suburban school districts that enroll far fewer low-income, Black, and Latino children. The choice to limit benefits to the public school district—private and charter schools are excluded—suggests that the Kalamazoo Promise is less about college affordability or workforce development than it is about reversing out-migration and strengthening the systems that serve the region's low-income students and students of color. The insistence on long-term attachment to KPS through enrollment and residency requirements also suggests an interest in revitalizing the urban core, although this assumption is problematic because the school district is larger than the

→ ROY'S STORY

Roy Almaguer is the first to admit he was not a great high-school student. "Art was my saving grace, it's what got me to school every day," he says, sitting in his airy studio on the second floor of the Park Trades Center in downtown Kalamazoo. Paintings cover the walls, and four tattoo stations stand at the ready. Roy, whose given name is Rogelio, offers "full sleeve" tattoos of lions and other ornate designs. Customers pay up to $1,200 for one of his more elaborate creations, and he employs a handful of other tattooists who share his space. Roy is a graduate of Michigan's top art school, the Kendall School of Art and Design, and he got there because of the Kalamazoo Promise.

"We were migrant workers. My family came from Mexico, but we moved around a lot," Roy explains. From Washington State to the Texas border region to West Michigan—Roy's father followed the work. "When things got really bad in 2007, we had to stay in Mexico with our grandparents while our parents figured it out." That's when they decided to come to West Michigan.

Roy's older brothers and sisters attended high school in Kalamazoo but did not graduate. "They missed so much school due to all the moves, and no one was sure how the credits from Texas would transfer," so they joined their father in the fields. Roy was affected too—he attended thirteen different schools between kindergarten and high school—but by the time he started high school, the family had settled in Kalamazoo.

"Art was my thing for as long as I can remember. My parents always said, 'You're talented, you should keep doing it,' but they didn't know how to shape and mold it into a career." His teacher Cindy Van Lieu did. Van Lieu has taught art and design at Loy Norrix High School since 2000 and has been an art educator since 1971. She spotted Roy's talent immediately, admitting him to her AP art class for three years of high school, giving him summer assignments, and encouraging him to enter the local art museum's high school area show. Exhibiting there in his senior year, he won a scholarship from Kendall on the spot. The Kalamazoo Promise covered 65 percent of his tuition; between the two scholarships, Roy finished his bachelor's degree with $23,000 in debt. "Friends from college are $80,000, $100,000 in debt," he says, "so my situation is not the worst." But Kendall was a financial struggle. "We were evicted a few times, and our van had no heater. I remember driving through the winter while my wife's pregnant to get back home to try to make some money."

Roy met his wife, Gabby, in high school, and they have two young daughters. The family owns a house in Kalamazoo, and Roy's tattoo studio is located downtown. His older daughter attends the district's Spanish-language elementary. "I want to build something here, not just for myself but for the community," Roy says. The only person in his family with a high school diploma or college degree, Roy feels a sense of responsibility not just to his own family but also to Kalamazoo's Latino community. He has returned to his high school to speak with aspiring artists there. And his studio, Manifold Art, funds two $1,000 scholarships annually for Hispanic students and emerging artists. "For me, it was challenging to get through school, so if I can help someone who's in my shoes, I will. When I was given my scholarship, it made a big difference. It just feels good to give back."

city, extending into several suburban-type neighborhoods. The guarantee of perpetuity for the scholarship program signals to the community that the investment is here to stay.

Have these choices led to greater equity? To a degree. The Kalamazoo Promise has been used at roughly similar rates across all income and racial groups.[40] There has also been a meaningful increase in degree completion across population groups, from an admittedly low base; rigorous research shows bachelor's completion rising from about 30 percent to 40 percent over six years.[41] However, mirroring national trends, low-income students and students of color have been more likely to attend open-admission community colleges than four-year universities. This enrollment pattern has meant that nonpoor students have completed three times as many bachelor's degrees as students who are economically disadvantaged.[42] College-going patterns differ by race and income in Kalamazoo as in other places in part because of the impact of broader systemic racism that goes back decades and that has curtailed wealth accumulation for the community's Black families. In low-income communities, students may need to contribute financially to their families or assume caretaking responsibilities for relatives, while progress toward degree completion can be derailed by seemingly small unexpected financial burdens. The Kalamazoo Promise's ten-year time frame for usage is especially helpful in light of these patterns, with recent data suggesting that low-income and Black students are able to use this more generous time frame to complete degrees.

The Kalamazoo Promise has underpinned a dramatic reversal of decades of enrollment decline; since 2005, KPS enrollment has increased by about 25 percent, making it one of the few urban public school districts outside the Southwest showing double-digit growth. The larger number of students has brought financial resources to the school district because schools are funded by the state on a per-pupil basis and the marginal cost of adding one more student to a school district is far less than the per-pupil cost overall. The program also has severely curtailed the growth of charter schools in Kalamazoo compared to other communities in Michigan.[43] Equally important has been the creation of a more robust college-going culture in K–12 schools, with an emphasis on early literacy, college readiness, and high school graduation, and a significant expansion in AP course offerings, college visits, and SAT or ACT test preparation. As for out-of-school support, the Kalamazoo Promise has catalyzed a number of initiatives, although these remain fragmented and not all students with needs are served.

The most-pressing challenges facing the Kalamazoo Promise and the larger community are to increase high school graduation rates, reduce the rate of students who begin but do not complete a degree or credential (sometimes called the "stopout rate"), and draw students who retain Promise eligibility onto the postsecondary path.[44] These tasks require different forms of student support along various stages of the life course. In recent years, it became clear that the patchwork nature of existing initiatives was inadequate to this task, so the Kalamazoo Promise organization itself stepped in with a larger staff and more intentional engagement with schools and the community. Promise Pathways coaches employed by the Kalamazoo Promise are now found in each high school, while other staff members work to create employment opportunities for Promise students with area businesses. The evolutionary nature of student support in Kalamazoo can be contrasted with a different approach—that of Say Yes to Education.

Buffalo Public Schools fits the picture of a typical urban school district in a city facing industrial decline. School district enrollment dropped from forty-five thousand students in 1998 to thirty-one thousand twenty years later. Over the same period, the free and reduced-price lunch rate rose from 68 percent to 79 percent, while the population of white students fell from almost one-third (30 percent in 1999) to one-fifth of students today. The high school graduation rate is 65 percent (class of 2019), with pronounced gaps by race and income; this compares to a statewide rate of 83 percent.[45] An added layer of complexity came from a school board that historically did not always function well and rapid turnover in school superintendents. This was an unlikely setting for a Say Yes chapter to thrive, yet the district's challenges may be related to the program's success.

In a detailed study of Say Yes as a whole, researchers at the Brookings Institution describe Buffalo (the second communitywide site after Syracuse) as the most successful Say Yes initiative and the one where the core components of the approach have been implemented most faithfully.[46] In explaining why the community was receptive to the Say Yes approach, the authors identify several factors. Say Yes was proposed at a time when there was an uptick in business activity and the announcement of some major economic development investments in Buffalo and the wider region. The explicit connection between Say Yes and economic revitalization drew the attention of business leaders. Say Yes also enjoyed the support of powerful local leaders from the philanthropic and public sectors. An effective executive director with roots in the community was another important ingredient, and early enthusiasm for the program was amplified by positive national media attention.[47] The problems plaguing the schools contrasted with more positive news elsewhere and created a sense of urgency that allowed various community partners to embrace a new approach. (Happily, both the school board and district administration have functioned much better since the arrival of a new superintendent in 2015 and strong leadership from recent board presidents.)

The scholarship component of the Say Yes program is more complex and difficult to access than the Kalamazoo Promise. It is a last-dollar scholarship, meaning that students must complete their FAFSA and New York State Tuition Assistance Program applications to unlock other forms of grant aid and determine the remaining amount of the Say Yes scholarship. There are also distinctions between the type of school attended and the level of support received—tuition is fully covered at in-state public colleges and universities, but students can also apply to private partner colleges. In most cases, these colleges will cover tuition if family income is below $75,000. If it is not, a Say Yes student will receive a $5,000 scholarship to help defray a small portion of costs. In contrast, the Kalamazoo Promise covers full tuition and fees at any of the program's eligible institutions. The greater complexity of Say Yes Buffalo raises challenges around effective messaging; as the Brookings authors write, "As in other Say Yes sites and for other organizations offering a final-dollar scholarship, communicating how the scholarship works, and what it covers and does not cover, is an ongoing challenge."[48]

Both programs are structured to provide new support to low-income students. The Kalamazoo Promise is more generous in this regard because the first-dollar structure allows students to retain full use of their Pell Grants to help cover living expenses. Low-income Buffalo students whose Pell Grants cover the full cost of tuition may receive up to $2,000 a year in additional support. A minimum four-year residency and enrollment requirement is in place in both locations. In Buffalo, the charter school sector is covered, while in Kalamazoo, it is not.

Turning from scholarship money to student support, the Say Yes program takes a different approach from that of most Promise programs, including Kalamazoo's. Rather than use scholarship funds as a catalyst to leverage support services for students, the Say Yes model embeds these directly within the program. Buffalo is the only Say Yes site where almost all services are delivered under the Say Yes banner (at other Say Yes sites, support services are provided by existing community organizations). Chief among these are family support specialists (school caseworkers managed by Say Yes) covering all of the district's fifty-five schools. Their role is to connect students and families to outside resources, like mental health services or afterschool programs (a role played in Kalamazoo by Communities in Schools of Kalamazoo), provide mentoring to students and families, and help families navigate school processes. A key focus of their work is improving attendance and minimizing involvement in the child welfare system. The Buffalo Public Schools has designated twenty-one sites as community schools; in these settings, one may find additional Say Yes navigators, added learning time (such as weekly Saturday academies, college simulation experiences, and fitness classes), and/or parent centers. Preventive health care, both physical and mental, is delivered through mobile units. Other initiatives include free legal clinics, summer camps, college-readiness programs, career development internships, and a volunteer-run, school-based FAFSA completion initiative. Interestingly, many of these resources also exist in Kalamazoo, although they are more loosely connected and not delivered under the Kalamazoo Promise banner. The Brookings researchers conclude that "Say Yes has acted as the connective tissue in this [health services] initiative, linking schools to providers and, crucially, to the county," which is the provider of many of these services.[49]

Alignment is more intentional and structured in the Say Yes model than it has been in Kalamazoo, not just in the delivery of services but also in the overall governance of the program. As the Say Yes Buffalo website reads, "The breakthrough component of Say Yes Buffalo is the transparent, collaborative governance structure that guides all efforts and reports on progress to the public at large. This collaborative approach recognizes that Erie County, the City of Buffalo, and the Buffalo Public School District all hold pieces of the puzzle, that the solutions reside between and among these systems, and that improving academic outcomes for urban youth with [sic] scale demands a cross-sector, cross-government approach."[50] Partnerships among key constituencies are facilitated through a multisector operating committee that meets every three weeks to review progress, along with a higher-level community leadership council representing key community stakeholders that meets three times a year. Data sharing and provision of services are outlined in memoranda of understanding between various partners. "The whole community's united. It's hard to think of a major institution in the community that is not somehow involved in Say Yes," according to Richard Tobe, former deputy Erie County executive.[51]

The deep involvement of economic actors, such as the City of Buffalo, Erie County, and local businesses, suggest that there is an ultimate economic development rationale for the Say Yes program, as there are for many Promise programs, including Kalamazoo's. And, as in Kalamazoo, the path to development is seen to run through the health of the school district serving the urban core. As Say Yes puts it, "This education-based initiative aims to provide a powerful engine for long-term economic development through radically improving the life course of public-school students in the City of Buffalo."[52]

Is the Say Yes model working? Rigorous, quasi-experimental research into the impact of Say Yes Buffalo echoes findings from Kalamazoo. This is an interesting result given that the Kalamazoo Promise is a first-dollar scholarship and Say Yes awards its scholarships on a last-dollar basis. Researchers have found that eligibility for Say Yes is associated with an increase of 20 percent in the likelihood of entering college within one year of graduation and an increase in the likelihood of persisting into a second year of nearly 16 percent.[53] Enrollment increases are concentrated at four-year institutions, which means the financial resources provided by Say Yes are allowing qualified students to shift from two-year to four-year institutions, as they have done in Kalamazoo. Most of the gains are concentrated in the middle third of the income distribution, suggesting that Say Yes's main benefits are not flowing to the district's best-off students, but neither are they reaching the very poorest. The authors of this study conclude that universal, last-dollar scholarships can increase college going in a cost-effective manner while helping shift students' enrollment choices to postsecondary institutions they might have originally considered out of reach.[54] Other research has found that Say Yes is associated with an increase in enrollment in the Buffalo Public Schools, an increase that coincided with declining private school enrollments.[55] If strengthening public school districts that serve a region's urban core and enroll most of its poor students is one goal of Promise programs—and clearly it is—these goals are being met in Buffalo, although not as strongly as they have been in Kalamazoo.

The introduction of New York's statewide Excelsior Scholarship in 2017 raised a question for Say Yes Buffalo and Say Yes Syracuse. Were their scholarships still needed if the state would now be funding two-year and four-year public college attendance? The answer has been a resounding yes. The many requirements associated with qualifying for the Excelsior Scholarship (detailed in chapter 3) have kept usage rates down. Low-income students, who constitute the bulk of students enrolled in both Buffalo and Syracuse public schools, have an especially difficult time meeting the full-time credit requirements of the Excelsior Scholarship. For now, Say Yes Buffalo is directing almost all students to apply for Say Yes rather than the statewide scholarship.

In neither Buffalo nor Kalamazoo has the scholarship program or its attendant supports changed the demographics of the school district. The public schools in both cities remain high-poverty districts with large majorities of nonwhite students. They both continue to struggle with the demands that pervasive poverty places on schools and communities. They both seek to provide additional supports to provide basic needs, close achievement gaps, promote high school graduation, and smooth the transition from K–12 to the postsecondary realm. Yet the Kalamazoo Promise and Say Yes Buffalo have changed these districts and their communities. They have provided new resources for schools and students, and they serve as points of alignment around which actors in different sectors can coalesce. They have raised the stakes of failure and generated new partnerships born of necessity. The equity impacts of these programs are difficult to quantify, but each in its own way shows the potential of a place-based scholarship to reorient a high-poverty school district in a more positive direction. As the founding chair of Buffalo's scholarship board, Alphonso O'Neil White, has put it, "You are helping thousands, literally thousands, of children, all at once and securing the future of a couple of generations."[56]

Table 4.2 compares the Kalamazoo Promise and Say Yes Buffalo on the equity metrics discussed above. As was the case in the previous chapter, there are multiple ways to structure Promise programs to achieve similar goals. More research is needed to clarify whether there

TABLE 4.2 Equity metrics for selected community-based Promise programs

	KALAMAZOO PROMISE	SAY YES BUFFALO
Maximum award (as of 2020)	In-state tuition and fees at University of Michigan ($16,948 in 2020–2021).	In-state tuition and fees at SUNY/CUNY ($7,070 in 2020–2021).
Student eligibility	Universal.	Universal.
Structure of scholarship	First dollar, covers tuition and fees as they increase.	Last dollar, covers tuition; additional $2,000 a year for low-income students.
Simplicity of application process	One-page form.	Must fill out FAFSA and New York State TAP.
Flexibility of postsecondary program type	High (public, private, apprenticeships).	Very high (public, private, out-of-state options).
Time frame for usage	10 years after high school graduation.	6 years after high school graduation.
Additional services	Not embedded in program.	Embedded in program.

is a difference in outcomes for student supports that are catalyzed by a scholarship program and those where they are built in.

State Programs: Washington, New Mexico, and Virginia

Community-based Promise programs, or at least a small subset of them, have been studied for long enough that it is possible to draw conclusions about their impact on college going and completion by race and income. Much less is known about the equity impacts of statewide Promise programs largely because those focusing explicitly on equity are very new and there has been little serious evaluation of the model overall.

To date, state-level Promise programs have been animated mainly by workforce concerns (see chapter 5) and structured as last-dollar, community-college-only programs. This means that most low-income students do not receive any new funding from the scholarships because Pell Grants, for which they must apply, fully cover tuition and fees. The structure of these programs is regressive in that much of their funding goes to nonpoor students.[57] On the other hand, the argument that such programs are covering tuition for affluent students does not carry much weight because students from wealthy families rarely attend community college; of students in the highest fifth of the income distribution, fewer than one in five enrolls at a public, two-year institution.[58]

Even last-dollar, community college–only programs can benefit low-income students, although not as much as they would if they included new financial resources. These benefits come from system changes that make college going more attainable. For example, if a robust college-going culture emerges in K–12 school districts as the result of a statewide Promise program, then college aspirations become the norm. Similarly, statewide or district-based FAFSA completion campaigns make it easier for low-income students to access the Pell Grants to which they are entitled—sky-high FAFSA completion rates in Tennessee since the introduction of the Tennessee Promise suggest this is an important effect. And enhanced support for first-generation or low-income college goers embedded in statewide Promise programs, such as the mentorship services delivered through tnAchieves, can help low-income students be more successful once they reach college.

A few states have added stipends to their Promise programs to bring some new money to students whose Pell Grants cover tuition. As discussed in chapter 2, Oregon piloted this last-dollar-plus model, although its 2.5 GPA requirement works to the detriment of poorer students who tend to have lower GPAs. Virginia builds on this idea in a recently announced program, adding basic needs grants of $2,000 per student per year for low-income college goers.

Equity-oriented policy organizations have been highly critical of existing statewide Promise programs due to their distributional impacts; the Institute for Higher Education Policy singled out Tennessee's and New York's programs for criticism in 2018.[59] Other states have taken equity considerations to heart during the design phase; however, these programs are so new that it is impossible to assess their impact. Instead, the focus here is on program structure and how free-college initiatives in Washington State, New Mexico, and Virginia stack up on the equity considerations discussed above.

Washington State's program is described by some of its sponsors as a College Promise, but it is really an expansion and rebranding of the existing state need grant.[60] Almost every state offers some form of need-based aid to its residents, but the programs are often narrowly targeted and almost always under-funded, meaning that not every eligible student receives an award. Washington State was no exception, with funding for its need-based grant historically running short. In 2019, 18,000 eligible students missed out on funding due to budgetary shortfalls.[61] The new program, signed into law in May 2019, raises the income ceiling and provides guaranteed funding for everyone below it. Beginning in 2020, the existing state need grant was replaced by the Washington College Grant. The new grant is both innovative and equity oriented.

First, the Washington College Grant makes need-based aid a guarantee by embedding funding within the tax code. The program is funded by an increase in the state's main business tax, with the highest rates paid by its two largest employers, Amazon and Microsoft, both of which supported the increase.[62]

Second, the legislation expands eligibility while targeting benefits squarely on lower- and middle-income families. Eligibility for the previous grant was set at a maximum of 70 percent of median family income (MFI). The new program raises the guarantee of full funding to those earning up to 100 percent of MFI (just over $50,000 in 2019). Partial awards are available for those earning almost twice as much.

Beyond the income requirements, eligibility is exceptionally flexible. The grant can be used by any Washington resident who doesn't already have a bachelor's degree and can be applied to certificate and apprenticeship programs. Sixty-six in-state schools are covered, including many of the state's private universities. There are no minimum credit requirements or time limits for using the scholarship. Undocumented students are also eligible, which is not the norm in other states, although they must meet residency and other requirements.[63]

Third, the program awards tuition scholarships on a first-dollar basis, before other forms of financial aid. As explained above, this has strong equity impacts because low-income students retain access to their Pell Grants, allowing them to cover at least a portion of nontuition expenses.

This equity-oriented scholarship structure emerged as a result of strong advocacy from the business community based on projections of unfilled job openings and concern among employers about meeting workforce needs—a concern that predated the current recession and that is discussed in more detail in the next chapter. Along with business support, the proposal, which moved through the legislature rapidly (the bill was introduced and passed within the first few months of 2019), enjoyed the support of the higher-education sector and benefited from intensive student advocacy. Passage depended on Washington's blue-state government where both houses of the state legislature and the governor's office are firmly in Democratic hands.

Two other statewide programs, both proposed in 2019, also hold the potential for positive equity impacts. In New Mexico, the governor proposed the New Mexico Opportunity Scholarship in fall 2019, and it was partially funded in 2020. The program is simple—any New Mexico resident of any age may attend college tuition free (on a last-dollar basis) at any of New Mexico's twenty-nine two-year and four-year public institutions.[64] Many students already receive Pell Grants, and there is also a New Mexico Lottery Scholarship; however, as in Washington, resources from that grant fell short of covering all eligible students for the past several years. The new program would guarantee tuition and fees coverage. The state would enter into agreements with colleges and universities to ensure tuition rates do not rise in response to the new scholarship resources and that schools invest in proven student success initiatives to ensure that the new cohort of incoming students will be successful in completing degrees.[65] While designed to cover both the two-year and four-year sectors, budget constraints have narrowed the program's scope to two-year institutions, at least for now.

The governor of Virginia has proposed yet another version of a statewide Promise program called the "Get Skilled, Get a Job, Give Back," or G3 program. Under the proposal (yet to be enacted into law), students would receive last-dollar funding to attend community college in the state tuition free. While not a universal program, the proposed income ceiling is generous, covering families earning up to 400 percent of the federal poverty level, or about $100,000 for a family of four in 2019. The grant would also be available to adult learners without college degrees. One innovative component of the proposal is that low-income students would receive an additional "basic needs grant" of $1,000 a year, along the lines of the Oregon Promise. Two provisions in the Virginia proposal create added complexity and should be expected to hold down usage. First, the scholarship is available only to students majoring in designated high-demand fields chosen based on economic projections, employer input, and the number of job openings; the list currently includes health care, information technology, public safety, early childhood education, and skilled trades. This is an unwieldy structure especially in light of pandemic-induced labor market dislocation and will undoubtedly muddy the "free college" message. There is also a community engagement requirement for a set number of service hours for every credit hour a student is enrolled—again, a confusing requirement that complicates messaging.

It is difficult to predict which of these new, equity-focused statewide programs will succeed in narrowing income and racial gaps in postsecondary attainment. Each falls short in a different way: New Mexico's is a last-dollar program, and Virginia's basic need grants are undercut by narrow eligibility requirements for field of study. Washington State comes closest, but we still await the true equity-oriented statewide Promise program. Such a program would be expensive, which is why it has not yet been created.

If one were to build a Promise program with racial and economic equity goals at its core, it should be designed to reach as many potential college goers as possible. This means eligibility needs to be broad, ideally universal, and include learners of all ages. Program rules should be simple and clear, and funding easy to access. All these program attributes would help support the notion of affordable college access as a public good, although questions remain about the degree to which a statewide Promise program untethered to local, community-based supports can catalyze cultural change in schools and neighborhoods.

Equity goals require that students have access to new financial resources to help them meet rising college prices. Last-dollar programs that restrict attendance to community college funnel resources to students above the Pell cutoff leaving low-income students to struggle with managing the full cost of attendance. An equity-focused program must ensure that new resources are available to help meet the cost of attendance, through either a first-dollar program structure or the provision of additional aid. Expecting students to behave differently without offering them incentives to do so is not likely to yield results.

An equity-focused Promise program would also acknowledge that money alone is not enough and would strive to change the public mindset around college going. Low-income and first-generation college goers need access to robust support services both to navigate their way to the right college with adequate financing and to succeed once enrolled. Planning for a local or statewide Promise program must from the beginning consider not just the cost of the scholarship but the expense of delivering support to students who need it.

These principles are written with equity in mind, but it turns out they are also critical to meeting another key goal of the free-college movement: the ability of employers to access a skilled workforce. It is to that motivation we now turn.

CHAPTER

5

Employment

WHEN THE CORONAVIRUS crisis erupted in March 2020, several states were in the process of designing their own statewide Promise programs. In other states, governors had already introduced tuition-free college initiatives and were seeking legislative approval and funding. Most of these initiatives were designed to include adults, based on a shortage of skilled workers and employer support for more training. All that changed, seemingly in a moment, as the US economy ground to a halt, millions of workers were laid off, and unemployment claims shot up. State fiscal priorities shifted as well, with all available resources going to coronavirus response needs and large budget deficits looming.

It is difficult to overstate the speed at which the labor market reversed itself. In the early months of 2020, the key challenge for businesses was how to hire workers in an exceedingly tight labor market; the national unemployment rate had been below 5 percent for several years, and in February 2020, it was 3.5 percent, a fifty-year low. A month later, unemployment had skyrocketed to its highest levels since the Great Depression, with increases so steep that monthly statistics could not keep up.[1] As the dust settled, the landscape looked very different than it had before the crisis. Instead of employers competing to hire qualified workers, workers found themselves needing to reskill to meet remaining pockets of demand and prepare for employment in future growth industries.

This chapter addresses the role of Promise programs in meeting employment needs, whether these arise from a tight labor market and employer concerns about hiring or from workers' needs to access better jobs in a more competitive environment. While most statewide tuition-free college programs were forged in the first setting, existing programs can serve as valuable resources for states seeking to reemploy their workforce—provided the financial resources to sustain them remain in place.

There is a strong connection between the employment and equity rationales for Promise programs. Business support for free-college initiatives is driven by the need for skilled workers. Writing about the Tennessee Promise for Politico, journalist Benjamin Wermund explained, "From the beginning, free college in Tennessee was framed not as a form of personal betterment, or social welfare, but in terms of economic development. State leaders found that companies considering locating in Tennessee wanted a broad base of skilled workers more than just about any financial incentive they could offer."[2] Yet the program's architects also understood that the workforce conversation was inexorably tied to issues of equity. Kenyatta Lovett, the former head of a college completion organization who is now with the Tennessee Department of Labor and Workforce Development, put it this way: "Employer voice helped community leaders and postsecondary institutions understand why equity was a necessity. Better college completion outcomes for all our students regardless of what they look like benefits the community overall."[3]

While the business imperative for reaching potential workers underserved by postsecondary education and training may be less pressing in light of the pandemic-induced recession, it has become more important thanks to greater public understanding of and support for social movements for racial justice. Many businesses are eager to pursue more equitable hiring practices, and there is a growing body of research that increased diversity in the workplace is tied to stronger economic growth.[4] Promise programs designed to meet workforce needs will expand the talent pipeline only if it is broadened to include more first-generation and low-income individuals, as well as more racial and ethnic minorities. Effective employment-based Promise programs thus will also have positive impacts on economic and racial equity.

THE NEED FOR SKILLED WORKERS

Throughout this book, I argue that Promise programs yield both individual and collective benefits, making them a unique, dual-value proposition that enjoys support from a variety of constituencies. The benefits of going to college for individuals have been clear for decades. As education levels rise, so do incomes. Degrees also cushion people's livelihoods when times are hard.

As figure 5.1 shows, the more education one has, the higher the income and the lower the unemployment rate.[5] (The differences would be even more stark if the graph included part-time workers.)

Figure 5.1 predates the pandemic-induced economic crisis, but the relationship also holds in difficult times. In 2010–2011, at the peak of the Great Recession, unemployment for those with bachelor's degrees was around 4 percent and those with associate degrees around 7–8 percent, while it was in the 14–15 percent range for workers without a high school diploma.[6] And, even as layoffs rose to record levels in the weeks after the COVID-19 outbreak, college-educated workers were the least likely to experience unemployment; in April 2020, the unemployment rate for those with bachelor's degrees was 8.4 percent, half that of high school graduates.[7]

The wage premium and cushion against layoffs provided by a college degree are such valuable goods that individuals and their families

FIGURE 5.1 Unemployment rates and earnings by educational attainment, 2019

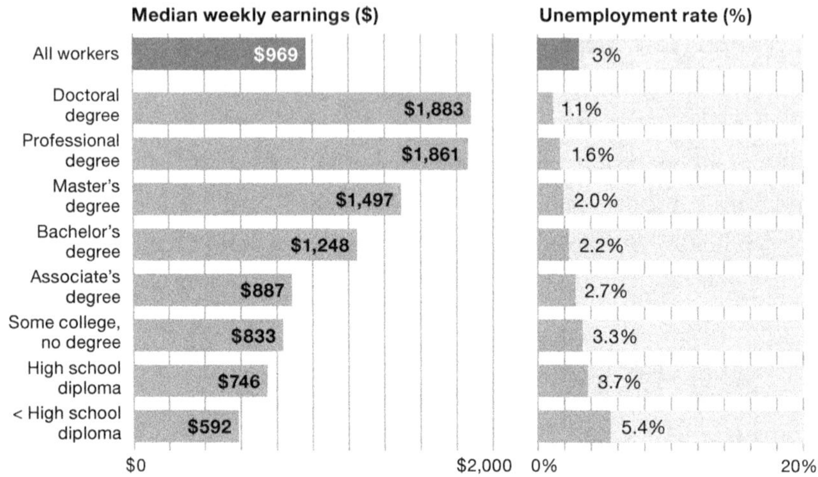

Note: Data are for persons age 25 and over. Earnings are for full-time wage and salary workers.
Source: Current Population Survey, US Department of Labor, US Bureau of Labor Statistics.

have gone to great lengths to invest in higher education, often accumulating more student loan debt than they are able to manage. And while it is well established that cities and states with highly educated populations are more economically successful than those without, the cost of acquiring education has for decades been seen as largely an individual responsibility.[8]

Until the 1970s, public funding for higher education reflected a consensus that degrees were also good for society. Affordable public higher education and a financial aid system that covered a large share of its price made college accessible for most families, the middle class expanded, and the nation steadily increased its stock of educated workers. That consensus gave way amid shifting views of government, political polarization, and a deteriorating fiscal climate for states. It is only in the past decade or so that some state leaders have again made the argument that paying for higher education is a worthwhile investment. In doing so, they mainly cite employment concerns.

Business-based or economic rationales for free college have been part of the Promise movement from the beginning. Inherent in the place-based scholarship idea is the concept of community transformation. For local Promise programs, community benefits include the creation of stronger K–12 school districts, a more educated population, and a greater ability to attract and retain residents and employers. Leaders of community-based Promise programs, however, recognize that students may attend college outside their home communities and not return or may leave for better job opportunities elsewhere; this undermines the business case for investing in local youth. As a result, the rationale for community- and institution-based Promise programs usually rests on some combination of arguments about college access, equity, and making places more attractive.

In contrast, state leaders almost always cite workforce development as the main rationale for investing in tuition-free college. From New Jersey to Michigan to Virginia to Tennessee, the free-college discussion is filled with references to workers' skills and a state's economic competitiveness:

- "The battle for talent is THE critical contest of the twenty-first century economy and keeping more people in-state is essential to building out New Jersey's workforce of tomorrow," said Tim Sullivan, New Jersey's chief education officer, in announcing the Garden State Guarantee.[9]
- "It is time to get aggressive in addressing our state's skills gap," reads a letter from Michigan's business leaders in support of the Michigan Reconnect program.[10]
- Speaking about the state's proposed "Get Skilled, Get a Job, Give Back" or G3 program, Virginia governor Ralph Northam claimed, "This initiative will improve access to training and education programs while preparing more Virginians to get jobs in high-need fields. We can bring skills to jobs."[11]
- When the Tennessee Reconnect program was announced in 2013, former Governor Bill Haslam commented, "We know that by 2025

> at least half the jobs in this state will require a college degree or certificate. Mathematically, there's no way to reach that goal just by equipping high school graduates with degrees."[12]

While all these comments emphasize the needs of business, most also make the point that education is not just of benefit to individuals but a societal good as well.

Claims of a skills gap go back decades, but discussion intensified as the nation recovered from the 2008 recession and businesses struggled to fill job openings in fields like advanced manufacturing, information technology, health professions, and the skilled trades.[13] Much of their concern centered on what are often called "middle-skill" jobs that require credentials, certificates, or associate degrees—in other words, postsecondary training that falls short of a bachelor's degree.[14] But any clarity in understanding whether and why there is a skills gap is hampered by the use of the term in widely different contexts.

Sometimes the skills-gap argument is framed as a failure of educational institutions to produce the type of workers the economy needs, as in this 2014 Economist Intelligence Unit summary based on a survey of businesses: "The overwhelming consensus among employers is that too many graduates lack critical-thinking skills and the ability to communicate effectively, solve problems creatively, work collaboratively and adapt to changing priorities."[15] In other contexts, the skills gap is defined as a mismatch between the number of jobs available in a given field and the number of trained workers available to fill them. Deloitte, for example, has carried out multiple studies of manufacturing jobs, forecasting (in 2018) a possible shortage of 2.4 million workers due to skills gaps, driven in part by retirements, between 2018 and 2028.[16]

Measuring a skills shortage is difficult and rests heavily on definitions. Sometimes, educational attainment is used as a proxy for skills—the more advanced the degree, the higher the skills. This simple definition is problematic because education does not necessarily impart the specific skills required by employers. Others take a different approach. Economist David Autor, one of the leading researchers in the field, has looked at occupational titles to capture specific job skills and how they are changing. Autor and his colleagues focus on the distinction between routine and nonroutine tasks, finding that computerization is increasingly assisting with routine tasks (think ATMs, parking garages, and self-checkouts). This has left high-skill and lower-skill nonroutine jobs to the humans.[17] In this formulation, middle-skill jobs may be just another term for nonroutine work that can be done without a four-year degree. Harry Holzer, another economist active in this field, finds that traditional middle-skill jobs in construction, production, and clerical work have indeed declined, but have been replaced by a new set of similar skill-level jobs in health care, maintenance and repair, and some services.[18] Economists also argue that recessions can exacerbate this type of job polarization. Brad Hershbein and Lisa Kahn have shown that the 2008 recession accelerated the restructuring of production toward more skilled workers and routine-labor saving technologies.[19] Of course, it is too soon to know, but the current recession may do the same.[20]

The skills gap idea has itself been challenged. Some of its critics are affiliated with left-leaning think tanks like the Economic Policy Institute (EPI) and the Washington Center for Equitable Growth.[21] They argue that job openings are going unfilled not because of a skills mismatch, but because employers are unwilling to pay the wage premium necessary to entice the workers they need. Employers also hesitate to spend on the kind of on-the-job training they delivered in earlier times, while employers counter that investing in an employee is a riskier proposition than it used to be because of greater job mobility. An analysis of job postings during and after the 2008 recession provides evidence for the importance of employer behavior, showing that businesses made their job descriptions and requirements stricter while unemployment was high but relaxed them as unemployment rates fell.[22] Critics like EPI make the compelling argument that if unions were stronger and firms found it more difficult to move overseas or outsource their business, firms themselves would invest more in on-the-job training.

Some question the skills gap at a more fundamental level. Nobel Prize-winning economist Paul Krugman calls the skills gap a prime example of a "zombie idea"—something that should have been killed by evidence but that "everyone knows to be true because everyone they know says it is true."[23] Krugman believes that by promoting the myth of the skills gap, public policy is "blaming workers for their own plight . . . [and] shift[ing] attention away from the spectacle of soaring profits and bonuses even as employment and wages stagnate."[24] University of Wisconsin professor Matthew T. Hora believes skills-gap language is used to undermine the value of a liberal education, replacing it with a "vocationalist framing" that is not in the interests of students, employers or society.[25] "[T]he skills-gap frame is inaccurate and incomplete. It misdiagnoses the nature of valued skills, ignores the critical role of teaching, and glosses over problematic aspects of employers' hiring practices," he writes.[26]

Skills gaps, if they exist, may be easiest to see at a local or regional level—in Nashville, for example, corporate and city leaders agree there are not enough information technology workers to meet the area's near-term business needs.[27] Ultimately it may not matter how a skills gap is defined or measured. As long as business leaders believe there is a shortage of qualified workers, and as long as their recruitment and hiring experience supports this belief, the business sector may be enthusiastic about state-funded workforce training activities, including Promise programs. In a few rare cases, as in Washington State today, they may even be willing to help pay for them.

As the pandemic drove unemployment rates to historic highs, concern about a skills gap seemed beside the point. By mid-2020, the overriding problem was a lack of demand for workers, not business hiring needs. Yet Promise programs continued to garner attention. In a weak labor market, degrees and credentials in high-demand fields are arguably more valuable than ever. Some industries will undoubtedly expand in the post-coronavirus economy, and training in these fields, much of which will take place at the sub-bachelor-degree level, could be a smart investment for both individuals and states. Michigan legislators recognized this by restoring funding for the Michigan Reconnect program that serves adults without college degrees in the state's 2021 budget, even amid tremendous fiscal uncertainty.

Tuition-free college can also help address some of the equity concerns that were laid bare by the pandemic. Michigan's Governor Gretchen Whitmer used federal recovery dollars to support a year-long, free community college program for the state's essential workers without college degrees. The Futures for Frontliners program was framed as a "GI Bill" for low-skilled individuals who had provided essential services during the early months of the pandemic. Needless to say, many of the tens of thousands of applicants for the program are low-income people of color.

CAN FREE COLLEGE HELP MEET EMPLOYMENT NEEDS?

Employment concerns are central to the participation of states in the free-college movement. In a tight labor market, a Promise program that sends a state's young people—and sometimes its adults—to college to acquire certificates, associate degrees, and other credentials can help states fill the middle-skill jobs that employers are concerned about. In a slack labor market, ample and affordable opportunities for higher education can create pathways for retraining and upward mobility that can help the workers most hurt by a downturn. But the argument for free college goes beyond this notion that education is mainly of value to individuals or firms. If the benefits of Promise programs accrue only to specific workers or businesses, why should states or localities invest in them? The reason is that higher levels of education help not just those with that education but their fellow citizens and the states and localities in which they live. Spillover effects from higher education are well documented by economists like Enrico Moretti, who has shown that adding more college-educated workers to a state actually boosts everyone's wages, with most of the gains going to noncollege-educated workers.[28] My colleague Tim Bartik has made a similar spillover argument about the economic development benefits of universal high-quality prekindergarten education.[29] In a slack economy, enabling workers to retrain for job openings in emerging fields will help support consumption and economic growth.

In addition to generating more skilled workers, Promise programs serve the important function of signaling to employers that a state or region is a good place to locate. Traditionally, being "open for business" has meant low corporate tax rates, light levels of regulation, weak unions, and a willingness to grant business subsidies. It is now beginning also to mean that a state or region invests in its residents' education and will partner with businesses to ensure they have a skilled, ready workforce.

Promise programs can be catalysts for cross-sector alignment, bringing together different systems and creating tighter connections between them. A good example is the many partnerships already in place between community colleges and technical training institutions on the one hand and employers on the other.[30] Such partnerships are seen regularly at the local level, but a statewide Promise program can scale up collaboration. Promise programs can also serve to strengthen those institutions providing technical training and associate degrees, not simply by bringing them new enrollees (this can actually be a negative for institutions if they are not equipped to serve them) but by stimulating creative thinking about how better to serve students.

The four questions of program structure that occur throughout the book provide a useful framework for examining how Promise programs can contribute to better employment outcomes for workers and business alike.

Who benefits? Promise programs focused on employment should be widely available and easy to access—hence, universal eligibility with minimal requirements is ideal, as is the inclusion of adults without college degrees. If stakeholders are serious about expanding the workforce, it is not sufficient to focus on the population already going to college. Instead, the pool must be broadened.

What are the postsecondary options? In employment-related Promise programs, it is appropriate to emphasize community colleges and other technical training institutions. While it is always an advantage for students to have more choice about what type of institution to attend, faster returns in the form of trained workers are more likely when programs direct students to shorter-term training, such as credentials and certificates, or associate degree–granting institutions. One corollary of this approach is the need to develop strategies to avoid the undermatching that can occur when academically qualified students shift attendance from four-year to two-year institutions in light of scholarship rules.

How much funding is involved? In a perfect world, funds for Promise programs would be delivered on a first-dollar basis. However, this is not the world we live in, and almost all Promise programs are structured as last-dollar programs, layered on top of existing federal and, in some cases, state need-based aid. In order to broaden the population accessing Promise funding, employment-focused scholarships should have FAFSA completion built into the application process and provide sufficient outreach and support to ensure that all Pell-eligible students receive their full allotment of federal funds. Additional financial support should also be available to help low-income students who do not receive new resources through the scholarship manage living costs and emergencies.

Are student support resources included? If the talent pipeline is to be broadened, whether to meet business needs, enhance equity, or enable workers to retrain in a turbulent economy, it is not enough to bring students to college; they must be supported through completion. Some of the students entering this larger pipeline will be less prepared to succeed in postsecondary settings than previous cohorts. These students, whether recent high school graduates or adults, need help at two critical stages—first, navigating the transition from high school or the workforce into college,

> and second, ensuring college persistence and degree or credential completion. Without robust support services at both stages, the expanded pipeline will narrow along the way as students drop out. Of course, effective interventions are also required during the preK–12 years to ensure that students are prepared in the first place to move on to higher education.

How do these design considerations play out in practice? Local Promise stakeholders face a dilemma mentioned earlier: students receiving scholarship funds may opt to leave the community to attend college, provided nonlocal postsecondary options are available. Even if they stay nearby for college, students may move away once their degrees are completed. More education gives people greater mobility, which is good news for individuals but less so for local stakeholders, funders, and businesses seeking employees. The mobility issue is not as acute when the focus of a Promise program is on local institutions, especially community colleges, since most community college attendees remain in or near their home communities.[31]

Employment-oriented Promise programs make greater sense at the state level where even if students do relocate after graduation, they are likely to remain in the state.[32] In this sense, these policies are an echo of the earlier generation of statewide merit-based programs that sought to retain the best and brightest. The difference is that the new programs are serving students who historically have not pursued postsecondary education. Statewide Promise programs tailored to employment needs thus represent a welcome recognition that human capital development should not be restricted to high-achieving students, as it was under the merit-based scholarship model, and that there is a postsecondary path that is right for almost every student.

The remainder of this chapter explores three Promise programs, one local and two statewide, that show how the employment rationale for tuition-free college naturally connects to equity concerns. The key provisions of these programs are summarized in table 5.1. These case

TABLE 5.1 Characteristics of selected employment-focused Promise programs

	DETROIT PROMISE (2-YEAR TRACK)	TENNESSEE PROMISE	TENNESSEE RECONNECT*
Date established	Announced 2011; implemented for Class of 2014.	Announced 2014; implemented for Class of 2015.	Announced 2017; implemented in 2018.
Student eligibility	Graduates of any high school in the City of Detroit who have attended school and lived in the city for at least the last two years of high school.	Tennessee resident/US citizen/eligible noncitizen who graduates from an in-state high school or homeschool, or earns a GED/HISET before 19th birthday.	Tennessee resident for at least one year who does not already have an associate or bachelor's degree; must be deemed an independent student.
Eligible postsecondary institutions	One of six community colleges in Southeast Michigan.	Two-year degree and credential programs at in-state community colleges, colleges of applied technology, and four-year institutions (with amount capped at community college tuition rate).	Two-year degree and credential programs at in-state community colleges, colleges of applied technology, and four-year institutions (with amount capped at community college tuition rate).
Structure of scholarship	Last dollar	Last dollar	Last dollar
Funding	Funded by Michigan Education Excellence Foundation and Detroit Promise Zone tax capture mechanism	Funded by lottery reserve fund and lottery proceeds	Funded by lottery proceeds
Other requirements	FAFSA completion; participate in Detroit Promise Path coaching	FAFSA completion; participate in high school mentoring, complete community service requirements; must enroll full-time.	FAFSA completion; must enroll half-time at community college or full-time at TCAT; must participate in an approved advising program

*There was an earlier program by the same name limited to older students enrolling in Tennessee Colleges of Applied Technology (TCATs). It was later expanded to include community colleges.

studies also illustrate the rationale for public investment in higher education—Detroit and Tennessee have invested in a pathway to free college not only to help the direct beneficiaries of these programs but to benefit the city and state themselves.

Community-Based Program: The Detroit Promise

The history of the Detroit Promise is complex. In 2011, Governor Rick Snyder announced the goal of providing all Detroit high school graduates with a tuition-free path to an associate degree or technical certification as part of a larger commitment to improving educational outcomes in Michigan's largest city. The setting was challenging—the Detroit Public Schools had been struggling for years, in part because of vigorous advocacy of charter schools in Michigan, and faced issues related to enrollment, finances, and infrastructure.[33] Detroit had been designated one of ten Michigan Promise Zones (there are now fifteen) under 2009 legislation enacted by Snyder's predecessor, Governor Jennifer Granholm, but local politics and the advent of the nation's largest municipal bankruptcy had hindered progress in forming and launching the Promise Zone. Many school-improvement efforts were underway, supported by local foundations, but there was no overarching citywide or regional approach to improving college readiness or access. At the same time, the business community, organized through the Detroit Regional Chamber, was focused on talent development for its eleven-county region and recognized that graduates of the area's largest school district were lagging in postsecondary attendance and career readiness.

Beginning with the class of 2013, the governor committed funding from the Michigan Excellence in Education Foundation to support a two-year scholarship for City of Detroit high school graduates. Based at the chamber, the Detroit Scholarship Fund allowed any high school graduate in the City of Detroit to attend one of five (now six) regional community colleges tuition free on a last-dollar basis. Students must have resided in and attended high school in the city for at least two years. Because Detroit has such a high poverty rate, most applicants to the program qualified for full Pell Grants that in turn covered most of the tuition at a community college, which meant the program was relatively inexpensive.

Two years later, Snyder collaborated with Detroit's mayor Mike Duggan to expand the scholarship and rebrand it the Detroit Promise. An earlier initiative called the Detroit Compact was retooled to provide a four-year option for Detroit high school graduates with GPAs of 3.0 and above. This option relies on the state's four-year universities to fund last-dollar scholarships for the students they admit. Some institutions have provided an open-ended commitment to accept an unlimited number of applicants who meet Detroit Promise academic requirements, while others have capped their commitment at a set number. Eighteen institutions, including most of the state's fifteen public universities, participate.

In practice, most graduates do not meet the terms of the four-year track, which include a 3.0 high school GPA requirement, a college-ready SAT or ACT score, and four years attendance or residency within the city. GED recipients are not eligible. Apart from these academic requirements, many students find it hard to manage living expenses if they move away from home (some colleges have responded to this quandary by providing additional scholarships from their own resources). As a result, roughly twice as many Detroit Promise recipients attend a community college under the two-year track as those who attend four-year institutions.[34] These are the students most likely to remain in the region after completing a degree or credential, and they include many who were not on any postsecondary path before the creation of the Detroit Promise.

The Detroit Promise Zone authorized back in 2009 under the Michigan Promise Zone legislation was also finally launched in 2015. As a result, the Detroit Promise has begun to receive state resources through a tax-increment financing structure that directs a portion of the increase in the State Education Tax to the scholarship. There are fourteen other Michigan Promise Zones that have the same financing structure.[35]

The Detroit Promise has two defining characteristics. First, it is administered and operated by the Detroit Regional Chamber, the state's leading business organization, and is just one aspect of the chamber's work on college access and success. The Detroit Regional Chamber, along with other chambers of commerce across the nation, including those in Austin, Dallas, Nashville, and Los Angeles, have embraced education as a pivotal component of their mission—to serve their business constituency by expanding the talent pipeline. It is no surprise to find many of these organizations also engaged in local and statewide college Promise programs.

The Detroit Regional Chamber's work on education begins with the understanding that most of Michigan's future jobs will require some kind of postsecondary education and training, and that as degree attainment rates rise, so will per capita income. Michigan performs poorly on most measures of educational attainment. The state ranks thirty-third in adults with an associate degree or higher, and the Detroit region ranks thirty-eighth among the nation's fifty largest metropolitan areas. It is in this context that Governor Gretchen Whitmer announced in 2019 a statewide educational attainment goal of 60 percent of residents with degrees or credentials by 2030; the rate in 2019 was 45 percent, up from 36 percent in 2010.[36] The chamber advances this goal through the Detroit Drives Degrees initiative—a collective impact effort to improve the talent pipeline in the region by increasing access to postsecondary opportunities, boosting student success, and attracting and retaining local talent.

The mantra of the Promise movement has changed over time from getting students *to* college to getting them *through* college. The second major contribution of the Detroit Promise comes in this area of student support. While the scholarship in its early years had increased the number of students in community college, many of them were insufficiently prepared and struggled with persistence and degree completion. In 2016, MDRC, a leading educational evaluation firm, began a pilot intervention called the Detroit Promise Path. Under the plan, a group of randomly selected scholarship recipients participated in a support model based on the City University of New York's Accelerated Study in Associate Program (ASAP). The intervention has four elements.[37] First, students connect with a *campus coach* who provides academic and personal support.

This is sometimes called "intrusive" advising as coaches reach out to students through multiple modes of contact and support students on a range of issues that can hinder degree completion. In the case of the Detroit Promise Path experiment, students were required to meet with their coach twice a month to retain monthly *monetary incentives* of $50 to help offset expenses, like transportation and food, that are not covered by financial aid. In a third program element, coaches promote *summer engagement*, which covers enrollment in summer courses or employment through a local job program. The fourth element is *data collection* and the issuing of regular reports to track student progress and underpin continuous improvement efforts by the program overall.

Final results of the randomized experiment are not yet available, but preliminary findings showed that students receiving Promise Path services were more likely to return for their second semester, attend full-time, enroll in summer courses, and be on track for degree completion than their peers.[38] The results were so compelling that the Detroit Promise now extends Promise Path support services to all its community college participants. These core support elements have been adopted by other Promise communities interested in improving student outcomes at community colleges. In 2018, a foundation-funded College Promise Success Initiative was launched by MDRC in partnership with College Promise and the State Higher Education Executive Officers Association; it works with five Promise programs (local, institutional, and statewide) to implement some of the findings of the Detroit experience. Interventions like these are essential if students attending community college are to complete degrees and enter the workforce with more valuable credentials.

The good news is that the Detroit Promise Path supports can be delivered at relatively low cost. One factor that had deterred widespread adoption of the ASAP model was its high cost—ASAP services initially cost over $10,000 per student, with the cost falling in subsequent cohorts to about $4,000 per student per year.[39] A similar demonstration project in Ohio had per-student costs of around $3,000.[40] In both these cases, ASAP was covering not only administrative, staffing, and incentive costs, but also paying for tuition waivers for program participants. In Promise communities, tuition is already paid for, so only coaching and incentives must be provided; the lower cost of living outside New York City has also been helpful in reducing costs. In Detroit, the chamber was able to deliver services at a per-student cost of $1,027, roughly the same amount as what it was spending on last-dollar tuition coverage.[41] This is a more manageable figure for a Promise program interested in providing effective student support; however, costs will vary depending on where and how program services are delivered.

There are even lower-cost models of student support emerging in some Promise communities, although they have not been rigorously evaluated. One example is volunteer mentorship to help guide students through the high school to postsecondary transition, such as the career-focused mentorship program offered to all recipients of the Richmond Promise.[42] Sending more students to college to enhance their value in the local workforce will benefit those students, their employers, and the city as a whole only if effective, affordable systems are in place to support student success and degree completion.

State Programs: Tennessee Promise and Tennessee Reconnect

Tennessee is at the forefront of the free-college movement. It was the first state to make community college tuition free for all high school graduates through the Tennessee Promise, announced in 2014. Four years later, Tennessee Reconnect was expanded from its modest roots to allow any adult in the state without a college degree to pursue an associate degree or other credential, also tuition free. The two initiatives were enacted in a deeply red state by a Republican governor with the support of the legislature's Republican majority, and both programs have sparked dramatic upticks in postsecondary enrollment. The Tennessee Promise operates as a public-private partnership, with money from the state and a nonprofit organization, Tennessee Achieves (tnAchieves), as its operating arm. The Ayers Foundation also facilitates student applications, FAFSA help, and mentor matching in the rural communities it serves.

The Tennessee Promise embodies the marriage of employment and equity goals. Only by reaching out to populations that have not attended college can a scholarship program hope to affect employment outcomes. To serve low-income, first-generation college goers well, such programs must include strong elements of navigation, FAFSA preparation, coaching, and other forms of student support. Tennessee has been a leader in innovating in this area, taking a volunteer mentorship program developed as part of a small free-college program to scale statewide and developing a variety of other strategies to promote student success.

The origin story of the Tennessee Promise has been told before.[43] One of its interesting elements is that many of the individuals present at the beginning are still involved more than a decade later, even as the program has grown from serving a few hundred students to tens of thousands (in October 2020, tnAchieves marked its 100,000th student to enroll in college). The story begins with Mike Ragsdale, a first-generation college goer who earned a PhD from the University of Tennessee and served as county mayor of Knoxville from 2002 to 2010. In 2006, Ragsdale hired Krissy DeAlejandro, another first-generation student (see the sidebar "Krissy's Story"). "Everyone was talking about workforce development," says DeAlejandro, recalling the political climate at the time.[44] Working with the Knoxville Chamber of Commerce, the county hired a vice president of workforce development, and the mayor began giving speeches about how East Tennessee needed a more skilled workforce. "One-third of students from Knox County were completing high school and pursuing no type of postsecondary training," continues DeAlejandro. "These were disproportionately low-income, first-generation, academically weaker students. The mayor asked, 'What if we tried to build a program for that one-third?'" Ragsdale's time as a community college dean had given him firsthand experience with this population and helped him formulate the idea of creating a scholarship through private dollars combined with Pell Grants.

The plan that emerged, which would become Knox Achieves, was a last-dollar scholarship with required mentorship and community

→ KRISSY'S STORY

Krissy DeAlejandro leads an enviable life. The mother of three and wife of a chef and restaurateur, the family lives in the Old City, Knoxville's historic district. Krissy can walk to her office located in a 1900s-era building shared with a restaurant and upscale condos. There she oversees a staff of two dozen people charged with making the Tennessee Promise work.

Krissy grew up worlds away in the small town of McMinnville, seventy miles southeast of Nashville. McMinnville's factories closed in the late 1990s, bringing joblessness and increased poverty. Krissy's parents did not attend college; in fact, her mother did not finish high school. The family lived in a tiny house but was happy and close knit. In first grade, Krissy was identified as academically talented and was tracked into advanced classes with a small group of other children. "I was a super nerd," she recalls. "The thirty of us were on a very different path from our schoolmates. Those thirty tended to be from college-going cultures, the kids of the doctors, the lawyers. I never really mixed with the other 370 of my peers," apart from her stint as a high school cheerleader, something encouraged by her mother to help her fit in socially.

In eleventh grade, Krissy's math skills took her to a competition at Sewanee: The University of the South, a liberal arts college with ivy-covered walls and a chapel with stained-glass windows. Knowing nothing about college, Krissy decided this was the school she would attend. "I came home and told my parents that's where I'm going. I had no idea what it cost, or anything about it." It was the only college she applied to. "It never dawned on me that I wouldn't get in, and my parents didn't know enough to say, 'What happens if it doesn't work out?' We talk about the Tennessee Promise now as a 'Plan B' for many students," Krissy explains. "Even if it's not your first choice, hang in there with it in case you need a fallback plan."

The passion Krissy brings to her work supporting students draws on her own experience as a first-generation college goer. These experiences began day one when her parents dropped her off for orientation weekend and then drove the hour back to McMinnville. Only when she got to the opening day picnic did she realize parents were supposed to have stayed and that an entire weekend of activities had been planned for them. Too proud to call and ask them to return, Krissy muddled through the weekend, one of the few students on her own. When Krissy found herself enrolled in a math class that was too advanced for her, she did not know that she could insist on a course change. Instead, she took no for an answer and struggled with a difficult first semester. Only through mentorship and weekly tutoring by her chemistry professor did she make it through her first year of college. Krissy ended up excelling at Sewanee. She studied abroad at Oxford University and moved to Knoxville to pursue a PhD at the University of Tennessee.

Transitioning to local government work when the opportunity arose, she helped create and now leads the Tennessee Promise's support organization, tnAchieves.

When Krissy talks today about supporting these students as they transition from high school to postsecondary education, these are the kinds of experiences she has in mind. She and her staff are continually exploring ways to impart that amorphous "college knowledge" about unwritten norms and rules to students whose families, like Krissy's, cannot provide it.

service components that would help high school students navigate the transition to higher education. Both Ragsdale and DeAlejandro had benefited from close mentoring relationships on their higher-education pathways and understood that the students they were hoping to reach would need support. To raise funds, Ragsdale turned to his friend and neighbor Randy Boyd, CEO of Radio Systems and, since 2020, president of the University of Tennessee system. "Randy came in for a one-hour meeting and asked a lot of questions to which we didn't have answers," recalls DeAlejandro. "When he left the meeting, we both felt good about it. A few hours later my desk phone rang. It was Randy, and he said, 'I've raised $2.3 million in cash and pledges. How quickly can we get this off the ground?'" Boyd had asked donors for a three-year commitment so when the scholarship was offered to a class of incoming students, funds were in place to see that class through to degree completion. "I remember walking into Ragsdale's office and saying, 'He's in,'" continues DeAlejandro. "That was July 2008; we announced [Knox Achieves] in October."

Timing and luck played a part in the creation of the Tennessee Promise. During Mayor Ragsdale's tenure, another Republican, Bill Haslam, was mayor of the city of Knoxville. The Haslam family owns the Pilot Flying J chain of gas stations and truck stops that accounts for Bill's and his brother Jimmy Haslam's inclusion on *Forbes*'s annual list of the nation's billionaires.[45] The county mayor and city mayor worked in the same building, and it was natural for Ragsdale to stop by Haslam's office and share his idea for Knox Achieves. Haslam's first reaction—"This is too simple"—mirrored that of many who heard about the program, but the city mayor soon came to understand that the program's simplicity was central to its power. Speaking years later about the Tennessee Promise, Haslam explained, "We wanted it to be an easy thing to sell and describe . . . Free was an easy discussion so we could say, 'If you walk across that high school stage, then you could go to college free.' And that was a conversation we wanted people to have around their dinner tables."[46]

Two other leading businesspeople soon joined Boyd and Ragsdale in launching Knox Achieves. More than a decade later, all four were on the board of tnAchieves, with DeAlejandro serving as executive director. The continuity in leadership represented by this group, even as the program has expanded across the state, has been important to its success, creating a framework of trust within which program leaders have been given the flexibility to innovate. The public-private structure under which the state funds the Tennessee Promise while tnAchieves leads operations has also insulated the program from political pressures and created broad buy-in across many sectors.

Other states have looked at Tennessee when considering whether and how to structure their own statewide Promise programs. In thinking about why Tennessee Promise has become such a powerful national model, five factors come to mind.

1. State leaders built the Tennessee Promise on a base of knowledge acquired from an earlier, smaller-scale program

Knox Achieves was part of the wave of innovation that took place in the years following the introduction of the Kalamazoo Promise. The program initially allowed high school graduates in the Knoxville region to attend one of three community colleges tuition free.[47] In its first year, 2008–2009, 496 high school seniors applied. Most were low-income or first-generation college goers, and to facilitate their success, 180 volunteer mentors were recruited to guide and support them through the application process. From this modest beginning, the program grew rapidly, three years later serving students in twenty-three counties under the tnAchieves name.

Haslam had been elected governor in 2010 and immediately sought to respond to employer concerns about the availability of skilled workers. The state economy was recovering from the 2008 recession, and businesses were clamoring for trained employees. But Tennessee's college attainment rate among adults was below the national average at both the associate and bachelor's degree levels. The Complete College Tennessee Act, passed under Haslam's Democratic predecessor in 2010, had been designed to raise postsecondary attainment rates. Haslam built on that effort, introducing the "Drive to 55" statewide attainment goal that sought to increase degree attainment to 55 percent by 2025. The figure came from Georgetown University's Center for Education and the Workforce estimates of what percentage of jobs by state would require some college education by 2020.[48] In 2014, the year the Tennessee Promise was announced, associate degree and certificate attainment stood at 39 percent[49]; by 2019, it was 43 percent.[50] Tuition-free community college for high school graduates was part of this effort. The core components of Knox Achieves were preserved in the statewide program: tuition-free two-year degrees, now offered at thirteen community colleges and twenty-seven Tennessee Colleges of Applied Technology (TCATs), as well as by some four-year institutions; mentorship, now carried out at a huge scale; and community service.

Just as the Tennessee Promise built on Knox Achieves, so did Tennessee Reconnect incorporate lessons learned from the Tennessee Promise. The program, known as Reconnect, is available to all adults in the state who do not have college degrees, and enrollment options are limited to associate or certificate programs. At the same time, Reconnect was adapted to accommodate some of the unique challenges adult learners face. Full-time attendance is not required (the minimum credit load is six credits per semester, or half-time), there are no community service requirements, and the mentorship model, which works well in the high school environment but less so with adults, was replaced by a largely online navigation system (see below).

2. Tennessee opted for a relatively simple, inclusive program structure with strong messaging and outreach

As argued elsewhere in this book, universal-eligibility programs are the best approach for reaching new college goers, and a simple, clear message facilitates this effort. The Tennessee Promise message was relatively simple and its approach inclusive: if you graduate from high school (or receive a GED or homeschool certificate by age nineteen), file a FAFSA, attend a mandatory orientation (generally held at your high school), pair up with a volunteer mentor, and perform eight hours of community service before the term the award is received, you will qualify for a last-dollar scholarship covering tuition and fees for a two-year degree or credential program. There are no merit- or financial-need requirements. The community service requirement is arguably a distraction that adds complexity and screens out students who fail to meet it; however, it helps program supporters show that students are giving back and dilutes criticism from the right that the scholarship is an entitlement or a "free ride."[51] Qualitative work by RAND researcher Jenna Kramer has shown that scholarship recipients see the scholarship as a contractual relationship, with community service requirements as their side of the bargain.[52]

These inclusive eligibility rules, coupled with energetic messaging, mean that almost every high school student in the state applies for the program. In some cases, schools or districts themselves will apply on behalf of their students. Most recent figures show 90 percent of public high school students and 80 percent of high school students overall begin the application process.[53] Not all will go on to use the scholarship—some will attend four-year or private institutions, while others will defer college attendance—but the Tennessee Promise serves as plan A for many and a backup for many others. These application rates have also vaulted Tennessee to its current position as the state with the nation's highest FAFSA filing rates.[54]

The impact of the rise in FAFSA filing rates has been profound. As a last-dollar scholarship that covers degree or credential programs of two years or less, the Tennessee Promise brings little or no new money to low-income, Pell-eligible recipients. This has made it a target of criticism from advocacy organizations concerned about whether free-college programs provide additional financial resources to low-income students.[55] However, the Tennessee Promise has brought many more low-income students into the college-going process by embedding FAFSA completion within its application and eligibility requirements. These students may have their college tuition funded by Pell Grants, but before the Tennessee Promise, they were not attending college at all. This means that the Tennessee Promise is in fact reaching new students—statewide, 40 percent of Promise recipients are first-generation college goers, while 52 percent qualify for Pell Grants.[56]

Tennessee Reconnect was designed for a different purpose—to reach adults without college degrees and offer them a tuition-free path to a credential or degree. The program has even fewer requirements than the Tennessee Promise, although adults are encouraged to connect with a navigator and make use of support resources provided by their postsecondary institutions. Participants attending a TCAT must go full-time when the rules of a specific program require it, but community college attendance under Reconnect can be half-time. Effective messaging and buy-in from employers, who help connect their own workers to the new postsecondary opportunities, have underpinned the program's success.

In its first year, Tennessee Reconnect surpassed state projections to enroll eighteen thousand scholarship recipients. Over 70 percent are female, and more than half have children. One-half of those applying make less than $25,000 a year. Essentially, the program is serving working poor mothers, many with children, illustrating how a program designed to build a talent pipeline to serve employer needs also promotes upward mobility for an historically disadvantaged population.

3. Both Tennessee Promise and Tennessee Reconnect embed student support to improve outcomes

From the earliest days of Knox Achieves, program stakeholders understood that first-generation, low-income college goers would need support on their journey to and through higher education. The mechanics of the mentorship program that served the initial class of Knox Achieves students have changed, but the core elements remain: every student eligible for the Tennessee Promise has access to an individual who can answer questions, provide encouragement, and connect the student to other resources. A mentor is paired with a small group of students in their senior year and meets them once or twice in person. Continued communication takes place through text or phone conversations. Mentors are recruited via an active social media campaign; in 2019, the campaign signed up 9,777 mentors. The top four entities contributing mentors were the Shelby County (Memphis) schools, the state's Department of Human Services, Blue Cross Blue Shield, and the Tennessee Department of Corrections, each of which contributed more than a hundred mentors from among their employees. Thirty-four percent of the mentors come from businesses. In 2018, mentors sent 9 million emails and 1.5 million text messages; two of the data points collected to underscore the reach of the mentorship program.[57]

When it came to creating Tennessee Reconnect, state policy makers recognized that a mentorship model geared toward high school students could not easily be adapted to the adult-learner population. Instead, the state experimented with locally based navigation resources in the form of Tennessee Reconnect Communities, then moved to a centralized program called Navigate Reconnect. This program is operated and funded by the state, unlike the mentorship component of Tennessee Promise run by tnAchieves and the Ayers Foundation, and paid for with philanthropic dollars. The state employs a team of sixteen navigators located in different regions that serve as an initial point of contact for adults considering enrolling in college. Tennessee partnered with The Graduate Network, a nonprofit organization focused on increasing college completion among adults, to design support services that recognize the unique challenges adult learners face. In addition, every student receiving a Reconnect grant is required to participate in a college success program. Most often, these are coaching programs based at community colleges. The legislation establishing Reconnect gave the

Tennessee Higher Education Commission (THEC) flexibility in designing support programs. The result has been innovative approaches, such as the Reconnect Cafés found on several campuses in the Nashville region that create an informal, nurturing environment in which students can connect with a coach.[58]

4. Program leaders have shown a commitment to continuous improvement to support better outcomes and operations

This mind-set of innovation and adjustment has been part of Tennessee's tuition-free college work from the beginning. Even in its earliest incarnation, Knox Achieves partnered with researchers at the University of Tennessee to carry out rigorous evaluations of its impact. THEC has invested in data tools like Salesforce, a customer relationship management software system, to track participation in Tennessee Reconnect, and has a dedicated staff in its policy and research unit tasked with collecting and analyzing data about effectiveness. TnAchieves, too, has been empowered to experiment with outreach mechanisms and support services. Robust data analysis coupled with flexibility has created room for innovation. Interventions that yield results have been scaled up, while those that are less effective have been phased out. As new needs have arisen, new approaches have been tried.

In 2019, a pilot program was introduced in the Knoxville region with $6.2 million in funding from The Haslam Foundation. It provided high-impact support services to all Tennessee Promise participants graduating from Knox County high schools in 2019 and 2020. The services include access to a dedicated "completion coach" who provides high-touch support to students throughout their college years; a summer support program to boost year-to-year retention; a textbook stipend; and access to "completion grants," emergency aid designed to meet needs that interfere with completion, such as transportation or car repairs.[59] If results are positive—that is, if they pay off with added degrees—the model may be scaled up to serve other regions.

Innovation does not always require new funding. In my earlier study of the Kalamazoo Promise, I argue there are two parts to an effective place-based scholarship program—funding and alignment.[60] Alignment refers to the reorientation of effort by multiple actors in support of program goals (see the sidebar "Fred and Dan's Story"). Without both elements, Promise programs will fail to be transformative. The architects of Tennessee Promise and Reconnect have taken the alignment lesson to heart and much of the program's innovation centers on enlisting individuals and organizations outside the educational sphere in the project of increasing degree attainment. One example is the training of Reconnect Ambassadors, individuals working in state agencies, corporations, or other position where they have contact with potential Reconnectors. In Nashville, the chamber trained 160 people throughout the city to serve as ambassadors, while the state delivered training to hundreds of public employees, including six hundred at the Department of Human Services and five hundred at American Jobs Centers. Reconnect Ambassadors are able to reach potential Reconnectors with plain-language messaging and handoffs to other resources.[61]

The combination of secure, statewide funding with flexibility for local experimentation has worked well for the program. With robust data collection integrated into the program, managers can determine where additional interventions are needed. And if results are uneven across communities or population groups, targeted initiatives can support outreach, student success, or even mentorship recruitment.

5. A final critical advantage concerns the program's funding

In its earliest days, Knox Achieves was funded by private donations and foundation grants; however, such privately funded models are not viable at the state level. Haslam and the legislature granted the Tennessee Promise and Reconnect financial security when they opted to fund these programs through the state's lottery. The Tennessee Education Lottery has been generating money for college scholarships since 2004. Under the legislation establishing the lottery, the state is required to preserve $100 million in a reserve fund, but over a decade, the fund accumulated about $400 million. Of this reserve, $300 million was used to create a Tennessee Promise endowment within the lottery

→ FRED AND DAN'S STORY

In a cozy room behind the admissions office at Nashville State Community College, Fred Frazier Jr. offers students who drop by a beverage, a snack, relaxing music, and a comfortable couch. Part taskmaster, part motivational coach, Fred also dispenses a unique blend of college advising that draws on his twenty-year career in the US Navy and another twenty as a career coach. Fred's job is to help adults returning to college through the Tennessee Reconnect program navigate their reentry and succeed in completing a degree or credential. He and a colleague serve as student success advisers, staffing Reconnect Cafés on three Nashville State campuses and supporting nine hundred adults who are returning to school or completing their degree or credential. They reach out regularly through email and text, with a special focus on critical moments in the semester, such as registration deadlines or midterm grading. For those who visit the café, Fred provides high-touch coaching, a handoff to other college resources, and a nurturing place to take a break from the pressures of being an adult learner. For students struggling to balance work-life demands or feeling anxious about their skills, having an advising relationship with someone who understands their challenges can make all the difference in whether or not they remain enrolled.

Thirty minutes away sits the Smyrna campus of the Tennessee College of Applied Technology (TCAT), a training facility serving Tennessee Promise and Reconnect students along with employees who work at the sprawling Nissan Smyrna Assembly Plant across the road. (The plant is the largest assembly facility in the nation, with maximum production capacity of 640,000 cars and trucks a year.) This is a different world than Fred's Reconnect Café. Spotless, airy, and filled with millions of dollars of state-of-the-art equipment donated by area manufacturers, here TCAT students and Nissan workers learn to operate the robotic assemblies and computers found on the factory floor. Dan Caldwell, a thirty-year veteran of Nissan and now vice president of collective impact and strategic initiatives at the area's United Way, gives the tour, explaining that the facility is a public-private partnership owned by the State of Tennessee on land bought by Nissan and donated to the state. The facility is split sixty-forty between the college and Nissan. Two hundred students, many of them receiving Tennessee Promise or Reconnect grants, learn automotive skills, welding, and machining. On the Nissan side, all 8,400 plant employees rotate through at some point to gain new skills. Nissan hires about 10 percent of the TCAT's graduates, and the other 90 percent go to work for suppliers or other companies in the area. "It's a win for everyone," explains Caldwell, who has also served for years as a Tennessee Promise mentor: as a public entity, the TCAT can accept donated equipment from automotive companies, Nissan employees and TCAT students can train on that equipment, vendors put their machines into the hands of their future workforce, and the community benefits as home to the facility and the human capital it represents.

The two settings may be worlds apart, but Fred and Dan are engaged in the same endeavor—ensuring that Tennessee residents are able to gain meaningful employment at a family-supporting wage, that Tennessee's employers have access to trained workers, and that Tennessee itself reaps the benefits of a cohesive system of training and education that runs from preK through adulthood. This is alignment in action, as disparate sectors work together for a common goal, and it is both an essential part of and a product of effective free-college programs.

reserve fund. Tennessee Reconnect is funded slightly differently, with resources coming directly from net lottery proceeds that fund thirteen scholarship programs overall. The annual cost of the Tennessee Promise is about $30 million a year to serve almost thirty thousand students, an amount easily covered by interest on the reserve fund plus new lottery proceeds. Tennessee Reconnect costs about the same amount, although it reaches fewer students—eighteen thousand in its first year. The cost for the adult program is higher on a per-student basis because Reconnect participants have a lower rate of Pell eligibility than recent high school graduates.

This secure funding stream became critically important as the nation entered the COVID-19-induced recession in 2020. While other states with adult-learner programs in the works, including New Jersey, New Mexico, and Virginia, put their efforts on hold, Tennessee Reconnect was prepared to support a surge of laid-off workers in need of retraining. The fate of several other statewide Promise programs remained uncertain, as governors' budgets were retooled in light of the crisis. These cutbacks and pauses hold important lessons for architects of Promise programs—that secure funding is essential for a Promise to be kept.

For all these reasons—a commitment to learning from experience, an inclusive model coupled with powerful messaging, built-in student support, and secure funding—Tennessee serves as a best-practice example for other states considering tuition-free college. It is also instructive to see how tuition-free college can be carried out in a conservative political climate. The emphasis on practical, short-term training delivered through the state's TCATs and community colleges makes the societal benefits of free college—a better-trained workforce, a more competitive state economy—easier for the public to see and creates enthusiasm for the effort among the business community and their legislative supporters.

Table 5.2 compares the provisions of the Detroit Promise and Tennessee programs when it comes to the employability metrics discussed above. Has the strategy worked? Have investments in college going by traditionally underserved populations in Detroit, Tennessee, and elsewhere led to the employment outcomes hoped for by the stakeholders in these programs? The honest answer is we do not know yet. Evidence around the impact of Promise programs on employment, earnings, and debt is still limited. In part, this is an issue of timing—these outcomes take many years to show up in the data—and in part it is a reflection

TABLE 5.2 Employment metrics for Promise programs

	DETROIT PROMISE (2-YEAR TRACK)	TENNESSEE PROMISE	TENNESSEE RECONNECT
Student eligibility	Universal; all high school graduates are eligible.	Universal; all high school graduates are eligible.	Universal; all adults without college degrees are eligible.
Flexibility of usage (postsecondary program type)	Can be used at one of 6 area community colleges.	Can be used at any community college or college of applied technology in the state.	Can be used at any community college or college of applied technology in the state.
How is funding delivered?	Last dollar, covers full tuition after other sources of grant aid including Pell Grants.	Last dollar, covers full tuition after other sources of grant aid including Pell Grants.	Last dollar, covers full tuition after other sources of grant aid including Pell Grants.
Support services	Embedded in program; coaches funded by Detroit Regional Chamber.	Mentorship a required component of the program (funded privately).	Students must participate in an approved advising program (no additional funding from the state).
Connection with employers	High. Detroit Regional Chamber leadership; program is part of a broader talent development strategy.	Medium. Businesses participate as mentors.	High. Employers refer students to programs; program is part of a broader talent development strategy.

of the limited resources devoted to rigorously evaluating this aspect of Promise programs. Such research is also methodologically challenging, as not every state has a data system that tracks students through the educational system and into the workforce. It is far easier to study what happens to Promise students in postsecondary settings than it is to determine what happens to them once they enter the workforce. We know from studies of some of the more mature Promise programs that tuition-free college leads more students to enroll in postsecondary education and more students to receive degrees or credentials. We also know from decades of research that individuals with degrees or credentials earn more and experience greater job security than those without. Even so, it is difficult to draw a straight line from free-college programs to positive employment outcomes. If free-college programs attract more high- school graduates to college, it is very possible that the earnings of these individuals in their late teens and early twenties will actually be lower than they would have been otherwise, as students focus on completing their education. It is also possible that the students induced to attend college through these scholarships face other barriers, such as more limited social networks, that make it difficult for them to translate their degrees and credentials into higher earnings. And for programs that offer scholarships to four-year institutions, it can take a decade before employment and earnings impacts show up in the data.

We are on the cusp of learning more. With funding from Strada Education Network and the Upjohn Institute, researchers from several communities are examining whether there is a link between Promise programs and employment or earnings. Research on Knox Achieves by Celeste Carruthers and colleagues shows that participants had higher earnings in the seven years after high school and are more likely to be employed in an unemployment insurance–covered job than a comparison group.[62] Brad Hershbein and colleagues have found that Kalamazoo Promise recipients are more likely than a comparison group to remain in or near Kalamazoo in the early years of their career, but that, to date, the Kalamazoo Promise has not had a significant positive impact on earnings.[63] Additional workforce findings should become available in 2021, but this early research suggests the importance of the local context. The employment and earnings impact of Promise programs may rest in part on the job opportunities available in the local labor market. As Hershbein and colleagues write, "As more states adopt explicit education goals to reach a certain share of their working-age population with post-secondary education credentials, our results serve as a cautionary reminder that greater educational attainment by itself may not be sufficient to lead to better workforce outcomes, and that additional measures to promote job development may be necessary."[64]

For now, the employment rationale for free college remains twofold: businesses need more skilled workers than what most states' educational systems are producing, and workers will do better in terms of lifetime earnings and job security if they complete some form of postsecondary education and training. For these outcomes to be achieved, employment-related Promise programs must be inclusive and embed strong navigation and student support components. If they do, both employment and equity goals will be served.

CHAPTER

6

Toward Free College for All

> Today's debate about free college tuition does something extremely valuable. It reintroduces the concept of public good to higher education discourse.
>
> —*Tressie McMillan Cottom*[1]

TUITION-FREE COLLEGE AVAILABLE to all will not happen without a significant federal investment and leadership from the top. Over many years and numerous reauthorizations of the Higher Education Act that became law in 1965, a patchwork system of college financial aid has developed. Several hundred localities and about half the states provide a range of financial benefits to their residents through Promise programs that vary in design. The federal Pell Grant system undergirds this movement, with most Promise programs awarding scholarships on a last-dollar basis, after other forms of grant aid. Without this federal investment, all but a few Promise programs would be unsustainable.

These interlocking local, state, and federal financing mechanisms help many students but leave many others behind.

Free college delivers benefits not just to individuals but also to society, whether in the form of a better-trained workforce, more equitable college access, or the strengthening of school districts and communities. As a public good that makes the economy more productive and society more just, it is in the nation's interest to ensure that everyone can afford to earn a credential or degree. The dramatic events of the spring of 2020—the COVID-19 pandemic, its economic fallout, and America's awakening to long-simmering racial injustice—have made such national action more likely and, indeed, more needed than ever.

Chapter 2 showed how the Promise movement has followed a typical path of policy diffusion, with the model evolving as it spread among localities, then making the leap to the states, where the evolution and replication process has continued at a larger scale. The logical culmination of this diffusion is consideration of similar policies at the federal level, but in the education sphere, there are barriers to national action in the form of local control of education and the existence of what are essentially fifty different state systems of higher education. These must be addressed if a national free-college plan is to become a reality.

The relationship between the state and local Promise movements and national free-college plans is not widely understood. State policy has certainly affected national efforts. President Obama's "America's College Promise" proposal in 2015 was influenced by the Tennessee Promise unveiled the previous year, as well as local initiatives like the Kalamazoo Promise, the Long Beach Promise, and Chicago's free-community-college program for higher-achieving students. But other factors played a role, too, including deep interest within the Obama administration in strengthening the nation's community college system. The emergence of a leading populist candidate of the left in 2016 in the person of Senator Bernie Sanders contributed another strand to the conversation, drawing on the example of other countries and the United States' own history.[2]

The biggest difference between national free-college proposals and the landscape of state and local Promise programs is, not surprisingly, politics. The local Promise movement from the beginning was apolitical, with stakeholders spanning the left-right continuum. Even statewide Promise programs have been a bipartisan effort, with the most well-known program, Tennessee's, enacted under Republican leadership, and more limited statewide programs found in other red states like Oklahoma and Arkansas. On the other hand, national public conversations about tuition-free college have taken place exclusively within the Democratic Party, while generally being derided by the right.[3]

If tuition-free college is to become national policy, it will need to be a bipartisan effort. Even with a Democratic president, Republican votes in the House and Senate will be required to sustain a free-college initiative or related endeavors such as student loan debt relief. There is public enthusiasm for the free-college idea across the political spectrum, as discussed below, and the issue has moved from the left wing into the mainstream of the Democratic Party, but there is a long way to go before a national consensus exists around publicly funded college for all.

This chapter examines the origins and evolution of the national debate over free college, with a focus on how it intersects with continued state and local action. It also takes on the question of how a national free-college strategy can be designed to draw broad political support and public funding at a time of economic and social unrest.

NATIONAL POLITICS AND THE FREE-COLLEGE DEBATE

Tuition-free public higher education is not a new idea. For much of the twentieth century, most public colleges and universities were free or inexpensive. That changed beginning in the 1970s as demand for higher education soared and state funding failed to keep pace. Advocates for free college often cite other developed countries' policies when pressing for a national, publicly funded, higher-education system. While it is true that universities are tuition free in many European countries, these systems tend to serve a smaller and more select group of students and educational systems are more centralized than in the United States.[4]

Current free-college proposals at the national level are very recent. Beginning with America's College Promise in 2015, they intensified with the presidential campaign pledges of senators Bernie Sanders and Hillary Clinton and multiplied during the 2020 Democratic primary season. During this time, the free-college idea moved from the left to the center of the Democratic Party.

In his 2015 State of the Union address, President Obama proposed making community college tuition free. The centerpiece of the America's College Promise proposal was a federal-state partnership to eliminate tuition at the nation's community colleges. A second component was a technical training fund geared toward adults to help states promote high-quality work-based learning and employer partnerships. President Obama's proposal was cast first and foremost as an employment readiness program: "By 2020, an estimated 35 percent of job openings will require at least a bachelor's degree and 30 percent will require some college or an associate's degree." But the plan embedded several equity-enhancing provisions. To begin with, the focus on community college emphasized the needs of lower- and middle-income students, as the percentage of affluent students that attend community college is small. In addition, the program would be open to anyone, whether recent high school graduate or adult; it would require only half-time attendance, making it manageable for working people; and most important, students would retain use of their Pell Grants to help cover living expenses. The proposal also emphasized quality, performance, and shared responsibility on the part of community colleges and states. Only high-quality programs would qualify, students would need to maintain a 2.5 GPA in college (a provision at odds with Pell Grant eligibility and most colleges and universities' requirement of a 2.0 GPA to remain in good standing), and states would need to contribute funding and other resources to align K–12, two-year, and four-year educational systems. Performance-based funding for community colleges was also part of the plan. States' differing higher-education system structures and tuition rates were addressed only vaguely: "States that already invest more and charge students less can make smaller contributions, though all participating states will be required to put up some matching funds."[5] Obviously, many details remained to be addressed, as is typical with State of the Union pronouncements.

The Obama proposal specifically referenced the Tennessee Promise and the Chicago Star Scholarship, both of which had launched in 2014. The latter was a project of Chicago mayor Rahm Emmanuel, who had served as President Obama's chief of staff from 2008 to 2011. (The Star Scholarship provides free community college tuition to all Chicago Public Schools graduates—and since 2019, some Catholic school graduates—who have 3.0 high school GPAs, making it an excellent example of a program that excludes students with lower GPAs and undermatches students who could qualify for four-year institutions. [6]) But there were other factors beyond these state and local examples driving the America's College Promise proposal. Since the beginning of President Obama's first term, there had been interest within the administration in supporting community colleges. As early as 2009, the administration had proposed the $12 billion American Graduation Initiative to support community colleges in improving performance and generating an additional 5 million graduates.[7] There were a number of people within the administration who had long been advocates for the nation's community colleges. These included Dr. Martha Kanter who now leads College Promise and who had served as a community college chancellor before joining the Obama administration as undersecretary of education in 2009, and the vice president's wife, Dr. Jill Biden, a community college English instructor since the early 1990s and now First Lady. Finally, there was support for a free-college proposal from key policy staff in the Department of Education. These various strands combined to make a free-college proposal an attractive option when planning for the State of the Union began in the months before 2015.

This proposal was also influenced by research on what such a plan would cost. In 2014, two associate professors at the University of Wisconsin–Madison released a report they had written with support from Lumina Foundation. In "Redefining College Affordability: Securing America's Future with a Free Two Year College Option," Sara Goldrick-Rab and Nancy Kendall argued that the reallocation of existing federal financial aid, for example, from private colleges, could cover two years of tuition for all students at public colleges and provide additional performance-based funding for those that did an especially good job serving low-income students.[8] The proposal went much further than advocating for free two-year degrees. It included four-year public institutions, acknowledged that living expenses constitute a major barrier to college attendance for low-income students, and proposed a state/local stipend to provide students with work-study opportunities at a living wage. It also stressed simplicity and powerful messaging as critical elements of any free-college plan. Goldrick-Rab brought these ideas to the White House in the spring of 2014. [9] Around the same time, Mark Huelsman of the progressive think tank Demos was reporting on the negative impacts of student loan debt on racial equity and promoting the idea of debt-free college.[10] The work of both Goldrick-Rab and Huelsman helped shape thinking around America's College Promise.[11]

There was never much expectation that the president's proposal would become law, especially since the 2014 midterm elections had cemented a House and Senate majority firmly opposed to any of the Obama administration's priorities. The administration's hope was that a free-college plan tied to employment and economic growth would attract some bipartisan support, but a resounding lack of interest on the part of legislative majorities in both houses put that idea to rest. Instead, in September 2015, an independent advisory board was named to move forward the tuition-free college movement through a nonlegislative path.

The College Promise Advisory Board was a coalition of community college leaders, educators from K–12 and a leading university system, politicians, foundations, nonprofits, students, and businesses co-led by

Jill Biden and former Wyoming governor Jim Geringer. Martha Kanter was its executive director. The vision was that the group would advance the free-college idea by working with local Promise initiatives and the Tennessee Promise to support more communities and states interested in developing their own Promise programs. This is the moment when national and grassroots efforts were first explicitly joined, but the connections were tenuous—only one representative of an existing local Promise program was named to the thirty-plus member advisory board, though many of the board members were working to launch programs in localities and at the state level.[12] Over time, the advisory committee evolved to become College Promise, an umbrella organization that gathers, disseminates, and supports high-impact practices, policies, research, networking, and advocacy efforts.

A second national organization, the Campaign for Free College Tuition (CFCT), had been launched even earlier. Led by Morley Winograd, a senior adviser to Vice President Al Gore, CFCT grew out of conversations that began in 2013 among former elected officials of both political parties committed to supporting economic growth through access to higher education. The organization, which ties its mission explicitly to the principles of universality reflected in the Kalamazoo Promise, promotes the idea that the nation's public colleges and universities should be tuition free. Through policy meetings, advisory work, and a sustained effort to collect polling data on public attitudes toward free college, CFCT has helped disseminate the free-college idea to state policy makers and build public support for it nationwide.

A more ambitious plan had followed on the heels of the Obama proposal. Bernie Sanders's "College for All" bill introduced in May 2015 proposed making the nation's four-year public colleges and universities tuition free, with two-thirds of funding from the federal government and one-third from the states. The federal share of spending would be offset by a tax on Wall Street transactions. In promoting his plan, Sanders referenced the employment rationale for free college: "We live in a highly competitive global economy. If our economy is to be strong, we need the best educated work force in the world." But it was affordability and equity concerns that drove his policy: "That will not happen if every year hundreds of thousands of bright young people cannot afford to go to college and if millions more leave school deeply in debt," Sanders said.[13] The free-tuition plan was accompanied by proposals to reduce student loan debt through cuts to federal student loan rates, the expansion of work-study programs, and other incentives to help colleges and universities hold down costs. The bill included provisions to reduce the use of low-paid adjunct faculty members and specified that "[n]o funding under this program may be used to fund administrator salaries, merit-based financial aid, or the construction of non-academic buildings like stadiums and student centers."[14]

The proposal was one of several major reforms proposed by Sanders as he launched his campaign for the Democratic presidential nomination in the spring of 2015. Staking out a position well to the left of establishment candidate Hillary Clinton, the free-college proposal echoed Sanders's plans for a single-payer health care system and a $1 trillion jobs and infrastructure program in representing a dramatic expansion of federal spending and leadership of key sectors. What is striking today is how many of Sanders's ideas, once considered outside the mainstream of the Democratic Party, became central to its education policy priorities.

Hillary Clinton had announced her candidacy for president in April 2015 and proposed a series of education reform measures, including tuition-free community college and student loan debt refinancing. As the primary election heated up, it was clear she would need to go further to address demands for more far-reaching change. Early on, she had criticized the Sanders free-college proposal as politically unrealistic and too expensive, noting (accurately) that Republican governors who were busy cutting money from higher education would be unlikely to pony up $28 billion in support of free college.[15] She also took issue with the idea of paying for wealthy students to attend college, claiming memorably (but inaccurately, since the children under discussion attended private institutions): "I am not in favor of making college free for Donald Trump's kids."[16] In July 2016, on the eve of her official nomination, Clinton introduced her own free-college plan, adopting many of Sanders's ideas but adding a $125,000 family income ceiling, with reduced benefits above the $85,000 income level. The program would be paid for by closing loopholes for high-income taxpayers.[17]

Both the Sanders and Clinton plans came in for criticism from various quarters. Some commentators took issue with the lack of detail or the political hurdles to passage.[18] But others zeroed in on the most contentious aspect of Promise programs: who benefits and who pays? Clinton's critique of the Sanders proposal—that it would send children from wealthy families to college with taxpayer money—was echoed in headlines like this one: "Sanders' free college plan would take from the rich to give to the rich."[19] But even Clinton's income ceiling failed to quell concern that low-income students who are more likely to attend cheaper two-year institutions would receive smaller subsidies than middle-class students enrolled in four-year universities. There was concern about the nation's many private colleges being left out of both plans, while some noted that elite public flagships, like the University of Michigan or the University of Virginia, while technically public, function much more like highly selective private universities such as those of the Ivy League. The nation's fifty-state system of higher education also came in for discussion, as a promise to make tuition free using federal dollars would reward those states that had historically underinvested in their higher-education system (and where tuition rates are higher) while possibly also creating incentives for raising tuition rates.[20]

TRADE-OFFS IN A CHANGING LANDSCAPE

The body of criticism of national free-college proposals is too wide-ranging to catalog in detail here. It comes from the left and the right, from experts and laypeople, from think tanks and journalists. Taken together, it reveals some of the key program design considerations discussed throughout this book. One of these is the trade-off between universalism and targeting, a long-standing area of debate in the formulation of social welfare programs all over the world.[21] Simple, universal free-college programs are easier to administer and explain to the public, but it is unavoidable that such programs will end up serving some students who can afford to attend college without them. Targeting programs to certain groups of students is more efficient but creates complexity around messaging and screens out parts of the population that could benefit from being served. Narrow targeting of financial aid also rests on unrealistic assumptions about how price influences behavior.[22] Perhaps most damaging, it dilutes political support for free-college initiatives, especially if they are designed to help the poor or students of color.

A second trade-off concerns the impact of free-college funding on racial and economic equity. The equity impacts of Promise programs will depend on the broader context as well as on how a program is designed. A community-based scholarship that serves all students from a high-poverty school district will reduce equity gaps even if some middle- or upper-income students are included. Programs with high academic thresholds in similar school districts will disproportionately advantage higher-income students who are more likely to have better grades. If limited to community colleges, such programs may also encourage students to undermatch. First-dollar structures will bring added resources to Pell-eligible students but be more costly to launch and sustain. Paradoxically, the most generous free-college programs that provide coverage for four-year degrees may lead to the most unequal distribution of benefits, since low-income students are less likely than middle- or higher-income students to attend more expensive four-year institutions.[23] In making choices about program structure, stakeholders—even those at the national level—are well advised to begin with key goals and then build a free-college program that supports these.

A third trade-off involves how dollars are used. Most Promise programs emphasize tuition and contribute very little to student support or navigation, not to mention living expenses, which are generally assumed to be the responsibility of the student. Many free-college proposals (and existing local and state programs) gloss over the fact that covering tuition leaves a large proportion of college expenses unaddressed. Living costs are for many the biggest-ticket item when it comes to college, disproportionately keeping low-income students off the pathway to a degree. To succeed in moving more students to and through college, Promise programs must also figure out how to pay for student support at key transition points (through high school to college, and then through college). Without an investment in student success, low-income and first-generation college goers may go to college, but they may not complete a degree or credential.

A final trade-off concerns the efficacy of national versus state versus local leadership around the free-college issue. Local solutions, such as the many community-based Promise programs already operating, have powerful advantages when it comes to meeting local needs. States, too, have found a way to respond to their most-pressing priorities through free-college initiatives. Will attention to the local or state context be lost if design decisions are made at the national level? This, too, is a perennial debate in the US federal system. Flexible federal funding that gives states freedom to meet their priorities while building on their unique higher-education assets—essentially the model envisioned by America's College Promise—may be a solution worth pursuing.

But almost no one is having these conversations. One interesting element of both the Sanders and Clinton proposals is that they made little reference to ongoing experimentation with free-college programs at the state and local levels. These proposals came from a different place, where national political figures were responding to growing concern about affordability with sweeping reform proposals that stood little chance of passage.[24] All the while, the work of creating and implementing state and local Promise programs continued. Seventeen communities introduced Promise programs in 2015 and thirty-one new free-tuition programs were created, many by California's community colleges, in 2016.[25]

National, state, and local movements became more closely aligned over time, as reflected in the October 2016 convening of PromiseNet, the annual gathering of Promise stakeholders discussed in chapter

2. Hosted by College Promise and organized by a virtual committee of Promise program representatives from around the nation, it was the largest PromiseNet meeting to date, drawing about four hundred attendees. The conference itself was followed by a meeting at the White House to discuss the free-college movement and luncheon at the vice president's residence where guests heard from Vice President Joe Biden and Dr. Jill Biden. Two weeks later, Donald J. Trump was elected president of the United States and national momentum around free college ground to a halt.

While a federal free-college program would be off the table for the next four years, expansion at the state and local levels continued apace. This movement was supported by polls showing 63 percent of US adults in favor of free tuition at public colleges; young people, Blacks, and Latinos are especially supportive.[26] It was also backed by an infrastructure of advocacy organizations like College Promise and the CFCT. These groups were joined in 2017 by Rise Inc., a grassroots advocacy organization that added student voices to the movement.[27] The youth-centered research and advocacy organization Generation Progress has also staked out a progressive position on student debt through its "Higher Ed Not Debt" campaign.[28] In the run-up to the 2020 presidential election, the free-college idea, widely popular and increasingly well known, became a must-have position for Democratic candidates.

In 2008, the last time a large field of Democratic presidential hopefuls had competed, not one had a plan for free college. In 2020, every candidate offered primary voters some version of it.[29] The front-runner and eventual nominee, former vice president Joe Biden, began his campaign emphasizing free community college along the lines of the America's College Promise proposal, but by March 2020 had adopted most of Sanders's ideas about free four-year public college degrees, with the proviso that any program be restricted to families with household incomes below $125,000.[30] This aligned his approach with that of Hillary Clinton during the 2016 campaign, as well as the plan of his former primary-season rival Pete Buttigieg.[31] Biden also put forward an income-based repayment plan to address the student loan debt crisis, although it was less sweeping than the almost-complete elimination of student loan debt that had been proposed by Senator Elizabeth Warren during the 2020 primary campaign.

When it was implemented in Tennessee in 2014, the free-college idea had been driven by the need for skilled workers and drew support and funding from Republican legislators. A few years later, the idea had become better known but also more politicized, tied tightly to the policy goals of the Democratic Party. In fact, some Republican officials who helped create Tennessee Promise acknowledge such a program would not be politically viable in the current environment. One reason is increased polarization around the notion of college itself. In 2019, the Pew Research Center released data tracking a sharp turn in Republican views toward college; the poll showed 59 percent of Republicans saying colleges have a negative effect on the United States, up from 35 percent in 2012.[32] Gallup polling backs this up, with a 2019 report showing that only 51 percent of Americans believe a college education is very important, down from 70 percent in 2013. The decline is steepest among young people, possibly reflecting concerns about rising college prices and the prospect of high student loan debt. Support has also fallen among Republican, male, and white respondents, while women, Blacks, and Latinos continue to believe a college education is very important.[33]

The free-college landscape has also become more complicated as new ideas about what is required for college success have entered the mix. Early discussions of free college focused on tuition. Gradually, the message has taken hold that tuition is but one component of the price of college and a relatively small one at that, especially for community college students. Living expenses are a crucial barrier for low-income students seeking degrees, and almost no Promise program pays for these. In addition, many more college students than is commonly believed struggle with food and housing security.

The understanding of basic needs challenges has been driven forward by the work of the Hope Center for College, Community, and

Justice now based at Temple University and led by Sara Goldrick-Rab. Among its other research and advocacy activities, the Hope Center regularly surveys college students about their food and housing status. While these are voluntary, nonrandom surveys, they draw a large number of respondents and reveal an underrecognized problem. Over five years, the surveys have collected data from 330,000 students at 411 institutions. On average, 43 percent of respondents reported food insecurity, 48 percent said they had faced some level of housing insecurity, and 16 percent reported being homeless at some point in the previous year.[34]

Based on such findings, Goldrick-Rab's 2016 book, *Paying the Price*, laid out recommendations for tuition-free college supplemented by enhanced safety net provisions for students. Attention to this work in the popular media, as well as a steady stream of data and advocacy, have begun to reshape public perceptions of the financial challenges facing students and families.[35] Growing awareness of students' basic needs shortfalls has also improved policy makers' understanding, providing a more nuanced picture of the barriers low-income students face in completing degrees where tuition and living expenses both play a role.

OPTIONS FOR ACTION

What are the options for action on free college? The America's College Promise Act outlived the Obama administration, having been reintroduced in the 115th and 116th sessions by a variety of Democratic legislators. Similarly, a Debt-Free College Act has been introduced repeatedly, garnering support from dozens of members of Congress, including many 2020 Democratic presidential candidates.[36] And a version of the Obama proposal—a federal-state partnership to make community college tuition free—became part of the Higher Education Act reauthorization bill in 2019, with cosponsorship and support from Tennessee's Republican senator Lamar Alexander, now retired.

Even if bipartisan agreement can be forged over the value of postsecondary education and training for all, free college as the preferred path is not a foregone conclusion. In fact, the Bipartisan Policy Center in its work on higher education stopped short of calling for free college, although it proposed dramatic increases in Pell Grant funding and a federal-state partnership structure.[37] Other options include debt-free college legislation, increasing the value of Pell Grants, and restoring funds for higher-education institutions to allow them to reduce tuition.

"Debt-free college" is a slippery term. Debt-free plans can be cheaper or more expensive than tuition-free college depending on how they are defined, and they lack the simple structure and message of free-college initiatives. The phrase is sometimes used to describe the most generous free-college efforts that cover living expenses as well as tuition, but it has also been heard in connection with more limited programs that leave current financial aid practices, such as the Expected Family Contribution (EFC), intact, while directing additional funds to low-income students. Senator Warren has gone the furthest, addressing debt for both current and past students through the canceling of up to $50,000 of an individual's student loan debt.[38] Senator Brian Schatz's (D-HI) debt-free college proposal, in contrast, works through a one-to-one federal match that channels funds to states to help them cover the price of attending a public institution beyond a student's EFC.[39]

In a 2018 Century Foundation report, Jen Mishory examined other federal-state partnerships to draw lessons about how a debt-free college plan could be structured. This proposal has several important elements, including the idea of creating a tiered system where states could buy in to the program at different levels and existing initiatives could be added to rather than replaced.[40] In a similarly practical vein, Mark Huelsman of Demos issued "A Blueprint for College Without Debt," setting forth various design options and focusing on how to build a powerful message behind the debt-free college movement while maintaining flexibility for states.[41] Unfortunately, none of the current debt-free college proposals address the problem of credit card debt, used by many to cover college costs and adding another component to the problem of student loan debt.

A second alternative to free-college initiatives is much simpler—an increase in Pell Grant funding to restore its purchasing power. As advocates point out, Pell Grants are already targeted toward those students most in need, and the structure for delivering them is well established.[42] They are also well liked by many Republicans. In addition to increasing the maximum grant amount, existing proposals include restoring automatic inflation adjustments that expired in 2017–2018 and increasing the number of semesters students are eligible to receive the grants. Reforms along these lines are included in current and recent legislative proposals, and before he embraced a more ambitious free-college plan, candidate Biden, as well as several other more moderate primary contenders, emphasized massive Pell Grant increases to address the college affordability crisis.[43]

While an increase in Pell Grants would be welcome by most everyone concerned about college affordability, pinning all hopes on such a strategy has real drawbacks. First, it keeps the focus on a confusing and complex FAFSA application process, whereas free-college programs lead with the message and make FAFSA just a step in the process (see chapter 5). Second, Pell Grants, lacking a middle-class constituency, have faced the fate of many programs targeted toward the poor, at times being racialized and attacked as welfare, even though most recipients are white. Third, Pell Grants leave out a population deeply affected by rising tuition prices—middle-income students with family incomes above the Pell cutoff. These students are not well off enough to afford rising college prices, yet they have incomes too high to qualify for need-based aid. Fourth, an increase in Pell Grants is a reformist, status quo move that is unlikely to lead to major changes in college affordability or college-going patterns. Even President Obama's efforts to increase the value of Pell Grants failed to restore their purchasing power.[44] Pell Grants are popular, but changes in their structure are unlikely to create the kind of widespread public excitement that tuition-free college programs engender. Experience in Tennessee and elsewhere has shown that a simple, free-college message delivered early and often is a more effective tool for bringing new students onto a higher-education pathway than leading with a FAFSA application process that doesn't even begin until a student's senior year of high school.

Another option, rarely discussed and difficult to achieve, would be for states to restore funding to their higher-education sectors. As noted in chapter 3, even ten years after the 2008 recession, state funding for colleges and universities had failed to return to its prerecession levels. And well before that, public higher education had been subject to a sustained period of defunding, chronicled by Christopher Newfield in two books, *Unmaking the Public University: The Forty-Year Assault on the Middle Class* and *The Great Mistake: How We Wrecked Public Universities and How We Can Fix Them*.[45] It is no wonder, then, that tuition increases—the main avenue through which colleges and universities compensate for state funding cutbacks—and accelerating student loan debt eventually reached crisis proportions.

Restoring funding for higher education may be the simplest approach to reducing tuition rates, but it is also highly unlikely, especially following the pandemic-induced fiscal crisis. A majority of state legislatures are Republican-dominated, and raising new revenue was off the table in most places even before the recession hit. The reluctance to re-fund higher education underscores the appeal of the free-college message. While legislatures continue to cut education spending (or, at a minimum, fail to restore previous spending levels), in some states, public resources continue to be invested in tuition-free college. This suggests that the political appeal of a simple college affordability message can transcend political divisions—something that increased state funding for education cannot do.

Of course, the approaches discussed here can be combined. For example, the College Affordability Act (H.R 4674), introduced in October 2019 as part of the Higher Education Reauthorization bill, included provisions both for increasing Pell Grants and for limited free college.

There is a final option that bears mention. The federal government commits a huge amount of money annually to various forms of student aid, mainly through Pell Grants but also through tax credits and support for states that get passed on to their higher-education sectors. Many observers, including Robert Samuels in his 2013 book, *Why Public Higher Education Should Be Free: How to Decrease Cost and Increase Quality at*

American Universities, and Goldrick-Rab and Kendall in the 2014 report cited above, have noted that the total of these amounts is sufficient, or close to sufficient, to cover tuition for everyone to attend public colleges or universities.[46] The biggest losers if such a redeployment of funds were to take place would be students at private colleges, both nonprofits and for-profits, who would no longer have access to Pell Grants. (Of course, for-profit institutions have long gained from the defunding of public higher education, as sociologist Tressie McMillan Cottom shows in her book, *Lower Ed: The Troubling Rise of For-Profit Colleges in the New Economy.*)[47] And there are major logistical and political challenges to such a policy change. Even so, if the arguments for free college are powerful enough to create momentum for new spending at the federal and state levels, a reallocation of existing resources to create this universal opportunity is also worth discussing.

When a national free-college program was last proposed by a US president back in 2015, the world looked very different. Community- and institution-based Promise programs were spreading, but statewide Promise programs were in their infancy. National advocacy organizations were new, and there were few connections among these different levels of activity. Today, a robust advocacy framework exists. Deeper connections have been forged among states seeking to reduce college costs and between state and local Promise programs. More research and consulting organizations have entered the arena, providing an exchange of ideas around best practices in design and student support, and expanding the base of knowledge around the impact of Promise programs. The COVID-19–induced recession also lent greater urgency to states' efforts to retrain adults, giving energy to free-college initiatives originally designed to address employer needs in a tight labor market.

Where does this leave us? As the fallout from the COVID-19 crisis played out in the overall economy and higher-education institutions, the free-college conversation continued. An oft-cited reason for not pursuing a free-college initiative—its high price tag—was undermined by the billions of dollars spent on relief and recovery, as well as the Trump administration's massive 2017 corporate tax cut. Widespread protests around racial injustice shone a spotlight on systemic racism and the hurdles Black, Latino, Native American, and other people of color face when it comes to upward mobility. Public understanding of inequality as a fundamental feature of the American economy continued to grow. Social conditions have never been more conducive to a free-college program. There are many more examples of state and local free-college programs to learn from and more evidence of impact. There is also a far higher profile for the free-college idea than there was in 2015, and large majorities of voters support the idea, so progress is not out of the question.

If such a program were to materialize, what should it look like? Instead of offering specifics here, I focus on four design principles that should be embedded in any tuition- or debt-free initiative. These principles hold the key to impact.

1. ***Simplicity.*** Fine print is the enemy of effective social programs. Any free-college initiative must be easy to understand and easy to access. At the state level, the Tennessee Promise is a good example of a fairly straightforward program with clear rules. At this point, almost all of the state's high school graduates apply, although fewer use it. New York State's Excelsior Scholarship is the opposite—on paper more generous than Tennessee's program, it is harder to access due to its many requirements and the possibility of its conversion into a loan, and usage is limited.
2. ***Strong messaging.*** Active public messaging can promote understanding and uptake. This messaging should rest on the word "free," which is a powerful motivator. One piece of evidence for the importance of messaging is the University of Michigan's HAIL Scholarship that essentially repackaged existing financial aid resources for low-income students and delivered them in a new and simpler way; the result was a large jump in the number of low-income students applying to the university.[48] The Tennessee Promise's high application rates are also driven by clear branding and repeated communication through multiple avenues.

3. *New money.* If better outcomes are wanted, new financial resources will be needed. Last-dollar (after Pell) programs that cover two-year institutions mean that most low-income students receive little or no new money from the scholarship. This type of scholarship can still have benefits, even for low-income students, but these are indirect.[49] For example, strong messaging and support for FAFSA completion mean that more low-income students will use their Pell Grants to go to college, but they will still struggle to cover the full price of attendance. America's College Promise was structured as a first-dollar program, but most current proposals are not and existing federal financial aid arrangements, including rules governing Pell Grants, make first-dollar statewide programs unworkable. Last-dollar-plus awards or supplemental need-based grants are alternate ways of directing new funds to all participants. At a minimum, there must be careful consideration and clear understanding of how the benefits of a free-college program are distributed; a last-dollar program that brings no new money to those most in need of it could fail to meet its objectives and lose legitimacy.
4. *Student support.* Money matters, but it is not all that matters. Evidence from the most generous community-based Promise programs—those in Kalamazoo and El Dorado—show that first-dollar scholarships that allow low-income students to use Pell Grants to cover a portion of living expenses increase degree completion across income groups. But robust navigation and support resources are also required, especially if a program's goal is to expand the population of college goers to include more first-generation and low-income individuals. Support is needed at two critical junctures—first, the transition from high school to college when students need help preparing for, applying to, and seeking additional financial resources for college; and, second, once in college to ensure successful degree or credential completion. There are many potential models, including mentorship, high-touch coaching, stipends, and data-driven nudges. But none of these are

free, and the free-college discussion has not paid sufficient attention to the costs and value of student support.

In answering the "big three" questions of program design discussed in chapter 2—who gets the benefit, where can it be used, and how is funding delivered—it is important to reiterate that any free-college program should be structured to align with its goals. As explored in chapters 3, 4, and 5, there are at least three goals animating Promise stakeholders—college affordability, racial and economic equity in postsecondary access and completion, and employment needs. Each of these has its own design implications. For example, affordability has been the most diminished in the four-year sector, so a program that aims to promote it should include four-year institutions. If equity is the overriding goal, bringing new money to low-income students is essential. If employability is the priority, limiting a scholarship to two-year institutions is more defensible than if the focus is on affordability.

Ideally, a free-college program would check all these boxes, but in practice, there will be trade-offs, and of course there are political and financial constraints. One huge challenge, as noted above, is the structure of the nation's higher-education system, which is decentralized and lacks standardization across states. Tennessee has applied colleges of technology; other states do not. California has a centralized, tripartite system governed from the top, while many states are a higher-education free-for-all with every institution competing for funding and setting its own tuition rates. Community colleges are reasonably priced in most states, but expensive in a few, such as Vermont, where tuition actually exceeds the Pell Grant maximum. This tremendous variability poses big issues for a national program. For this reason, the most practical path forward may be a federal/state partnership along the lines advocated by President Obama in 2015 or the option for states to buy in at various levels of support, as proposed by the Century Foundation.

A free-college program that covers two years of college and is tied to workforce readiness is more realistic than one that includes four-year institutions. If financial constraints were not an issue, including both two-year and four-year public institutions would broaden choice for students and mitigate the problem of undermatching. Under no circumstances should private for-profit institutions be included, but it is likely that some provision would need to be made for private, not-for-profit colleges. An income ceiling or scaled-down benefits as incomes rise could also be a political necessity, but it would need to be different from state to state to account for variations in median incomes and the cost of living. It is difficult to envision such a fifty-state system without injecting a high level of complexity into the process.

What threads the needle of viability and impact would be a first-dollar program that covers two-year degrees, very much along the lines of the 2015 America's College Promise proposal. In fact, the Biden administration is on record in support of such a strategy, along with a more ambitious goal of covering four-year degrees that is politically a tougher sell. Such an initiative would lead to more equitable outcomes, as low-income students would retain use of their Pell Grants to cover some of their living expenses. It would also be congruent with some of the preK through grade 14 public education commitments that are emerging in a handful of states (Oklahoma and Oregon among them). In the twentieth century, the argument for making high school compulsory and free was an economic one—young people needed more skills in the new economy—and the same holds true in the twenty-first. A high school diploma is not enough; some kind of postsecondary education or training is needed to succeed.

THE WAY FORWARD

In 2020, the tectonic plates underpinning American life slipped. It took a virus and the killing of George Floyd to lay bare what many people already knew or suspected—that the United States had failed in its promise to provide liberty and equality for all. That dream had been illusory from the beginning—a democracy founded on the legality of slavery that failed ever to fully grapple with its consequences obviously had fundamental shortcomings. But in the twentieth century, the power of government had been used to narrow the gap between rich and poor, while social movements drove forward the rights of women, Black and Latino people, the LGBTQ+ community, and people with disabilities. Higher education was democratized and many more people from all social classes went to college. It was possible to share the optimism behind Martin Luther King Jr.'s oft-quoted comment that "the arc of the moral universe is long, but it bends toward justice."[50]

The COVID-19 pandemic called this progress into question. As the United States failed to contain the virus and suffered consequences far beyond those of other rich countries, serious questions were raised about the state of the nation's social safety net, the resilience of its educational systems, and the disparate impact of the pandemic across racial and economic lines. The chaos also opened space for a new narrative. Low-paid service industry employees, many of them people of color, were recast as essential workers and frontline heroes. Policies that had seemed long shots just a few months earlier drew greater attention, opening the way for new approaches to policing, reparations, and access to health care.

Free college is a part of this conversation. At a time of cataclysmic economic and social change, policies that help both individuals and societies are undeniably attractive. In the 1940s, my own family was set on a path to the middle class because a twist of fate had brought my grandmother and her children to California at a time when college there was free. In 2005, a group of rich people in Kalamazoo placed a bet that paying for other people's children to go to college would help not just those young people but also their hometown, in the process inspiring many other communities to do the same. In the 2020s, tuition-free access to postsecondary education can support economic recovery while providing disenfranchised groups greater access to the American dream.

Earlier in the book, I noted that successful local Promise programs are those that are embedded in a community's ethos, respond to its needs, and enjoy its support. It is difficult to replicate these factors at the national level, but a nation committed to widespread economic opportunity and a reversal of racial injustice could do worse than make free college a part of its plan.

NOTES

CHAPTER 1

1. Tammy E. Kim, "What Free College Really Means," *New York Times*, June 30, 2019.
2. Beth Akers and Matthew M. Chingos, *Game of Loans: The Rhetoric and Reality of Student Debt* (Princeton, NJ: Princeton University Press, 2016); Kevin W. Connell, *Breaking Point: The College Affordability Crisis and Our Next Financial Bubble* (Lanham, MD: Rowman and Littlefield, 2016); Sara Goldrick-Rab, *Paying the Price: College Costs, Financial Aid, and the Betrayal of the American Dream* (Chicago: University of Chicago Press, 2016); Joseph Stiglitz, "Student Debt and the Crushing of the American Dream," The Great Divide series, *New York Times*, May 13, 2013.
3. Goldrick-Rab, *Paying the Price*.
4. Charles T. Clotfelter, *Unequal Colleges in the Age of Diversity* (Cambridge: Harvard University Press, 2017); Caroline M. Hoxby and Christopher Avery, "The Missing 'One-Offs': The Hidden Supply of High-Achieving, Low-Income Students," Brookings Papers on Economic Activity, Spring 2013, https://www.brookings.edu/wp-content/uploads/2016/07/2013a_hoxby.pdf.
5. Jonathan Rothwell, "The stubborn race and class gaps in college quality," Brookings Social Mobility Papers, December 18, 2015, https://www.brookings.edu/research/the-stubborn-race-and-class-gaps-in-college-quality/; Doug Shapiro et al., *Completing College: A National View of Student Attainment Rates by Race and Ethnicity—Fall 2010 Cohort*, Signature Report No. 12b, National Student Clearinghouse Research Center, April 2017, https://nscresearchcenter.org/wp-content/uploads/SignatureReport12.pdf.
6. Timothy J. Bartik and Brad Hershbein, "Degrees of Poverty: The Relationship between Family Income Background and the Returns to Education" (Upjohn Institute Working Paper 18-284, W.E. Upjohn Institute for Employment Research, 2018).
7. John Bridgeland, Jessica Milano, and Elyse Rosenblum, "Across the Great Divide: Perspectives of CEOs and College Presidents on America's Higher Education and Skills Gap" (US Chamber of Commerce Foundation Report, March 2011), https://www.uschamberfoundation.org/sites/default/files/publication/edu/Great%20Divide%20Final%20Report%20.pdf.
8. James Bessen, "Employers Aren't Just Whining—the Skills Gap is Real," *Harvard Business Review*, August 25, 2014, https://hbr.org/2014/08/employers-arent-just-whining-the-skills-gap-is-real#:~:text=Every%20year%2C%20the%20Manpower%20Group,%2C%2039%25%20of%20employers%20did; Harry Holzer, "Higher

Education and Workforce Policy: Creating More Skilled Workers (and Jobs for Them to Fill)," *Economic Studies at Brookings*, April 2015, https://www.brookings.edu/research/higher-education-and-workforce-policy-creating-more-skilled-workers-and-jobs-for-them-to-fill/; Matthew T. Hora, "Beyond the Skills Gap: How the Vocationalist Framing of Higher Education Undermines Student, Employer, and Societal Interests," address given at the Annual Meeting of the American Association of Colleges and Universities, January 2018, https://www.aacu.org/liberaleducation/2018/spring/hora.

9. Lauren Bauer and Jay Shambaugh, "Workers with low levels of education still haven't recovered from the Great Recession," *Up Front* (blog), Brookings Institution, September 6, 2018, https://www.brookings.edu/blog/up-front/2018/09/06/workers-with-low-levels-of-education-still-havent-recovered-from-the-great-recession/.
10. Isabel Sawhill and Christopher Pulliam, "Americans Want the Wealthy and Corporations to Pay More Taxes but Are Elected Officials Listening?," *Up Front* (blog), Brookings Institution, March 14, 2019, https://www.brookings.edu/blog/up-front/2019/03/14/americans-want-the-wealthy-and-corporations-to-pay-more-taxes-but-are-elected-officials-listening/.
11. Patrick Murray, "National: Protestors' Anger Justified Even If Actions May Not Be," Monmouth University Poll, June 2, 2020, https://www.monmouth.edu/polling-institute/documents/monmouthpoll_us_060220.pdf/.
12. Lauren Gambino, "Calls for Reparations Are Growing Louder. How Is the US Responding?," *Guardian* (US Edition), June 20, 2020, https://www.theguardian.com/world/2020/jun/20/joe-biden-reparations-slavery-george-floyd-protests; Christian Weller, "Getting Serious About Closing Racial Wealth Gap Means Looking for New, Large Solutions," *Forbes*, January 14, 2020, https://www.forbes.com/sites/christianweller/2020/01/14/getting-serious-about-closing-racial-wealth-gap-means-looking-for-new-large-solutions/.
13. Brent Budowsky, "Bernie Sanders' Great Idea: Free Public College," *The Hill*, June 9, 2015, https://thehill.com/blogs/pundits-blog/presidential-campaign/244462-bernie-sanderss-great-idea-free-public-college.
14. Michelle Miller-Adams, *The Power of a Promise: Education and Economic Renewal in Kalamazoo* (Kalamazoo, MI: W.E. Upjohn Institute for Employment Research, 2009), 59–61.
15. Michelle Miller-Adams et al., "Promise Programs Database," W.E. Upjohn Institute for Employment Research, 2017, updated 2020, https://www.upjohn.org/promise/.
16. Michelle Miller-Adams, *Promise Nation: Transforming Communities Through Place-Based Scholarships* (Kalamazoo, MI: W.E. Upjohn Institute for Employment Research, 2015).
17. Laura W. Perna and Elaine W. Leigh, "Database of College Promise Programs," University of Pennsylvania, Alliance for Higher Education and Democracy, http://ahead-penn.org/creating-knowledge/college-promise.
18. "Mann, Horace," *Encyclopaedia Britannica Online*, https://www.britannica.com/biography/Horace-Mann.
19. Claudia Goldin and Lawrence Katz, *The Race Between Education and Technology* (Cambridge, MA: Belknap Press for Harvard University Press, 2008).
20. Stuart v. School District No. 1, 30 Mich. 69 (1874), https://cite.case.law/mich/30/69/.
21. Claudia Goldin, "America's Graduation from High School: The Evolution and

Spread of Secondary Schooling in the Twentieth Century," *Journal of Economic History* 58, no. 2 (1998): 347.

22. *The Condition of Education 2018* (Washington, DC: IES/NCES, updated May 2019), https://nces.ed.gov/programs/coe/indicator_coi.asp.
23. Thomas D. Snyder, ed., *120 Years of American Education: A Statistical Portrait* (Washington, DC: IES/NCES, January 1993), https://nces.ed.gov/pubs93/93442.pdf.
24. "Fast Facts," IES/NCES, https://nces.ed.gov/fastfacts/display.asp?id=372#College_enrollment.
25. "Digest of Education Statistics: 2017 Tables and Figures," IES/NCES, https://nces.ed.gov/programs/digest/d17/tables/dt17_302.60.asp.
26. John Aubrey Douglass, *The California Idea and American Higher Education: 1850 to the 1960 Master Plan* (Palo Alto, CA: Stanford University Press, 2000), 4.
27. *Colleges of Agriculture at the Land Grant Universities: A Profile* (Washington, DC: National Academy Press, 1995), https://www.nap.edu/read/4980/chapter/2.
28. Caldwell Titcomb, "Key Events in Black Higher Education: JBHE Chronology of Major Landmarks in the Progress of African Americans in Higher Education," *Journal of Blacks in Higher Education*, https://www.jbhe.com/chronology/.
29. Jen Mishory, Mark Huelsman, and Suzanne Kahn, "How Student Debt and the Racial Wealth Gap Reinforce Each Other," Century Foundation Report, September 9, 2019, https://tcf.org/content/report/bridging-progressive-policy-debates-student-debt-racial-wealth-gap-reinforce/.
30. Douglass, *The California Idea*, 198.
31. Suzanne Gould, "Why the Higher Education Act Matters," American Association of University Women, November 11, 2015, https://www.aauw.org/2015/11/12/higher-education-act/.
32. *Two Decades of Change in Federal and State Higher Education Funding*, Fiscal Federalism Initiative (Philadelphia: The Pew Charitable Trusts, 2019), https://www.pewtrusts.org/en/research-and-analysis/issue-briefs/2019/10/two-decades-of-change-in-federal-and-state-higher-education-funding.
33. Douglass, *The California Idea*, 170.
34. Gerard J. De Groot, "Ronald Reagan and Student Unrest in California, 1966–1970," *Pacific Historical Review* 65, no. 1 (1996): 107–129, https://online.ucpress.edu/phr/article/65/1/107/79345/Ronald-Reagan-and-Student-Unrest-in-California.
35. Campbell Gibson and Kay Jung, "Historical Census Statistics on Population Totals by Race, 1790 to 1990, and by Hispanic Origin, 1970 to 1990, for the United States, Regions, Divisions, and States" (US Census Bureau, Population Division Working Paper #56, September 2002), https://www.census.gov/content/dam/Census/library/working-papers/2002/demo/POP-twps0056.pdf.
36. "Tuition & cost of attendance 2020–2021," University of California, https://admission.universityofcalifornia.edu/tuition-financial-aid/tuition-cost-of-attendance/.
37. Nicole Freeling, "UC Regents declare their support for an end to race-blind admissions," *University of California News*, June 25, 2020, https://www.universityofcalifornia.edu/news/uc-regents-declare-their-support-end-race-blind-admissions.
38. James Traub, *City on a Hill: Testing the American Dream at City College* (Reading, MA: Addison-Wesley, 1994), 21.
39. Traub, *City on a Hill*, 24.
40. Traub, *City on a Hill*, 9.
41. "Two CUNY Alumni Win 2019 MacArthur Awards," September 30, 2019, City University of New York, https://www1.cuny.edu/mu/forum/2019/09/30/two-

cuny-alumni-win-2019-macarthur-awards/.
42. Traub, *City on a Hill*, 10.
43. Traub, *City on a Hill*, 24.
44. Stephen Brier, "Why the History of CUNY Matters: Using the CUNY Digital History Archive to Teach CUNY's Past," *Radical Teacher* 108 (2017), http://radicalteacher.library.pitt.edu/ojs/radicalteacher/article/view/357.
45. Traub, *City on a Hill*, 67.
46. Paul Attewell and David E. Lavin, *Passing the Torch: Does Higher Education for the Disadvantaged Pay Off Across the Generations?* (New York: Russell Sage Foundation, 2007).
47. Jennifer R. Delaney and William J. Doyle, "State Spending on Higher Education: Testing the Balance Wheel over Time," *Journal of Education Finance* 36, no. 4 (2011): 343–68.
48. Matthew Chingos, "50 Reasons the Idea of Free College Is Misunderstood," *The Upshot* (blog) *New York Times*, December 20, 2019, https://www.nytimes.com/2019/12/20/upshot/50-reasons-free-college-misunderstood.html?searchResultPosition=1.
49. Miller-Adams, *Power of a Promise.*

CHAPTER 2

1. Michelle Miller-Adams et al., "Promise Programs Database," W.E. Upjohn Institute for Employment Research, 2017, updated 2020, https://www.upjohn.org/promise.
2. Dallas County Promise, https://dallascountypromise.org/about.
3. Dallas County Promise.
4. Chuck Wilbur, Michigan Promise Zones Association, in discussion with the author.
5. Blake Alsup, "UM Efforts to Aid Lower-income Students Begin to Bear Fruit," *Detroit News*, June 28, 2018, https://www.detroitnews.com/story/news/local/michigan/2019/06/29/um-efforts-aid-lower-income-students-begin-bear-fruit/721229002/.
6. "Rochester Promise," University of Rochester, https://enrollment.rochester.edu/community-programs/#rochester-promise.
7. David L. Sjoquist and John V. Winters, "State Merit-Based Financial Aid Programs and College Attainment," *Journal of Regional Science*, September 24, 2014.
8. Susan M. Dynarski, "Hope for Whom? Financial Aid for the Middle Class and Its Impact on College Attendance," *National Tax Journal* 53, no. 3 Part 2 (September 2000): 629–62; Donald E. Heller and P. Marin, eds., *State Merit Scholarship Programs and Racial Inequality* (Cambridge, MA: The Civil Rights Project at Harvard University, 2004).
9. Jen Mishory, *The Future of Statewide College Promise Programs: A State Guide to Free College* (New York: The Century Foundation, 2018), https://tcf.org/content/report/future-statewide-college-promise-programs/.
10. Michael Wickline, "Grant Program Short on Takers: State Adding Money to Get Word Out to Qualifying Students," *Arkansas Democrat Gazette*, June 2, 2019, https://www.arkansasonline.com/news/2019/jun/02/grant-program-short-on-takers-20190602/?news-arkansas.
11. Tiffany Jones and Katie Berger, "A Promise Fulfilled: A Framework for Equitable Free College Programs," The Education Trust, September 6, 2018, https://s3-us-east-2.amazonaws.com/edtrustmain/wp-content/uploads/2018/09/05155636/A-

Promise-Fulfilled-A-Framework-for-Equitable-Free-College-Programs-9.6-18.pdf; and Alain Poutré and Mamie Voight, "Do Tennessee Promise and New York's Excelsior Scholarship Help Students with Limited Means Afford College?," Institute for Higher Education Policy, September 2018, http://www.ihep.org/research/publications/state-free-college-tennessee-promise-and-new-yorks-excelsior-scholarship.

12. Sara Goldrick-Rab and Michelle Miller-Adams, "Don't Dismiss the Value of Free-College Programs. They Do Help Low-Income Students," *Chronicle of Higher Education* 65, no. 3 (2018), https://www.chronicle.com/article/Don-t-Dismiss-the-Value-of/244468.
13. Monica Nickelsburg, "Tax hike on Amazon and Microsoft to fund higher ed in Washington state passes legislature," *GeekWire,* April 29, 2019, https://www.geekwire.com/2019/tax-hike-amazon-microsoft-fund-higher-ed-washington-state-passes-legislature/.
14. American Educational Research Association, "Research Finds That High School GPAs Are Stronger Predictors of College Graduation than ACT Scores," news release, January 28, 2020, https://www.aera.net/Newsroom/Research-Finds-that-High-School-GPAs-Are-Stronger-Predictors-of-College-Graduation-than-ACT-Scores.
15. Douglas N. Harris et al., *The Promise of Free College (and its potential pitfalls)* (Washington, DC: Brookings Institution, 2018), https://www.brookings.edu/research/the-promise-of-free-college-and-its-potential-pitfalls/.
16. *Digest of Education Statistics 2019* (Washington, DC: IES/NCES, 2019), https://nces.ed.gov/programs/digest/d19/tables/dt19_303.40.asp.
17. Andy Carlson and Sophia Laderman, "The Power of a Promise: Implications and Importance of Adult Promise Programs" (white paper, State Higher Education Executive Officers Organization, Boulder, Colorado, 2019), https://sheeoorg.wpengine.com/wp-content/uploads/2019/02/Adult-Promise-White-Paper-The-Power-of-a-Promise-copy.pdf.
18. The Intensity and Saturation indices are based on characteristics included in the Upjohn Institute's Promise Programs Database. See Miller-Adams et al., "Promise Programs Database," 2017.
19. Laura W. Perna and Elaine W. Leigh, "Understanding the Promise: A Typology of State and Local Programs," *Educational Researcher,* November 22, 2107, 155–80.
20. Everett M. Rogers, *Diffusion of Innovations,* 5th ed. (New York: Free Press, 2003), 17.
21. Charles R. Shipan and Craig Volden, "The Mechanisms of Policy Diffusion," *American Journal of Political Science* 52, no. 4 (October 2008): 840–57.

CHAPTER 3

1. Timothy J. Bartik, Brad Hershbein, and Marta Lachowska, "The Merits of Universal Scholarships: Benefit-Cost Evidence from the Kalamazoo Promise" (Upjohn Institute Working Paper 16-252, W.E. Upjohn Institute for Employment Research, 2016).
2. Brad Hershbein and Kevin Hollenbeck, *College Costs: Students Can't Afford Not to Know* (Indianapolis: Lumina Foundation, 2014).
3. Sara Goldrick-Rab and Nancy Kendall, "The Real Price of College, College Completion Series: Part Two" (New York: The Century Foundation, March 3, 2016), https://tcf.org/content/report/the-real-price-of-college/.
4. Robert Kelchen, Sara Goldrick-Rab, and Braden Hosch, "The Costs of College Attendance: Examining Variation and Consistency in Institutional Living Cost

Allowances," *Journal of Higher Education* 88, no. 6 (2017): 947–71.
5. Ben Myers, "How Colleges Give Students a Flawed Sense of Living Costs," *Chronicle of Higher Education*, July 10, 2017, https://www.chronicle.com/interactives/cost-of-living.
6. Erin Dunlop Velez and Laura Horn, *What High Schoolers and Their Parents Know About Public 4-Year Tuition and Fees in Their State* (Washington, DC: IES/NCES, October 2018), https://nces.ed.gov/pubsearch/pubsinfo.asp?pubid=2019404.
7. Scott Jaschik, "Senators Question College Board Data on Paying for College," *Inside Higher Ed*, July 10, 2017, https://www.insidehighered.com/admissions/article/2019/06/24/senators-urge-college-board-change-reports-paying-college.
8. *Federal and State Funding of Higher Education: A Changing Landscape*, Chartbook (Washington, DC: The Pew Charitable Trusts, June 2015), https://www.pewtrusts.org/-/media/assets/2015/06/federal_state_funding_higher_education_final.pdf, %203.
9. Michael Mitchell et al., *Unkept Promises: State Cuts to Higher Education Threaten Access and Equity* (Washington, DC: Center on Budget and Policy Priorities, October 4, 2018), 2, https://www.cbpp.org/sites/default/files/atoms/files/10-4-18sfp.pdf.
10. Mitchell et al., *Unkept Promises*, 8.
11. *Federal and State Funding of Higher Education*, Chartbook, 3.
12. *SHEF: FY2018*, State Higher Education Finance (New York: State Higher Education Executive Officers Association, 2019), https://sheeo.org/wp-content/uploads/2019/04/SHEEO_SHEF_FY18_Report.pdf.
13. Matt Gianneschi and Sarah Pingel, "A Hidden Cause of Rising Tuition: Tuition Discounting in Public Colleges and Universities," *Progress in Education Reform* 15, no. 4 (2014), https://www.ecs.org/clearinghouse/01/14/07/11407.pdf.
14. *2018 Tuition Discounting Study* (Washington, DC: National Association of College and University Business Officers, 2019).
15. Lucie Lapovsky, "Do Price Resets Work?," April 2019, https://lapovsky.com/wp-content/uploads/2010/07/Do-Price-Resets-Work-.pdf.
16. Caroline Simon, "Bureaucrats and Buildings: The Case for Why College Is So Expensive," *Forbes*, September 5, 2017, https://www.forbes.com/sites/carolinesimon/2017/09/05/bureaucrats-and-buildings-the-case-for-why-college-is-so-expensive/#77a16bcc456a.
17. Donna M. Desrochers and Steven Hurlburt, *Trends in College Spending: 2003–2013*, Delta Cost Project (Washington, DC: American Institute for Research, 2016), https://deltacostproject.org/sites/default/files/products/15-4626%20Final01%20Delta%20Cost%20Project%20College%20Spending%2011131.406.P0.02.001%20....pdf.
18. "Compliance Matrix," last modified July 30, 2019, Higher Education Compliance Alliance, https://www.higheredcompliance.org/compliance-matrix/.
19. Robert Kelchen, "Is Administrative Bloat Really a Big Problem?," *Kelchen on Education Blog*, May 10, 2018, https://robertkelchen.com/2018/05/10/is-administrative-bloat-a-problem/.
20. Simon, "Bureaucrats and Buildings."
21. Kellie Woodhouse, "Lazy Rivers and Student Debt," *Inside Higher Ed*, June 15, 2015, https://www.insidehighered.com/news/2015/06/15/are-lazy-rivers-and-climbing-walls-driving-cost-college.
22. National Student Clearinghouse Research Center, "Current Term Enrollment Estimates—Fall 2019," December 16, 2019, https://nscresearchcenter.org/tag/enrollment-trends/.

23. Donna Desrochers, *Academic Spending versus Athletic Spending: Who Wins?*, Delta Cost Project (Washington, DC: American Institute for Research, 2013), https://www.air.org/sites/default/files/downloads/report/Academic-Spending-vs-Athletic-Spending.pdf.
24. Robert Hiltonsmith, "Pulling Up the Higher-Ed Ladder: Myth and Reality in the Crisis of College Affordability," *Demos*, May 5, 2015, https://www.demos.org/research/pulling-higher-ed-ladder-myth-and-reality-crisis-college-affordability.
25. William R. Doyle and Jennifer A. Delaney, "Bouncebacks in Higher Education Funding: Patterns in Length of Time to Recover Following Cuts in State Appropriations" (Policy Brief, University of Wisconsin, August 30, 2011), https://files.eric.ed.gov/fulltext/ED524266.pdf.
26. National Conference of State Legislators (NCSL), State Partisan Composition, August 29, 2019, http://www.ncsl.org/research/about-state-legislatures/partisan-composition.aspx.
27. When adjusted for inflation, however, public university funding from the state has actually decreased 12 percent in nine years.
28. Mitchell et al., *Unkept Promises,* figure 1.
29. Emily Parker, "Coupling Incentives to Tuition Caps: A new path toward affordability?," *EdNote* (blog), *Education Commission of the States*, May 18, 2017, https://ednote.ecs.org/coupling-incentives-to-tuition-caps-a-new-path-toward-affordability/.
30. Education Commission of the States, "Postsecondary Tuition Capping and Freezing," Policy Snapshot, November 2018, https://www.ecs.org/wp-content/uploads/Postsecondary-Tuition-Capping-and-Freezing.pdf.
31. Ben Barrett and Iris Palmer, "New Research on How States can Control Tuition Growth," *Education Policy* (blog), *New America*, July 24, 2015, https://www.newamerica.org/education-policy/edcentral/states-control-tuition-growth/.
32. M. M. Kim and J. Ko, "The Impacts of State Control Policies on College Tuition Increase," *Educational Policy* 29, no. 5 (2015): 815–38.
33. Jennifer Barnett Reed, "Boomtown Once More," *Arkansas Times*, March 9, 2007, https://arktimes.com/general/top-stories/2007/03/09/boomtown-once-more.
34. Sarah Grant, "El Dorado, Arkansas's New Boom," *Rolling Stone*, October 13, 2018, https://www.rollingstone.com/music/music-features/el-dorado-arkansas-musicfest-murphy-arts-district-706972/.
35. Jennifer W. Ash and Gary W. Ritter, "Early Impacts of the El Dorado Promise on Enrollment and Achievement," *Arkansas Education Report* 11, no. 1, University of Arkansas Office of Education Policy, April 23, 2014; Elise Swanson and Gary Ritter, "Start to Finish: Examining the Impact of the El Dorado Promise on Postsecondary Outcomes" (EDRE Working Paper No. 2018-02, March 30, 2018), https://papers.ssrn.com/sol3/papers.cfm?abstract_id=3153153.
36. El Dorado Promise, "Community Report Card 2008," http://eldoradopromise.com/pdf/PromiseImpact2008.pdf.
37. El Dorado Promise, "A Decade of Promise," 2017, http://eldoradopromise.com/pdf/El_Dorado_Promise_Booklet.pdf.
38. Bill Bowden, "Murphy Oil Leaving Their Long-time Legacy, El Dorado," *Arkansas Democrat-Gazette*, May 9, 2020, https://www.eldoradonews.com/news/2020/may/09/murphy-oil-leaving-their-long-time-legacy-el-dorad/.
39. El Dorado Promise, Report to the El Dorado Public Schools Board Meeting, July 15, 2019 (provided to the author by the El Dorado Promise).
40. Swanson and Ritter, "Start to Finish."
41. Elizabeth Behrman, "Pittsburgh Promise scholarship program changes course

with new rules," *Pittsburgh Post-Gazette*, February 11, 2018, https://www.post-gazette.com/news/education/2018/02/11/Pittsburgh-Promise-Saleem-Ghubril-Max-King-scholarship-Pennsylvania-decrease-residency-requirement/stories/201802100004.

42. Eleanor Chute, "Pittsburgh Promise loosens scholarship restrictions for technical programs," *Pittsburgh Post-Gazette*, June 18, 2014, https://www.post-gazette.com/news/education/2014/06/19/Pittsburgh-Promise-loosens-scholarship-restrictions-for-technical-programs/stories/201406190071.
43. Lindsay C. Page et al., "The promise of place-based investment in postsecondary access and success: Investigating the impact of the Pittsburgh Promise," *Education Finance and Policy* 14, no. 4 (2019).
44. Oded Gurantz, "What Does Free Community College Buy? Early Impacts from the Oregon Promise," *Journal of Policy Analysis and Management*, July 10, 2019.
45. State of Oregon, Higher Education Coordinating Commission, *Senate Bill 81 Legislative Report: The First Term of the Oregon Promise*, December 2016.
46. State of Oregon, Higher Education Coordinating Commission, *Senate Bill 81 (2015): The Oregon Promise—Report from Year 3*, December 2018, https://www.oregon.gov/highered/research/Documents/Reports/SB-81-Oregon-Promise-2018.pdf.
47. State of Oregon, Higher Education Coordinating Commission, *Senate Bill 81 (2015)*.
48. Jesse McKinley, "Cuomo Adopts a Middle-class Mantra," *New York Times,* April 12, 2017, https://www.nytimes.com/2017/04/12/nyregion/andrew-cuomo-new-york-middle-class.html.
49. Sara Goldrick-Rab, "Dear Jimmy: Making 'Free College' Pay in New York," medium.com, April 11, 2017, https://medium.com/@saragoldrickrab/dear-jimmy-making-free-college-pay-in-new-york-f6ba6696e430.
50. Tom Hilliard, *Excelsior Scholarship Serving Very Few New York Students*, Report (New York: Center for an Urban Future, 2018), https://nycfuture.org/research/excelsior-scholarship.
51. Ryan Deffenbaugh, "Study: Small percentage of SUNY and CUNY students receive Excelsior Scholarship," Westfair Communications, August 14, 2018, https://westfaironline.com/105740/study-small-percentage-of-suny-and-cuny-students-receive-excelsior-scholarship/.
52. Melanie Kruvelis, "A Closer Look at New York's State Budget Year for Fiscal Year 2021," *YI Blog*, April 16, 2020, https://younginvincibles.org/a-closer-look-at-new-yorks-state-budget-for-fiscal-year-2021/; Larry Meyer, "Oregon Legislators Aim to Rebalance State Budget Following Revenue Losses," *Argus Observer,* July 17, 2020, https://www.argusobserver.com/news/oregon-legislators-aim-to-rebalance-state-budget-following-revenue-losses/article_b7f9cb30-c84d-11ea-bf54-f7b1e47df802.html.
53. State of Oregon, *Oregon Promise Report*, 2018, x.
54. Hilliard, *Excelsior Scholarship.*
55. Andrew Theen, "Oregon Promise Will Be 'Significantly' Changed 2 Years After It Started," *Oregonian/Oregon Live*, June 28, 2017.

CHAPTER 4

1. "College Admissions Scandal," Special online news section, *New York Times*, 2020, https://www.nytimes.com/news-event/college-admissions-scandal.
2. Kelly McLaughlin, "Here's everyone who has been sentenced in the college admissions scandal so far," *Insider,* July 15, 2020, https://www.insider.com/college-admissions-scandal-full-list-people-sentenced-2019-9#parent-devin-slone-

was-sentenced-to-four-months-in-prison-3.

3. Madison Malone Kircher, "College Admission Scam Involved Photoshopping Rich Kids' Heads Onto Athletes' Bodies," *New York Magazine*, March 12, 2019, https://nymag.com/intelligencer/2019/03/college-admissions-scandal-kids-photoshopped-as-athletes.html.
4. S. F. Reardon et al., "Is Separate Still Unequal? New Evidence on School Segregation and Racial Academic Achievement Gaps" (CEPR Working Paper No.19-06, Stanford Center for Education Policy Analysis, 2019); Emma Garcia and Elaine Weiss, "Education Inequalities at the School Starting Gate: Gaps, trends, and strategies to address them," Economic Policy Institute, September 27, 2017, https://www.epi.org/publication/education-inequalities-at-the-school-starting-gate/.
5. *Public High School Graduation Rates* (Washington, DC: IES/NCES, updated May 2020), https://nces.ed.gov/programs/coe/indicator_coi.asp.
6. *Digest of Educational Statistics 2018* (Washington, DC: IES/NCES, 2018), table 306.30, https://nces.ed.gov/programs/digest/d18/tables/dt18_306.30.asp?current=yes.
7. Population estimates, July 1, 2018 (v2018), US Census Bureau, https://www.census.gov/quickfacts/fact/table/US/PST045218.
8. This rate is known as the Immediate College Enrollment rate.
9. *College Enrollment Rates* (Washington, DC: IES/NCES, updated May 2020), https://nces.ed.gov/programs/coe/indicator_cpb.asp.
10. *College Enrollment Rates.*
11. *College Enrollment Rates.*
12. Paul Fain, "Feds Release Broader Data on Socioeconomic Status and College Enrollment and Completion," *Inside Higher Ed*, May 23, 2019, https://www.insidehighered.com/print/news/2019/05/23/feds-release-broader-data-socioeconomic-status-and-college-enrollment-and-completion.
13. "High School Benchmarks 2019," Annual Report, National Student Clearinghouse Research Center, October 7, 2019, https://nscresearchcenter.org/high-school-benchmarks-2019/.
14. Timothy J. Bartik, Brad Hershbein, and Marta Lachowska, "The Effects of the Kalamazoo Promise Scholarship on College Enrollment and Completion," *Journal of Human Resources*, May 6, 2019, http://jhr.uwpress.org/content/early/2019/05/01/jhr.56.1.0416-7824R4.abstract; Elisa Swanson and Gary Ritter, "Start to Finish: Examining the Impact of the El Dorado Promise Program on Postsecondary Outcomes," *Journal of Student Financial Aid* 49, no. 3 (2020), https://ir.library.louisville.edu/jsfa/vol49/iss3/2/; Lindsay C. Page et al., "The Promise of Place-Based Investment in Postsecondary Access and Success: Investigating the Impact of the Pittsburgh Promise," *Education Finance and Policy* 14, no. 4 (2019): 572–600, https://www.mitpressjournals.org/doi/abs/10.1162/edfp_a_00257; Robert Bifulco, Ross Rubenstein, and Hosung Sohn, "Evaluating the Effects of Universal Place-Based Scholarships on Student Outcomes: The Buffalo 'Say Yes to Education' Program," *Journal of Policy Analysis and Management* 38, no. 4 (2019): 918–43, https://onlinelibrary.wiley.com/doi/full/10.1002/pam.22139; Celeste Carruthers and William Fox, "Aid for all: College coaching, financial aid, and post-secondary persistence in Tennessee," *Economics of Education Review* 52, no. C (2016): 97–112, https://econpapers.repec.org/article/eeeecoedu/v_3a51_3ay_3a2016_3ai_3ac_3ap_3a97-112.htm; Celeste Carruthers, "Five Things to Know About The Tennessee Promise Scholarship," *Brown Center Chalkboard* (blog), Brookings Institution, May 6, 2019, https://www.brookings.edu/blog/brown-center-chalkboard/2019/05/06/five-things-to-know-about-the-tennessee-promise-scholarship/.

15. *Status and Trends in the Education of Racial and Ethnic Groups 2018* (Washington, DC: IES/NCES, 2018), https://nces.ed.gov/programs/raceindicators/indicator_red.asp.
16. *Status and Trends in the Education of Racial and Ethnic Groups 2018.*
17. Michelle Dimino, "How Outcomes Metrics Can Better Reflect Community College Performance," *Third Way,* October 8, 2019, https://www.thirdway.org/report/how-outcomes-metrics-can-better-reflect-community-college-performance.
18. Fain, "Feds Release Broader Data."
19. D. Shapiro et al., *Completing College 2019 National Report,* Signature Report 18 (Herndon, VA: National Student Clearinghouse Research Center, December 2019), https://nscresearchcenter.org/wp-content/uploads/Completions_Report_2019.pdf.
20. CJ Libassi, "The Neglected College Race Gap: Racial Disparities Among College Completers," Center for American Progress, May 23, 2018, https://www.americanprogress.org/issues/education-postsecondary/reports/2018/05/23/451186/neglected-college-race-gap-racial-disparities-among-college-completers/#fn-451186-1.
21. *The Condition of Education 2020* (Washington, DC: IES/NCES, 2020), https://nces.ed.gov/pubs2020/2020144.pdf.
22. *Status and Trends in the Education of Racial and Ethnic Groups 2018* (Washington, DC: IES/NCES, 2018), https://nces.ed.gov/programs/raceindicators/indicator_RFA.asp.
23. Bridget Terry Long and E. Riley, "Financial Aid: A Broken Bridge to College Access?," *Harvard Educational Review* 77, no. 1 (2007): 39–63.
24. Jessica F. Harding, Pamela A. Morris, and Diane Hughes, "The Relationship Between Maternal Education and Children's Academic Outcomes: A Theoretical Framework," *Journal of Marriage and Family,* January 14, 2015, https://onlinelibrary.wiley.com/doi/full/10.1111/jomf.12156.
25. *2018 State-By-State Student-To-Counselor Ratio Report: 10-Year Trends* (Arlington, VA: National Association for College Admission Counseling and American School Counselor Association, 2018), https://www.nacacnet.org/globalassets/documents/publications/research/state-by-state-ratio-report.pdf.
26. Anthony P. Carnevale et al., *Our Separate & Unequal Public Colleges* (Washington DC: Center on Education and the Workforce at Georgetown University, 2018), https://cew.georgetown.edu/cew-reports/sustates/.
27. Elaine M. Allensworth and Kallie Clark, *Are GPAs an Inconsistent Measure of College Readiness across High Schools? Examining Assumptions about Grades versus Standardized Test Scores* (Chicago: University of Chicago Consortium on School Research, 2019), https://consortium.uchicago.edu/sites/default/files/2019-01/Are%20GPAs%20an%20Inconsistent%20Measure-Jan2019-Consortium.pdf.
28. New York State's Excelsior Scholarship Program, discussed in chapter 3, is an anomaly in that the grant will convert to a loan if students do not meet the program's residency requirements.
29. Michelle Miller-Adams and Edward Smith, "Promise Scholarship Programs and Local Prosperity" (Upjohn Institute Policy Paper No. 2018-019, W.E. Upjohn Institute for Employment Research, 2018), https://research.upjohn.org/up_policypapers/19/.
30. Andrew P. Kelly, Jessica S. Howell, and Carolyn Sattin-Bajaj, eds., *Matching Students to Opportunity: Expanding College Choice, Access, and Quality* (Cambridge, MA: Harvard Education Publishing Group, 2016).
31. Donald E. Heller, "Should Wealthier Students Get Subsidized College Education?," *The Conversation,* March 3, 2106, https://theconversation.com/should-

wealthier-students-get-subsidized-college-education-55675; and Laura W. Perna and James S. Riepe, *Delivering On the Promise: Structuring College Promise Programs to Promote Higher Education Attainment for Students from Underserved Groups* (Philadelphia: Penn Ahead Alliance for Higher Education and Democracy, 2016), http://collegepromise.wpengine.com/wp-content/uploads/2016/10/Delivering-On-the-Promise_Perna.pdf.

32. Robert Kelchen, "The Political Attractiveness of Last Dollar Scholarships," *Kelchen on Education Blog*, April 17, 2014, https://robertkelchen.com/2014/04/17/the-political-attractiveness-of-last-dollar-scholarships/.
33. David J. Deming and Christopher R. Walters, "The Impact of Price Caps and Spending Cuts on U.S. Postsecondary Attainment" (NBER Working Paper 23736, National Bureau for Economic Research, August 2017), https://www.nber.org/papers/w23736; and Marco Lepe and Evan Weissman, *Looking Ahead Toward Equity: The College Promise Success Initiative* (New York: MDRC, January 2020).
34. Angela Johnson, Megan Kuhfeld, and Greg King, "Catching up or falling behind: Measuring middle school achievement trajectories for college readiness" (EdWorkingPaper No. 20-233, Annenberg Institute at Brown University, 2020), https://www.edworkingpapers.com/sites/default/files/ai20-233.pdf; and Daniel Collier and Isabel McMullen, "Modeling First Year Stop Out of Kalamazoo Promise Scholars: Mapping Influences of Socioeconomic Advantage and Pre-College Performance to College Performance and Stopping Out," a presentation for Student Financial Aid Research Network (SFARN) National Conference, June 12, 2020.
35. Tiffany Jones and Katie Berger, "A Promise Fulfilled: A Framework for Equitable Free College Programs," The Education Trust, September 2018, https://s3-us-east-2.amazonaws.com/edtrustmain/wp-content/uploads/2018/09/05155636/A-Promise-Fulfilled-A-Framework-for-Equitable-Free-College-Programs-9.6-18.pdf.
36. Say Yes To Education, https://sayyestoeducation.org/about/story/.
37. Richard V. Reeves, Katherine Guyot, and Edward Rodrigue, "Gown Town: A Case Study of Say Yes To Education," The Brookings Institution, June 12, 2018, https://www.brookings.edu/research/gown-towns-a-case-study-of-say-yes-to-education/.
38. Michelle Miller-Adams, *The Power of a Promise: Education and Economic Renewal in Kalamazoo* (Kalamazoo, MI: W.E. Upjohn Institute for Employment Research, 2009), 29–58.
39. Nisa Khan, "NeighborhoodScout Ranks 9 Most Dangerous Cities in Michigan," January 15, 2019, WUOM Michigan Radio website, https://www.michiganradio.org/post/neighborhoodscout-ranks-9-most-dangerous-cities-michigan.
40. Michelle Miller-Adams et al., "Promise Programs Database," W.E. Upjohn Institute for Employment Research, 2017, updated 2020, https://www.upjohn.org/promise/.
41. Timothy J. Bartik, Brad Hershbein, and Marta Lachowska, "The Effects of the Kalamazoo Promise Scholarship on College Enrollment and Completion," *Journal of Human Resources,* published ahead of print, May 6, 2019, http://jhr.uwpress.org/content/early/2019/05/01/jhr.56.1.0416-7824R4.abstract.
42. W.E. Upjohn Institute, "The Kalamazoo Promise: Data Collection," Table 16, https://www.upjohn.org/about/research-initiatives/promise-investing-community/kalamazoo-promise-data-collection.
43. Julie Mack, "Bucking trend, charter schools fail to gain foothold in Kalamazoo," MLive, last updated January 20, 2019, https://www.mlive.com/news/kalamazoo/2015/07/why_has_the_charter_school_mov.html.

44. Daniel Collier, Isabel McMullen, and Brad Hershbein, "An exploration of Kalamazoo Promise Scholars who stop out of college, and who may return," presentation for Association for Education Finance and Policy (AEFP), March 19, 2020.
45. All data from New York State Education Department, https://data.nysed.gov/profile.php?instid=800000052968.
46. Reeves, Guyot, and Rodrigue, "Gown Town," 83.
47. Reeves, Guyot, and Rodrigue, "Gown Town," 84–85.
48. Reeves, Guyot, and Rodrigue, "Gown Town," 87.
49. Reeves, Guyot, and Rodrigue, "Gown Town," 98.
50. Say Yes Buffalo, https://sayyesbuffalo.org/about/governance/.
51. "Say Yes Buffalo: The Future Isn't Waiting," October 7, 2015, video, https://www.youtube.com/watch?v=Jw-wm_nvStc&feature=youtu.be.
52. Say Yes Buffalo website, https://sayyesbuffalo.org/about/story-mission/.
53. Bifulco, Rubenstein, and Sohn, "Evaluating the Effects of Universal Place-Based Scholarships on Student Outcomes: The Buffalo "Say Yes to Education" Program."
54. Bifulco, Rubenstein, and Sohn, "Evaluating the Effects of Universal Place-Based Scholarships on Student Outcomes: The Buffalo "Say Yes to Education" Program."
55. Hosung Sohn et al., "Assessing the Effects of Place-Based Scholarships on Urban Revitalization: The Case of Say Yes to Education," *Educational Evaluation and Policy Analysis* 39, no. 2 (June 2017): 198–222.
56. "Say Yes Buffalo," video.
57. Kelchen, "The Political Attractiveness of Last Dollar Scholarship."
58. Paul Fain, "Wealth's Influence on Enrollment and Completion," *Inside Higher Ed*, May 23, 2019, https://www.insidehighered.com/news/2019/05/23/feds-release-broader-data-socioeconomic-status-and-college-enrollment-and-completion.
59. Alain Poutre and Mamie Voight, "Do Tennessee Promise and New York's Excelsior Scholarship Help Students With Limited Means Afford College?," Institute for Higher Education Policy, September 2018, http://www.ihep.org/sites/default/files/uploads/docs/pubs/ihep_state_free_college_intro.pdf.
60. Office of the Governor, State of Washington, "Washington College Promise," press release, February 2019, https://ofm.wa.gov/sites/default/files/public/budget/statebudget/highlights/budget19/WA_college_promise.pdf; "The New Washington College Grant," Washington Student Achievement Council, https://wsac.wa.gov/wcg.
61. "The New Washington College Grant," Washington Student Achievement Council, https://wsac.wa.gov/media-2019-04-30-WCG.
62. Ashley A. Smith, "Boosting Aid With a Tax on Business," *Inside Higher Ed,* May 28, 2019, https://www.insidehighered.com/news/2019/05/28/tax-hike-employers-will-help-make-college-free-many-students-washington-state.
63. "Financial Aid for Undocumented Students/DREAMers," Washington State Board for Community and Technical Colleges, https://www.sbctc.edu/paying-for-college/undocumented-students.aspx.
64. Office of the Governor, State of New Mexico, "Gov. Lujan Grisham Announces Plan To Make College Tuition Free for New Mexico Students," press release, September 18, 2019, https://www.governor.state.nm.us/2019/09/18/gov-lujan-grisham-announces-plan-to-make-college-tuition-free-for-new-mexico-students/.
65. Ryan Boetel, "Strings Attached: New Mexico Governor, Universities Discuss Proposed Opportunity Scholarship," *Las Cruces Sun News*, December 23, 2019, https://

www.lcsun-news.com/story/news/local/new-mexico/2019/12/23/new-mexico-opportunity-scholarship-would-come-strings-attached/2733694001/.

CHAPTER 5

1. Justin Wolfers, "The Unemployment Rate Is Probably Around 13 Percent," *New York Times,* April 16, 2020.
2. Benjamin Wermund, "The Red State That Loves Free College," *Politico*, January 16, 2019, https://www.politico.com/agenda/story/2019/01/16/tennessee-free-college-000867/.
3. Author's interview with Kenyatta Lovett, assistant commissioner of workforce services with the Tennessee Department of Labor and Workforce Development, March 30, 2020.
4. Estelle Slootmaker, "HireReach: Hiring Strategy That Reduces Biases Unexpectedly Increased Diversity," *Rapid Growth*, August 9, 2018, https://www.rapidgrowthmedia.com/devnews/080918HireReach.aspx; Ani Turner, *The Business Case for Racial Equity* (Battle Creek, MI: W.K. Kellogg Foundation, 2018), https://www.wkkf.org/resource-directory/resources/2018/07/business-case-for-racial-equity.
5. "Unemployment rates and earnings by educational attainment," US Bureau of Labor Statistics, September 14, 2019, https://www.bls.gov/emp/chart-unemployment-earnings-education.htm.
6. "Unemployment rates for persons 25 years and older by educational attainment," US Bureau of Labor Statistics Graphics for Economic News Releases, https://www.bls.gov/charts/employment-situation/unemployment-rates-for-persons-25-years-and-older-by-educational-attainment.htm, accessed June 1, 2020.
7. "Unemployment rates for persons 25 years and older by educational attainment."
8. Edward L. Glaeser and Jesse M. Shapiro, "Is There a New Urbanism? The Growth of US Cities in the 1990s" (Harvard Institute of Economic Research Paper No. 1925, June 2001); and Larry Good and Jannine La Prad, "Educational Attainment as an Economic Driver for States, Regions and Communities" (Lansing, MI: Michigan State University EDA University Center for Regional Economic Innovation, 2013), https://reicenter.org/upload/documents/colearning/good2013_report.pdf.
9. The Office of Governor Phil Murphy, State of New Jersey, "Governor Murphy Announces Historic $50 Million Investment in College Affordability with Tuition-Free 'Garden State Guarantee,'" news release, February 26, 2020, https://www.nj.gov/governor/news/news/562020/20200226a.shtml.
10. Detroit Regional Chamber, "Michigan Reconnect Letter To Legislature," August 20, 2019, https://michauto.org/michigan-reconnect-letter-to-legislature/.
11. Hannah Natanson, "Gov. Northam Proposes Making Community College Free for Some Job-Seekers in Virginia," *Washington Post*, December 12, 2019, https://www.washingtonpost.com/local/education/gov-northam-proposes-making-community-college-free-for-some-job-seekers-in-virginia/2019/12/12/8f2a25fa-1cdc-11ea-8d58-5ac3600967a1_story.html.
12. Governor Bill Haslam, "Tennessee lands a first among states in reconnecting adults to education," CNBC.com, November 7, 2017, https://www.cnbc.com/2017/07/11/tennessees-novel-plan-to-tie-education-to-jobs-gov-bill-haslam.html.
13. Thomas A. Kochan, David Finegold, and Paul Osterman, "Who Can Fix The 'Middle-Skills' Gap?" *Harvard Business Review*, December 2012, https://hbr.org/2012/12/who-can-fix-the-middle-skills-gap.
14. "The 'Middle Skills' Gap: Half of America's Jobs Require More Than High School

Diplomas but Less Than 4-Year Degrees. So Why Are They Under So Many Students' Radars?," the74million.org, https://www.the74million.org/article/the-middle-skills-gap-half-of-americas-jobs-require-more-than-high-school-diplomas-but-less-than-4-year-degrees-so-why-are-they-under-so-many-students-radars/.

15. The Economist Intelligence Unit, "Closing the skills gap: companies and colleges collaborating for change" (Indianapolis: The Lumina Foundation, 2014), https://www.luminafoundation.org/files/publications/Closing_the_skills_gap.pdf.
16. Craig A. Giffi et al., "The Jobs Are Here, But Where Are The People?" *2018 Deloitte and The Manufacturing Institute Skills Gap and Future of Work Study*, November 14, 2018, https://www2.deloitte.com/us/en/insights/industry/manufacturing/manufacturing-skills-gap-study.html.
17. David H. Autor, Frank Levy, and Richard J. Murnane, "The Skill Content of Recent Technological Change: An Empirical Exploration," *Quarterly Journal of Economics* 118, no. 4 (2003):1279–1333.
18. Harry Holzer, "Job Market Polarization and US Worker Skills: A Tale of Two Middles," Economic Studies at Brookings (Washington, DC: Brookings Institution, April 2015), https://www.brookings.edu/wp-content/uploads/2016/06/polarization_jobs_policy_holzer.pdf.
19. Brad Hershbein and Lisa B. Kahn, "Do Recessions Accelerate Routine-Biased Technological Change? Evidence from Vacancy Postings," *American Economic Review* 108, no. 7 (2018): 1737–1772.
20. Alana Semuels, " Millions of Americans Have Lost Jobs in the Pandemic—And Robots and AI Are Replacing Them Faster Than Ever," *Time*, August 6, 2020, https://time.com/5876604/machines-jobs-coronavirus/.
21. Heidi Shierholz and Elise Gould, "Why Is Real Wage Growth Anemic? It's Not Because of a Skills Shortage," *Economic Policy Institute, Working Economics Blog*, July 19, 2018, https://www.epi.org/blog/why-is-real-wage-growth-anemic-its-not-because-of-a-skills-shortage/; Paul Osterman and Andrew Weaver, "Why Claims of Skills Shortages in Manufacturing Are Overblown," Economic Policy Institute, Issue Brief #376, March 26, 2014, https://www.epi.org/publication/claims-skills-shortages-manufacturing-overblown/; Kate Bahn, "'Skills Gap' Arguments Overlook Collective Bargaining and Low Minimum Wages," The Washington Center for Equitable Growth, May 9, 2019, https://equitablegrowth.org/skills-gap-arguments-overlook-collective-bargaining-and-low-minimum-wages/.
22. Matthew Yglesias, "The 'Skills-Gap' Was A Lie," Vox.com, January 7, 2019, https://www.vox.com/2019/1/7/18166951/skills-gap-modestino-shoag-ballance.
23. Paul Krugman, "Jobs and Skills and Zombies," *New York Times*, March 30, 2014.
24. Rick Cohen, "Krugman—Public Policy Has Bought Into Skills-Gap Myth," *Nonprofit Quarterly*, April 7, 2014, https://nonprofitquarterly.org/krugman-charges-public-policy-has-bought-into-skills-gap-myth/.
25. Matthew T. Hora, Ross J. Benbow, and Amanda K. Oleson, *Beyond the Skills Gap: Preparing College Students for Life and Work* (Cambridge, MA: Harvard Education Press, 2016).
26. Matthew T. Hora, "Beyond the Skills Gap: How the Vocationalist Framing of Higher Education Undermines Student, Employer, and Societal Interests," *Liberal Education* 104, no. 2 (2018), https://www.aacu.org/liberaleducation/2018/spring/hora.
27. Nashville Area Chamber of Commerce, 2019 Tech Workforce Study, https://s3.amazonaws.com/nashvillechamber.com/PDFs/NACC_TECH_WORKFORCE_FINAL_FINAL.pdf.
28. Enrico Moretti, "Social Returns to Human Capital," *NBER Reporter: Research*

Summary, Spring 2005, https://www.nber.org/reporter/spring05/moretti.html.
29. Timothy J. Bartik, "The Economic Case for Preschool," TEDxMiamiUniversity, September 2012, https://www.ted.com/talks/timothy_bartik_the_economic_case_for_preschool.
30. Katie Brown, "Powerful Partners: Businesses and Community Colleges," National Skills Coalition, July 2018, https://m.nationalskillscoalition.org/resources/publications/file/Powerful-Partners-Businesses-and-Community-Colleges.pdf.
31. Rob Sentz et al., "How Your School Affects Where You Live," *Emsi*, May 2018, https://www.economicmodeling.com/how-your-school-affects-where-you-live/.
32. Sentz et al., "How Your School Affects Where You Live."
33. Ben Rooney, "Michigan approves plan to close half of Detroit schools," *CNN Money*, February 22, 2011, https://money.cnn.com/2011/02/22/news/economy/detroit_school_restructuring/index.htm.
34. Detroit Regional Chamber, "Education and Talent Strategies," PowerPoint presentation, Detroit, September 19, 2019.
35. Michigan Promise Zones Association, https://promisezonesmi.com/.
36. "Sixty by 30," Michigan College Access Network website, https://micollegeaccess.org/6030.
37. Detroit Promise Path, MDRC website, https://www.mdrc.org/project/detroit-promise-path#agenda-scope-goals).
38. MDRC, "Detroit Promise Path Boosts Full-time Enrollment, Persistence, and Credit Accumulation by Detroit Community College Students," press release, April 2019, https://www.mdrc.org/news/press-release/detroit-promise-path-boosts-full-time-enrollment-persistence-and-credit.
39. MDRC, "Frequently Asked Questions About CUNY's Accelerated Study in Associate Programs (ASAP)," memorandum, March 2015, https://www.mdrc.org/sites/default/files/FAQs_ASAP_020916.pdf.
40. MDRC, "Frequently Asked Questions About CUNY's Accelerated Study."
41. Alyssa Ratledge et al., "A Path from Access to Success: Interim Findings from the Detroit Promise Path Evaluation," MDRC, April 2019, 16, https://www.mdrc.org/sites/default/files/Detroit_Promise_Path_Report-Final_0.pdf.
42. "Career Mentoring," RichmondPromise.org, https://richmondpromise.org/mentorship/.
43. Wermund, "The Red State."
44. Quotes from Krissy DeAlejandro in this section come from author's interview, Knoxville, TN, March 10, 2020.
45. #1335 Bill Haslam," *Forbes Billionaire Profiles*, https://www.forbes.com/profile/bill-haslam/#575e9ca635af.
46. Wermund, *The Red State*.
47. "Knox Achieves to Assist 496 Knox County Students," City of Knoxville, press release, January 12, 2009, https://knoxvilletn.gov/archived_news_stories/2009/knox_achieves_to_assist_496_knox_county_students.
48. Anthony P. Carnevale, Nicole Smith, and Jeff Strohl, "Recovery: Projections of Jobs and Education Requirements Through 2020," *State Report* (Washington, DC: Georgetown Public Policy Institute, 2013), https://1gyhoq479ufd3yna29x7ubjn-wpengine.netdna-ssl.com/wp-content/uploads/StateProjections_6.1.15_agc_v2.pdf.
49. Tennessee Higher Education Commission (THEC), "Tennessee's Educational Attainment Rate" infographic, https://www.tn.gov/content/dam/tn/thec/d55_snapshot/infographics/EdAttainmentRates_2018.pdf.

50. Tennessee Higher Education Commission, "Enabling the Competitive Edge: Tennessee Higher Education in the New Economy," *Master Plan Update 2020*, https://www.tn.gov/thec/about-thec-tsac/master-plan/master-plan.html.
51. Mattie Quinn, "Tennessee's Free College Program Is Popular, But Will It Succeed?," *Governing*, October 2016, https://www.governing.com/topics/education/gov-tennessee-free-community-college-promise.html.
52. J. W. Kramer, "Bridging high school and college: Supporting enrollment for college-intending high school seniors in Tennessee" (PhD diss., Vanderbilt University, 2019).
53. Data shared with author by staff of Tennessee Higher Education Corporation, March 10, 2020.
54. "Current FAFSA Completion Rates by State," FAFSA Tracker—National, https://national.fafsatracker.com/currentRates.
55. Alain Poutre and Mamie Voight, "Tennessee Promise: Does it help students with limited financial means attend college?" Institute for Higher Education Policy, September 2018, http://www.ihep.org/sites/default/files/uploads/docs/pubs/ihep_state_free_college_tennessee_promise.pdf.
56. tnAchieves, 2019 Annual Report, https://tnachieves.org/lib/file/manager/Miscellaneous/2018-2019_Annual_Report.pdf.
57. tnAchieves, 2019 Annual Report.
58. Laura Ward, "Two unique programs are helping Nashville adults go back to school, *The Avenue* (blog), Brookings Institution, February 11, 2020, https://www.brookings.edu/blog/the-avenue/2020/02/11/two-unique-programs-are-helping-nashville-adults-go-back-to-school/.
59. tnAchieves, Knox Promise website, https://tnachieves.org/knoxpromise/.
60. Michelle Miller-Adams, *The Power of a Promise: Education and Economic Renewal in Kalamazoo* (Kalamazoo, MI: W.E. Upjohn Institute for Employment Research, 2009).
61. Tennessee Reconnect Ambassador Guidebook and Resources, https://www.tn.gov/content/dam/tn/thec/workforce/AmbassadorGuidebook_Complete_1.16.2018.pdf.
62. Celeste K. Carruthers, William F. Fox, and Christopher Jepsen, "Promise Kept? Free Community College, Attainment, and Earnings in Tennessee," University of Tennessee Working Paper, February 2020 (work in progress), https://www.frbatlanta.org/-/media/documents/news/conferences/2020/04/16/southeastern-micro-labor-workshop/Carruthers_Fox_Jepsen.pdf.
63. Brad Hershbein, Isabel McMullen, Brian Pittelko, and Bridget Timmeney, "Beyond Degrees: Longer-term outcomes of the Kalamazoo Promise," Upjohn Institute Working Paper (work in progress), November 2020.
64. Hershbein et al., "Beyond Degrees, 29.

CHAPTER 6

1. Tressie McMillan Cottom, "Why Free College Is Necessary, *Dissent Magazine*, Fall 2015, https://www.dissentmagazine.org/article/tressie-mcmillan-cottom-why-free-college-necessary.
2. Bernie Sanders, "Make College Tuition Free," news release, May 19, 2015, https://www.sanders.senate.gov/newsroom/recent-business/make-college-tuition-free.
3. Jason D. DeLisle, "Evidence against the free-college agenda: An analysis of prices, financial aid, and affordability at public universities," *Questioning the Cost of Free College* Series (Washington, DC: American Enterprise Institute, 2020), https://

www.aei.org/research-products/report/evidence-against-the-free-college-agenda-an-analysis-of-prices-financial-aid-and-affordability-at-public-universities/.

4. Jason Delisle and Preston Cooper, "What European Countries Sacrifice for Free College," *NationalReview.com*, August 15, 2019, https://www.nationalreview.com/2019/08/what-european-countries-sacrifice-for-free-college/.
5. The White House Office of The Press Secretary, "White House Unveils America's College Promise Proposal: Tuition-Free Community College for Responsible Students," news release, January 9, 2015, https://obamawhitehouse.archives.gov/the-press-office/2015/01/09/fact-sheet-white-house-unveils-america-s-college-promise-proposal-tuitio.
6. City Colleges of Chicago, "Mayor Emanuel and City Colleges Chancellor Juan Salgado Announce Big Shoulders Fund Partnership That Will Expand the Star Scholarship Program," news release, May 6, 2019, http://www.ccc.edu/news/Pages/Mayor-Emanuel-and-City-Colleges-Chancellor-Announce-BSF-Partnership-That-Will-Expand-Star-Scholarship-Program-.aspx.
7. The White House of President Barack Obama, "Investing in Education: The American Graduation Initiative," blog entry by Katherine Brandon, July 14, 2009, https://obamawhitehouse.archives.gov/blog/2009/07/14/investing-education-american-graduation-initiative; and Alan Berube, "The End of the American Graduation Initiative," *The Avenue* (blog), Brookings Institution, March 23, 2010, https://www.brookings.edu/blog/the-avenue/2010/03/23/the-end-of-the-american-graduation-initiative/.
8. Sara Goldrick-Rab and Nancy Kendall, "Redefining College Affordability: Securing America's Future with a Free Two-Year College Option," *The EduOptimists*, April 2014, https://www.luminafoundation.org/files/resources/redefining-college-affordability.pdf.
9. David Leonhardt, "Obama's Community College Plan: A Reading List," *The Upshot* (blog), *New York Times*, January 10, 2015, https://www.nytimes.com/2015/01/10/upshot/obamas-community-college-plan-a-reading-list.html.
10. Mark Huelsman, "The Case for Debt-Free College," Demos, August 10, 2015, https://www.demos.org/policy-briefs/case-debt-free-college.
11. Colin Lenton, "Politico50: The List," *Politico*, 2016, https://www.politico.com/magazine/politico50/2016/sara-goldrick-rab-adam-green-mark-huelsman.
12. Ashley A. Smith, "Obama Steps Up Push For Free Tuition," *Inside Higher Ed*, September 9, 2015, https://www.insidehighered.com/news/2015/09/09/obama-unveils-new-push-national-free-community-college.
13. Sanders, "Make College Tuition Free.
14. Summary of Sen. Sanders' College For All Act, https://www.sanders.senate.gov/download/collegeforallsummary/?inline=file.
15. Haley Sweetland Edwards, "The Toughest Critic of Hillary Clinton's College Plan? Herself," *Time*, July 7, 2016, https://time.com/4396456/hillary-clinton-free-college-tuition-cost/.
16. Nick Gass, "Clinton knocks Sanders' college plan: Trump's kids shouldn't get free ride," *Politico*, October 5, 2015, https://www.politico.com/story/2015/10/hillary-clinton-criticize-bernie-sanders-college-plan-214424.
17. Sam Frizell, "Hillary Clinton Adopts Major Bernie Sanders' Idea: Free College for (Almost) Everyone," *Time*, July 6, 2016, https://time.com/4394699/hillary-clinton-free-college-bernie-sanders-tuition/.
18. Laura Meckler, "Hillary Clinton's Free College-Tuition Plan Short on Specifics," *Wall Street Journal*, August 4, 2016, https://www.wsj.com/articles/hillary-

clintons-free-college-tuition-plan-coming-up-short-on-specifics-1471167001; David H. Feldman and Robert B. Archibald, "Why Bernie Sanders's Free College Plan Doesn't Make Sense," *Washington Post*, April 22, 2016, https://www.washingtonpost.com/news/grade-point/wp/2016/04/22/why-bernie-sanderss-free-college-plan-doesnt-make-sense/.

19. Emmanuel Felton, "Sanders' Free College Plan Would Take From the Rich to Give to the Rich," *Hechinger Report*, November 13, 2015, https://hechingerreport.org/sanders-free-college-plan-would-take-from-the-rich-to-give-to-the-rich/.
20. Kevin Carey, "The Trouble With Hillary Clinton's Free College Plan," *New York Times*, July 19, 2016, https://www.nytimes.com/2016/07/20/upshot/the-trouble-with-hillary-clintons-free-tuition-plan.html; and "The Free College Fantasy," *Chronicle of Higher Education*, December 9, 2019, https://www.chronicle.com/article/the-free-college-fantasy/.
21. Katia Savchuk, "Why Universalism Trumps Targeting in Social Policy," *The Polis Blog*, May 6, 2012, https://www.thepolisblog.org/2012/05/why-universalism-trumps-targeting-in.html.
22. Sara Goldrick-Rab and Tammy Kolbe, "A Matter of Trust: Applying Insights From Social Psychology to Make College Affordable," *Policy Insights from the Behavioral and Brain Sciences* 3 no. 2 (2016), https://journals.sagepub.com/doi/abs/10.1177/2372732216656457.
23. Matthew M. Chingos, "Who Would Benefit Most From Free College?," Brookings Institution, April 21, 2016, https://www.brookings.edu/research/who-would-benefit-most-from-free-college/.
24. Matthew Yglesias, "There's a Big Problem with Bernie Sanders's Free College Plan," *Vox,* March 14, 2016, https://www.vox.com/2016/3/14/11222482/bernie-sanders-free-college.
25. Michelle Miller-Adams et al., "Promise Programs Database," W.E. Upjohn Institute for Employment Research, 2017, updated 2020, www.upjohn.org/promise/.
26. Hannah Hartig, "Democrats Overwhelmingly Favor Free College Tuition, While Republicans Are Divided By Age, Education," Pew Research Center, February 21, 2020, https://www.pewresearch.org/fact-tank/2020/02/21/democrats-overwhelmingly-favor-free-college-tuition-while-republicans-are-divided-by-age-education/.
27. The website of Rise, Inc., https://risefree.org/how-we-work/.
28. The website of Higher Ed, Not Debt, https://higherednotdebt.org/about.
29. Douglas N. Harris, "The Central Role of Free College and Loan Forgiveness in the Democratic Primary," *Brown Center Chalkboard* blog, June 19, 2019, https://www.brookings.edu/blog/brown-center-chalkboard/2019/06/19/the-central-role-of-free-college-and-loan-forgiveness-in-the-democratic-primary/.
30. Bianca Quilantan, "How Joe Biden Would Make Community College Free and Fix Student Loans," *Politico*, October 8, 2019, https://www.politico.com/news/2019/10/08/joe-biden-2020-election-community-college-student-loans-plan-041634.
31. Kery Murakami, "Biden and Sanders Spar on Free College," *Inside Higher Ed*, March 16, 2020, https://www.insidehighered.com/quicktakes/2020/03/16/biden-and-sanders-spar-free-college.
32. Kim Parker, "The Growing Partisan Divide in Views of Higher Education," Pew Research Center, August 19, 2019, https://www.pewsocialtrends.org/essay/the-growing-partisan-divide-in-views-of-higher-education/.
33. Stephanie Marken, "Half in US Now Consider College Education Very Important,"

Gallup, December 30, 2019, https://www.gallup.com/education/272228/half-consider-college-education-important.aspx.

34. Christine Baker-Smith et al., "#RealCollege 2020: Five Years of Evidence on Campus Basic Needs Insecurity," *hope4college.com*, February 2020, https://hope4college.com/wp-content/uploads/2020/02/2019_RealCollege_Survey_Report.pdf.
35. Sara Goldrick-Rab, *Paying the Price: College Costs, Financial Aid, and the Betrayal of the American Dream* (Chicago: University of Chicago Press, 2016).
36. Brian Schatz, "Schatz, Pocan Reintroduce Legislation To End Student Loan Debt Crisis," news release, March 6, 2019, https://www.schatz.senate.gov/press-releases/schatz-pocan-reintroduce-legislation-to-end-student-loan-debt-crisis.
37. G. William Hoagland et al., *A New Course for Higher Education: Strengthening Access, Accountability, and Affordability* (Washington, DC: Bipartisan Policy Center: 2020), https://bipartisanpolicy.org/report/new-higher-ed/.
38. Ella Nilsen, "Elizabeth Warren Has the Biggest Free College Plan Yet," *Vox*, April 22, 2019, https://www.vox.com/2019/4/22/18509196/elizabeth-warren-debt-free-college.
39. Andrew Kreighbaum, "Senator Pushes 'Debt-Free' as Solution for College Costs," *Inside Higher Ed*, March 7, 2019, https://www.insidehighered.com/news/2019/03/07/schatz-reintroduces-debt-free-college-bill.
40. Jen Mishory, "Path To Debt-Free College: A Blueprint for Building a Successful Federal-State Partnership," Higher Education (New York: The Century Foundation, 2018), https://tcf.org/content/report/path-debt-free-college/?agreed=1Warren?.
41. Mishory, "Path To Debt-Free College."
42. Spiros Protopsaltis and Sharon Parrott, "Pell Grants—a Key Tool for Expanding College Access and Economic Opportunity—Need Strengthening, Not Cuts," Center on Budget and Policy Priorities, July 27, 2017, https://www.cbpp.org/research/federal-budget/pell-grants-a-key-tool-for-expanding-college-access-and-economic-opportunity.
43. Andrew Kreighbaum, "The Moderates' Alternative to Free College," *Inside Higher Ed*, October 9, 2019, https://www.insidehighered.com/news/2019/10/09/big-new-spending-pell-grants-catches-moderate-presidential-hopefuls.
44. Danielle Douglas-Gabriel, "Obama Breathed New Life Into Federal Grant Aid Yet It's Not Enough to Tackle College Costs," *Washington Post*, February 29, 2016, https://www.washingtonpost.com/news/grade-point/wp/2016/02/29/obama-breathed-new-life-into-federal-grant-aid-yet-its-not-enough-to-tackle-college-costs/.
45. Christopher Newfield, *Unmaking the Public University: The Forty-Year Assault on the Middle Class* (Cambridge, MA: Harvard University Press, 2008); *The Great Mistake: How We Wrecked Public Universities and How We Can Fix Them* (Baltimore: Johns Hopkins University Press, 2018).
46. Robert Samuels, *Why Public Higher Education Should Be Free: How to Decrease Cost and Increase Quality at American Universities* (New Brunswick, NJ: Rutgers University Press, 2013); Jordan Weissmann, "How Washington Could Make College Tuition Free (Without Spending a Penny More on Education)," *Atlantic*, March 8, 2013, https://www.theatlantic.com/business/archive/2013/03/how-washington-could-make-college-tuition-free-without-spending-a-penny-more-on-education/273801/; and Sara Goldrick-Rab, Lauren Schudde, and Jacob Stampen, "Making College Affordable: The Case for an Institution-Focused Approach to Federal Aid," in Sara Goldrick-Rab and Andrew P. Kelly, eds. *Reinventing Financial Aid: Charting a New Course to College Affordability* (Cambridge, MA: Harvard Education Press, 2014).
47. Tressie McMillan Cottom, *Lower Ed: The Troubling Rise of For-Profit Colleges in the*

New Economy (New York: The New Press, 2018), https://thenewpress.com/books/lower-ed.

48. Mandira Banjeree, "HAIL Promise Effectively Recruits Low-Income Students to U-M," *University Record*, December 11, 2018, https://record.umich.edu/articles/hail-promise-effectively-recruits-low-income-students-u-m/.
49. Sara Goldrick-Rab and Michelle Miller-Adams, "Don't Dismiss the Value of Free-College Programs. They Do Help Low-Income Students," *Chronicle of Higher Education*, September 7, 2018, https://www.chronicle.com/article/Don-t-Dismiss-the-Value-of/244468.
50. Mychal Denzel Smith, "The Truth About 'The Arc Of The Moral Universe,'" *Huffington Post*, January 18, 2018, https://www.huffpost.com/entry/opinion-smith-obama-king_n_5a5903e0e4b04f3c55a252a4.

ABOUT THE AUTHOR

Michelle Miller-Adams is a senior researcher at the W.E. Upjohn Institute for Employment Research and a professor of political science at Grand Valley State University. An expert on asset-building and economic development strategies, she received her PhD in political science and master of international affairs from Columbia University, and bachelor of arts in history from the University of California, Santa Barbara. Her professional career has spanned the fields of nonprofit management, finance, research, and academia.

Miller-Adams is the author of the first book on the Kalamazoo Promise, *The Power of a Promise: Education and Economic Renewal in Kalamazoo* (W.E. Upjohn Institute, 2009) and an e-book on the free-college movement entitled *Promise Nation: Transforming Communities through Place-Based Scholarships* (W.E. Upjohn Institute, 2015). She was the principal investigator for a Ford Foundation–sponsored research project that culminated in the publication of *Owning Up: Poverty, Assets, and the American Dream* (Brookings Institution Press, 2002). She is also the author of *The World Bank: New Agendas in a Changing World* (Routledge, 1999). Miller-Adams speaks regularly with local and national media about free-college programs and consults with states and communities designing their own Promise initiatives. Miller-Adams lives in Kalamazoo, Michigan, with her daughter and two dogs.

INDEX

AB 19 (College Promise bill), 19, 26, 39
academic requirements, 41–42
administrative budgets, 65–66
Almaguer, Roy, 110–111
Amazon, 39
amenities, 66–67
America's College Promise proposal, 160, 162–164, 172, 178, 180
Arkansas Future Grants, 38
attendance policies, 41
Autor, David, 130–131

balance wheel, 24
Biden, Joe, 4–5, 170–171, 180
Black people. *See also* equity; racial disparities
  college completion, 94–95
  college enrollment, 13, 19, 22–23, 91–92
  degree attainment, 97–98
  GI Bill access and, 13–14
  high school graduation rates, 90
  standardized test scores, 100
  systemic racism and, 19, 177
  wealth and income inequality, 4
"A Blueprint for College Without Debt" (Huelsman), 173
Boyd, Randy, 145

Caldwell, Dan, 153–154
California
  AB 19 (College Promise bill), 19, 26, 39
  free college experiment, 15–20
  state funding declines and, 63
California state university system, 18–19
Campaign for Free College Tuition (CFCT), 50–51, 165
Chicago Star Scholarship, 163
City College (Free Academy), 20–21
City University of New York (CUNY) system, 22–23
Clinton, Hillary, 4, 166–167, 169
college access, inequality in, 89–100. *See also* equity
college admission scandal, 87–88
college affordability. *See also* first-dollar funding; last-dollar funding; Promise programs
  cost compared, 56
  politics and, 175
  price of college, 56–62
  reasons for increasing costs, 62–69
  timing of focus on, 55

College Affordability Act, 175
College Board, 57–61
College Bound program, 8
college completion, equity and, 83–84, 89–90, 94–100
college education
  federal government role in, 12–15
  public opinion on, 171
  value of, 56
college enrollment
  decline of, 67
  equity and, 89–90, 91–93
  by people of color, 13, 19, 22–23, 91–92
College For All bill, 165–166
college funding
  balance wheel and, 24
  decline of state support for, 2, 63–64
  tuition and, 67–69
college majors, 97
College Promise, 164–165. *See also* Promise programs
College Promise Advisory Board, 164–165
College Promise Grant (CA), 19, 26, 39
College Promise initiative, 7
College Promise programs. *See* Promise programs
College Promise Success Initiative, 141
college selection factors, 99. *See also* undermatching for college selection
college wage premium, 25, 97, 127–128
college-going expectations
  El Dorado Promise, 73
  equity and, 88, 98, 101–102, 111–112, 123
  GI Bill and, 13
  Kalamazoo Promise and, 111–112
  Promise programs increasing, 99, 102, 119
color-blind admission, 19
common schools, 9
communication systems and policy diffusion, 47
community colleges
  in California, 18–19
  Obama administration and, 163
  purposes of Promise programs, 33–35, 36
  socioeconomic status and attendance, 118–119
community service requirements, 148
community-based scholarships. *See also specific programs*
  defined, 7
  equity and, 101, 106–118
  impacts of, 129
  income restrictions and, 71
  purposes of, 30–33, 52
  school districts strengthened by, 102–103
Complete College Tennessee Act, 147
Cooley, Thomas, 11
coronavirus, 125–126, 176–177, 181
cost of attendance, 56
cost of higher education. *See also* tuition inflation
  affordability compared, 56
  eligibility for program and, 43–44
  increases in, 2
COVID-19 pandemic, 125–126, 176–177, 181
Cuomo, Andrew, 80–81

Dallas County Promise, 8, 31
DeAlejandro, Krissy, 143–146
debt-free college, 173
Debt-Free College Act, 172
degree attainment
  affordability and, 83–84
  equity and, 94–100
  unemployment and, 127–128
  unemployment rates and, 127, 130
Democratic Party, 4–5
Denver Scholarship Foundation, 8, 42
Detroit Compact, 139
Detroit Promise
  characteristics of, 137
  employment metrics for, 155–157
  history of, 138–142
  postsecondary options in, 43
  private institutions and, 69
  purposes of, 27
  student supports, 140–142
  as universal, 40–41
Detroit Promise Path, 140–142
Detroit Promise Zone, 139
Detroit Regional Chamber, 139–140
Detroit Scholarship Fund, 138
discounts for tuition, 64–65
diversity in workplace, 127

Douglass, John Aubrey, 12
Drive to 55 campaign (TN), 147

economic competitiveness
as driving force of Promise programs, 126
education and, 17
free college and, 128–129
Say Yes Buffalo and, 116
spillover argument for, 133–134
economic equity, 2. *See also* equity
Economist Intelligence Unit summary, 130
economy
diversity in workplace and, 127
educational level of workers and, 127–128
free college and, 25–27, 161
state funding declines and, 63, 67–68
Educate and Grow scholarship, 33
education, as public or private benefit, 10–11, 29–30, 32, 85, 160
education gap, 90–91
The Education Trust report, 105–106
educational equity. *See* equity; income and wealth inequality; racial disparities
El Dorado Promise
affordability and, 77–78
characteristics of, 40, 71–72, 74
funding provided, 44
impacts of, 73–75
origins of, 72–75
private institutions and, 69
purposes of, 33
Emmanuel, Rahm, 163
employment. *See also* workforce readiness
nonroutine work, 131
unemployment rate, 125–126
equity. *See also* workforce readiness
overview, 87–89
college access and, 89–100
community-based programs, 106–118
ideal program design and, 105–106, 122–123
impacts of Promise programs generally, 100–106
social upheaval and, 180–182
state programs, 118–123
trade-offs about, 168
estimated living expenses, 56
Excelsior Scholarship, 25–26, 78–84, 117, 177

FAFSA completion, 119, 135, 148–149, 174
federal government. *See also* Pell Grant funding
contributions compared to states, 63–64
role in higher education, 12–15, 176–177, 179–180
financial aid. *See also* first-dollar funding; last-dollar funding; Pell Grant funding; Promise programs
college expense calculations and, 57
net price and, 59–61
tuition inflation and, 61
first-dollar funding
amount of funding and, 44, 104
defined, 24
equity and, 101, 178
who benefits from, 70, 74, 104
"Framework for Equity-Driven Free College Policy" (Education Trust), 105–106
Frazier, Fred, Jr., 153–154
Free Academy (City College), 20–21
free college. *See also* history of free education
action options, 172–180
benefits from, 160
in California, 15–20
debate over, 161–167
economic competitiveness and, 128–129
employment and, 155–157
momentum about, 170
in New York City, 20–25
program design for, 177–180
state/federal funding and, 159–161
support for, 4–5
systemic racism and, 14
trade-offs about, 167–172
workforce readiness and, 129–130, 162–164
free college movement
California's free-college experiment, 15–20
equity and, 88
high school movement similarity, 11

free college, *continued*
political and economic forces driving, 25–27, 161
reasons for, 1–4
free education. *See* free college; history of free education
Futures for Frontliners, 133

Georgia HOPE Scholarship, 36
Get Skilled, Get a Job, Give Back (G3) program, 121–122
GI Bill (Servicemen's Readjustment Act of 1944), 13–14, 15
Goldrick-Rab, Sara, 2, 164, 172
GPA, 100
Great Recession, 63, 67–68, 127, 130

HAIL Scholarship (MI), 177
Harris, Townsend, 20–21
Haslam, Bill, 145–146, 147
Hershbein, Brad, 131, 156–157
high school, 9–11, 90–91
Higher Education Act of 1965, 14–15
Higher Education Act reauthorization, 172
Hispanic people. *See* Latino/Hispanic people
Historically Black Colleges and Universities (HBCUs), 13
history of free education
overview, 8–9
California's free-college experiment, 15–20
college for some, 12–15
high school, 9–11
New York City's free college, 20–25
Holzer, Harry, 131
Hope Center, 171–172
HOPE Scholarship (GA), 36
Hora, Matthew T., 132
Huelsman, Mark, 164, 173

income and wealth inequality
affordability and, 62
college enrollment and, 92–93
college wage premium and, 97
educational attainment and, 127–128
high school graduation rates and, 90–91
postsecondary completion and, 95–96
reasons for, 97–100
social systems and, 3
innovation and policy diffusion, 47
institution-based programs, 33–36
intensity, 45
Ivy League institutions, 35, 67, 167

junior colleges, 16. *See also* community colleges

Kahn, Lisa, 131
Kalamazoo Promise
characteristics of, 107
earnings and, 156–157
eligibility for, 42
equity and, 106–112, 118
funding provided, 44
impacts of, 111, 117
postsecondary options in, 43
private institutions and, 69
purposes of, 5–6, 27, 33
Say Yes Buffalo compared, 113–115
as universal, 40
Kalamazoo Union High School, 10–11
Kendall, Nancy, 164
Knox Achieves program, 7, 36, 143–146, 151. *See also* Tennessee Promise
Krugman, Paul, 131–132

land-grant colleges, 12–13, 16
last-dollar funding
amount of funding and, 44, 104
defined, 34
equity and, 101, 123, 178
last-dollar-plus funding, 104, 119
Latino/Hispanic people. *See also* equity; racial disparities
college completion, 94–95
college enrollment and, 22–23, 91–92
degree attainment, 97–98
high school graduation rates, 90
standardized test scores, 100
systemic racism and, 19, 177
lifetime earnings, 56
living expense estimates, 56
living expenses, 61, 169, 171–172

Long Beach Community College, 34–35
Long Beach Promise, 34–35
Los Angeles College Promise, 31–32
Lovett, Kenyatta, 126
low-income students. *See also* equity; Pell Grant funding; racial disparities; undermatching for college selection; *specific programs*
college enrollment and, 93
college selection and, 96, 111, 168
first-dollar funding, 70, 74, 104
living expenses and, 61, 169
program requirements and, 46, 81, 117
residency requirements and, 40, 76
sticker prices and, 64

Mann, Horace, 9
MDRC, 51
mentorship model, 150
merit-based programs
equity and, 22, 36, 103
purposes of, 36
who benefits from, 41–42, 103
messaging, 174, 177
Michigan Reconnect, 26
Michigan's Promise Zones, 33, 139
Microsoft, 39
middle-class students
college enrollment and, 93
disadvantages of, 84
Oregon Promise, 79
Pell funding and, 70, 174
Washington College Grant program, 26, 120
middle-skill jobs, 130
Mishory, Jen, 173
Morrill Act of 1862, 12
Murphy Oil Corporation, 73

National Defense Education Act of 1958, 14
Native Americans, 19, 90, 177. *See also* equity; racial disparities
Navigate Reconnect, 150
need-based targeting, 103–104, 120
net price information, 59–61
new economics of college, 2
New Haven, 27
New Mexico Opportunity Scholarship, 38, 42, 121–122
New York City's free college, 20–25
nonroutine work, 131
Northeast State College (TN), 33

Obama, Barack, 160, 162–164
Operation Varsity Blues, 87–88
Oregon Promise, 78–84, 104, 119

pandemic, 125–126, 176–177, 181
parent education level, 98
Paying the Price (Goldrick-Rab), 2, 172
Pell Grant funding
community colleges and, 34
FAFSA completion and, 119, 135, 148–149, 174
first versus last dollar funding, 70, 101, 104
four-year public institutions, 61–62
historical support of, 15
increasing of, 173–174
last-dollar-plus funding, 119
number of, 80
PennAHEAD, 51
People's Initiative to Limit Property Taxation (Proposition 13), 18
Pittsburgh Promise
academic requirements, 41
affordability and, 77–78
characteristics of, 71–72, 75–76
Extension Program, 75
funding provided, 44
impacts of, 77
purposes of, 8, 27, 33
as universal, 40
place-based scholarships. *See* community-based scholarships
policy diffusion, 46–53
politics, 161–167
postsecondary completion, 83–84, 89–90, 94–100
postsecondary enrollment. *See* college enrollment
private four-year institution costs, 57–61, 64–65, 69
Promise Extension Program (Pittsburgh), 75

Promise movement, 5–8
Promise programs. *See also* supports for students to be successful; *specific programs*
  alignment and, 152, 179
  college affordability and, 69–85
  college enrollment and, 93
  degree attainment and, 83–84
  demographics and, 99–100
  differing definitions of, 7–8, 45
  diffusion of idea about, 46–53, 160
  economic benefits of, 133
  eligibility for, 40–42, 70–72
  employment outcomes with, 134–136
  evidence about lacking, 48–49
  Excelsior Scholarship, 25–26, 78–84, 117, 177
  funding of, 152–154
  funding provided, 44–46, 135, 168–169
  intensity versus saturation, 45
  number of, 7
  Oregon Promise, 78–84, 104, 119
  postsecondary options in, 42–44, 135
  public versus private benefit, 29–30, 32, 85, 160
  purposes of, 26–27, 30–39, 45–46
  research needed on, 51–52
  simplicity versus complexity of, 104
  structure of, 39–46
  variations in, 37
  who benefits from, 69–71, 103, 134
Promise wrapper effect, 34
PromiseNet, 49–51, 169–170
Proposition 13 (CA), 18
Proposition 209 (CA), 19
public four-year institution costs, 57–61
public two-year institution costs, 57–61
purposes of Promise programs. *See also* college affordability; equity; workforce readiness
  community-based programs, 30–33, 53
  design and, 45–46
  institution-based programs, 33–36
  local conditions as impetus for, 26–27

racial disparities. *See also* equity
  college attendance discrimination, 13
  college wage premium and, 97
  CUNY system, 22–23
  degree attainment, 97
  high school graduation rates, 90–91
  issues with, 2
  postsecondary enrollment, 91–92
  reasons for, 97–100
  well-being, 3–4
Ragsdale, Mike, 143–146
Reconnect. *See* Tennessee Reconnect program
Reconnect Ambassadors, 152
"Redefining College Affordability: Securing America's Future with a Free Two Year College Option" (Goldrick-Rab & Kendall), 164
redlining, 14
regulations, administrative costs of compliance, 65–66
residency requirements, 40–41, 76
Rhode Island Promise, 26
Richmond Promise, 8
Rochester Promise, 35
Rogers, Everett M., 46–47, 48

Sanders, Bernie, 4, 160, 165–166, 169
saturation, 45, 70
Say Yes Buffalo, 107–108, 112–118
Say Yes to Education, 106–108
Schatz, Brian, 173
School Counts! program, 33
Second Morrill Act of 1890, 13
Servicemen's Readjustment Act of 1944 (GI Bill), 13–14, 15
single-institution programs, 43
skills gap, 3, 130–132
social systems and policy diffusion, 47
spillover argument, 133–134
standardized test scores, 100
Star Scholarship, 163
state funding declines, 63–65, 67–69, 175
state programs. *See also specific programs*
  equity and, 118–123
  federal government and, 176–177, 179–180
  purposes of, 36–39, 53
sticker prices, 64–65
stopout rate, 112
Stuart, Charles, 10

supports for students to be successful
  design of, 114–115, 178–179
  Detroit Promise, 140–142
  employment and, 135–136
  merit-based programs and, 103
  need for, 104–105
  Tennessee Promise and Reconnect, 149–151
  trade-offs about, 169
systemic racism, 3–4, 14, 19, 177. *See also* equity; racial disparities

targeted programs, 38, 168
Tennessee Promise
  characteristics of, 137, 154–155
  employment metrics for, 155–157
  funding provided, 44
  history of, 143–146
  impacts of, 104, 148–149
  as place-based, 7
  political and economic forces driving, 25
  politics and, 171
  purposes of, 36–37, 38
  simplicity of, 148–149, 177
  student supports, 149–151
  success factors in, 146–155
Tennessee Reconnect program
  built on Tennessee Promise, 147
  characteristics of, 137
  eligibility for, 42
  employment metrics for, 155–157
  funding of, 154
  political and economic forces driving, 25
  requirements for, 149
  student supports, 150–151
test scores, 100
test-optional admissions, 100
time and policy diffusion, 47
tnAchieves, 143. *See also* Tennessee Promise
Traub, James, 21–22
tuition caps, 68–69
tuition discounting, 64–65
tuition inflation
  amount of, 57–61
  disproportionate impacts of, 2
  financial aid and, 61
  reasons for, 2
  state funding declines and, 63–65, 67–69, 175
tuition reset, 65
tuition-free college
  in Europe, 162
  living expenses not considered, 171–172
  pandemic and, 133
  support for, 170
  transformation with, 52

undermatching for college selection
  college application barriers and, 95
  postsecondary options and, 135, 168, 179–180
  program requirements and, 46, 163
  student supports and, 104–105
unemployment rate, 125–126, 127–128
universal programs
  defined, 8
  simplicity of, 148
  trade-offs about, 167–168
  who benefits from, 40–41, 103
University of California, 16, 18, 19
University of Michigan, 35
University of Rochester, 35
Upjohn Institute
  impacts of scholarship programs, 45, 51
  intensity and saturation, 45, 70, 78
  place-based programs, 7, 30–31
  program requirements, 41–43, 71
urban exodus, 6

Ventura College Promise, 33
Virginia. *See* Get Skilled, Get a Job, Give Back (G3) program
vocational training, 76

wage premium, 25, 97, 127–128
Warren, Elizabeth, 4, 66–67, 173
Washington College Grant program
  eligibility for, 42
  equity and, 120–121, 122
  uniqueness of, 26, 37–38
wealth and income inequality, 3

Wermund, Benjamin, 126
WestEd, 51
Wolverine Pathways, 35
workforce readiness. *See also* Detroit Promise; Tennessee Promise; Tennessee Reconnect program
  college degrees and, 3
  free college movement and, 129–130, 162–164
  need for skilled workers, 127–133
  skills gap and, 3, 130–132
  spillover argument for, 133–134
  Washington College Grant program and, 121